INTERNATIONAL ASSOCIATION F

OF EDUCATIONAL ACHIEVEMENT (IEA)

International Studies
In Evaluation IV

INTERNATIONAL ENGLISH COMMITTEE

E. Glyn Lewis (Chairman)
Ian Dunlop
Esther Heitner
Pierre Morette
Agnes M. Niyekawa-Howard
Rauno Piirtola
Clifford H. Prator

The Teaching of English as a Foreign Language in Ten Countries -

E. Glyn Lewis and Carolyn E. Massad

With Contributions by
Care Burstall and
John B. Carroll

and a Foreword by
Torsten Husén

Almqvist & Wiksell International
Stockholm, Sweden

A Halsted Press Book
John Wiley & Sons
New York—London—Sydney—Toronto

© 1975
International Association for the Evaluation of
Educational Achievement (IEA), Stockholm

First published by
Almqvist & Wiksell International
Stockholm, Sweden
ISBN 91-2200020-8

Design Dick Hallström

Printed in Sweden by
Almqvist & Wiksell, Uppsala 1975

Library of Congress Cataloging in Publication Data
Lewis, E. Glyn.
The teaching of English as a foreign language in ten countries.
(International studies in evaluation; IV) "A Halsted Press book."
1. English language—Study and teaching—Foreign students. I. Massad,
Carolyn E., joint author. II. Title. III. Series.
PE1128.A2L4   420'.7   74-20109
ISBN 0-470-53195-9

Contents

Foreword

Some ten years ago, when the Mathematics survey was close to its completion, IEA discussed the merits of a comparative study of the outcomes of the teaching of English as a Foreign Language. A background paper dealing with the rationale, feasibility and some of the ramifications of an international study of achievement in English and the social and didactic determinants of student competence was submitted to the 1965 IEA Council meetings in Chicago and Hamburg. At this point it was decided to include English as a Foreign Language in what has become known as the Six Subject Survey.

The English project—as was the case with the other five subject-area projects—was conducted in three steps.

Initially, an International Committee was appointed and charged with the task of specifying the hypotheses and designing the project. This was followed by the construction of internationally valid instruments whereby both the cognitive and the non-cognitive outcomes of the teaching of English could be assessed. As this was the first large-scale international study of its kind, it meant that considerable pioneering work, particularly in terms of instrument construction, had to be achieved. We were fortunate to enlist the support of Mr E. Glyn Lewis, renowned internationally as an expert on foreign language teaching, as the Chairman of the International Committee.

Secondly, the data collection had to be carefully planned and implemented. These plans had to include the selection of random probability samples of students, the administration of the achievement tests to the students and of questionnaires to principals, teachers, and students. All these procedures were tested in a "dry run" before the main data collection.

Thirdly, the unique set of international data obtained by employing uniform methods of collection had to be duly processed in order to become amenable to the statistical analyses that had been planned. In most instances, responses were made on optical scanning cards. These were read and entered on to magnetic tape at the MRC Center in Iowa. The editing, sorting, filing and scoring took place at the IEA Data Processing Unit established at Columbia University, New York.

This Center also produced the student and teacher univariates as well as the reports summarizing the results for the participating schools. The multivariate statistical analyses were conducted by a second IEA Data Processing Unit established in Stockholm.

The construction of the Listening and Reading tests had in many respects to follow conventional paths, although the items had first to be tested in various linguistic contexts. It was decided that IEA would pioneer international Speaking and Writing tests which lent themselves to objective scoring but that these should be included as international options. Since the Speaking tests had to be administered individually and required the use of tape recorders, it was not feasible to test samples of the same size as could be covered by group-administered tests. In the case of the Writing tests, financial constrants associated with the scoring prevented data being collected from the full original sample. The scoring of the tape recordings from the Speaking sample and the open-ended Writing scripts took place in London, where Dr Clare Burstall of the National Foundation for Educational Research in England and Wales had set up a panel of scorers.

Needless to say, because of the quantity and complexity of the data, we were repeatedly confronted with unprecendented problems in the data processing. It is to the credit of the two Data Processing Units and the International Staff that these problems were finally resolved.

A project of this size and complexity cannot be conducted without close-knit teamwork, where expertise from both the international and national level is drawn upon. The project had to proceed in a methodologically uniform way according to a agreed-upon time-table. As could be anticipated, one of the hardest technical problems was to achieve methodological consensus with regard to achievement tests that could yield comparable results. Considering the character of the highly coordinated teamwork, which was established, it is difficult to acknowledge all the contributions from within the IEA family. I shall therefore confine myself to mentioning those who as authors, members of the International Committee or coordinators in special capacities, were instrumental in contributing to the project reported in this volume of the *International Studies in Evaluation* series.

Mr Lewis has as the Chairman of the International Committee been with the project from its inception. He is also the senior author of this book. IEA is indebted to him for all the time that he has put into the project, in spite of demanding commitments in his home country.

Dr Carolyn E. Massad of the Educational Testing Service, Princeton, co-author of the book, spent a year at IEA as a visiting Spencer Foundation Fellow. Her competence in statistical analysis of achievement test data contributed substantially to the planning and completion of the multivariate analysis for which she took particular responsibility.

The major part of the Six Subject Survey took place when Dr T. Neville Postlethwaite was the Executive Director of the project. His successor, Mr Roy W. Phillipps, has been actively involved in the complicated and tedious work connected with the statistical analyses and the reporting of the project. The editing of the present report, including the extensive network of contacts with the National Centers, has been the responsibility of Mrs Clotye Larsson. The various drafts of the report have been submitted to the National Centers for comments and criticisms. Their reactions have as faithfully as possible been incorporated into the final version.

I would like to commend Dr John R. Schwille, Research Officer with the IEA and one of the first Visiting Spencer Foundation Fellows, for his dedicated work in preserving the extensive set of data from this study in the Data Bank.

I would also like to extend our thanks to the members of the International Committee who are listed opposite the front page of the report.

The present report, as with other studies within the framework of the Six Subject Survey, has been brought to a successful completion thanks to the financial support that IEA has obtained from various sources. The international operating costs have been met by generous grants from the Bank of Sweden Tercentenary Fund, the U.S. Office of Education, the Ford Foundation, the Stiftung Volkswagenwerk, the Leverhulme Trust and UNESCO. The Swedish Government has, through the Office of the Chancellor of the Swedish Universities, provided data processing time. The University of Stockholm has been serving as the host of the IEA International Secretariat since 1969. Since 1971, when the Institute for the Study of International Problems in Education was established, the project has been accommodated on its premises.

Finally, the publication of this report has been made possible by a grant from the Bank of Sweden Tercentenary Fund.

It would, indeed, be tempting to try to highlight some of the major findings from the present study. I shall, however, leave this to the reader himself. Let me, in this connection, confine myself to emphasizing what I have repeatedly pointed out, that the IEA survey is *not* intended to be and should not be read as an international contest. The overall purpose is to identify social, economic, and pedagogical factors which account for differences between students, schools and national systems of education in learning a particular subject. I think it is justified to say that the IEA research has widened our perspective on the effect of formal schooling and the constraints set by social and economic factors. Apart from its contribution to our knowledge of the educational process *per se*, it has provided us with evaluation instruments and established procedures which can be employed in the field of developmental education. A valuable by-product, that also deserves to be mentioned, is the competence in applied educational research that has been brought to countries where an "infra-structure" of this kind had not been built up prior to the participation in the IEA survey work.

The subject-wise reporting in the series *International Studies in Evaluation* is of a rather comprehensive character and therefore only scratches the surface of extensive areas of study. As was pointed out above, the major aim has been to identify salient factors which explain differences between students, schools and systems. But studies in depth of particular problems, such as sex differences in achievements or the effect of the age of school entry on later performance, require partly other techniques of statistical analyses than those employed in the overall reports. Thus, further analyses have been conducted by Robert Liljefors, the IEA National Technical Officer for Sweden, and by Ian Dunlop, member of the International English Committee. Several other studies are under way, and still others are contemplated. A grant from the Spencer Foundation makes provision to bring to Stockholm each year during a five-year period two post-doctoral and two pre-doctoral Fellows. During their stay at IEA International, Fellows are encouraged to conduct studies for which they draw upon the IEA Data Bank.

It was considered of great importance that the unique set of data collected by IEA should be made available to the international research community by the setting up of a Data Bank. This has been done under a grant from the Ford Foundation. It is our hope that the Bank, of which replicas will be placed at various research centers around the world, will become a major source of data for research workers in the future as well as an asset in the training of researchers. For reasons of economy, we have not been able to print the instruments used in this survey. The instruments can, however, be obtained from the Educational Resources Information Center (ERIC); detailed information about the coding and scoring of the items can be found in the IEA Data Bank Manuals, available from IEA, c/o the Institute for the Study of International Problems in Education, University of Stockholm, Fack, S-104 05 Stockholm 50, Sweden.

Torsten Husén
Chairman of IEA

Author's Preface

After nine years the completion of the study of English as a Foreign Language is a welcome opportunity for the author to record his profound indebtedness to many of those directly associated with IEA at all levels and to some not so deeply involved with the direction of the Six Subject Survey. In spite of occasional and inevitable frustrations the members of the International Committee and especially the author of this report are grateful to the Council of IEA and particularly its Chairman, Professor Torsten Husén, for enabling us to participate in this exciting aspect of IEA activities, and to benefit from its interdisciplinary orientation. The willingness of so many scholars from several countries to contribute to the promotion of the study of the place of the English language in the educational systems of ten countries, was a continuing inspiration to those of us who were more directly associated with English than with other subjects. Dr T. Neville Postlethwaite, the first Executive Director of IEA studies, was intimately involved in the early direction of the English study. He more than any other helped to design the investigation and especially the questionnaires and other non-cognitive measures. His enthusiasms as much as his experience and knowledge carried the study over some of its more difficult periods. His successor, Mr Roy W. Phillipps, has been no less helpful and assiduous in guiding the production of the report and in ensuring its ultimate appearance. To Gilbert Peaker, the statistical consultant for the IEA projects, the author's own long standing personal indebtedness is profound. His willingness to put his great knowledge, his statistical expertise as well as his experience of schools at the disposal of those involved with the English study gave us confidence.

The intricate and laborious processing of the data was the responsibility of John Hall, Paul Barbuto, Kevin Dolye and Richard Wolf in New York, together with Mats Carlid and Birgit Cedheim in Stockholm. Richard Noonan acted as the intermediary between the English Committee and IEA administration and was instrumental in facilitating the preparation of early drafts of tests and questionnaires as well as the graphic material. The co-operation of the National Centers and their English Committees was a *sine qua non* of any possibility of success. They were most helpful in their criticism of suggestions and drafts as well as in the supply of materials. The National Technical Officers of the ten countries and the staffs of the schools are entitled to be regarded as equal contributors to whatever success the study may have achieved. Nor should we ignore the many thousands of students who undertook the tests and completed the questionnaires.

The staff at IEA International, Stockholm, at all times eased the work of the English Committee. They were especially helpful to the author during his more extended stays in Stockholm. Mrs Clotye Larsson has competently undertaken the difficult task of editing the final report.

The main responsibility for the preparation and design of the English study was undertaken by the English Committee without whose varying and complementary competences the task of the Chairman would have been immeasurably more difficult. This Committee was small and for that reason it may be invidious to refer to any particular members. Nevertheless, the contribution of Professor Clifford Prator, especially in ensuring the preparation of satisfactory tapes for the Listening Tests, must be mentioned. The meticulousness of Mr Ian Dunlop, who replaced Mr Pierre Morette when he resigned early in the investigation because of ill health, in reading the drafts of the report and in making perceptive suggestions for the improvement of the tests, is also greatly appreciated. Two contributors to the report, Dr Clare Burstall and Dr Carolyn Massad, who were not members of the English Committee made invaluable contributions to the study over a period of some time. Dr Burstall, a member of the French International Committee, helped to design the Speaking and Writing tests. She undertook the overall responsibility for the scoring of those tests and prepared the chapter which reports some of the findings. Dr John B. Carroll, Chairman of the French International Committee, prepared the scoring model for the Speaking and Writing Tests. Without the assistance of my co-author, Dr Massad, first in Stockholm and then after her return to the United States the report could not have been produced in its present form. Although she is named as an independent author of only one chapter of the Report her assistance in interpreting the statistical data was invaluable throughout, and her knowledge and experience of language testing permeates the whole of the Report.

When he was invited to become Chairman of the English Committee the author was at the Ministry of Education for England and

15

Wales, whose agreement to his participating in the study, involving far more time than they had envisaged, is gratefully acknowledged. Finally, to the very many who concurred with the author's importunate requests for guidance and assistance and who cannot be named here, and to my wife for her uncomplaining acceptance of my lengthy immurement among print-outs and tests, I offer sincere thanks.

E. Glyn Lewis
Senior Author

Chapter 1

Introduction: Some General Considerations

The present investigation of the place of English in the educational systems of ten very different countries drawn from Asia, Asia Minor, South America, Eastern and Western Europe was undertaken as part of a much more comprehensive program of comparative studies planned and organized by the International Association for the Evaluation of Educational Achievement (IEA). In so far as the English study was part of the general project, the design and development of the instruments used in the English study were subordinate to more widely embracing considerations and aims. The achievement tests in English as well as the questionnaires were developed with the intention of allowing conclusions to be drawn which might not affect the teaching of English specifically though they would be relevant to that subject. This does not entail that the criteria by which the tests should be judged need to be less rigorous than would be the case if only the teaching of English was involved, nor that the theoretical bases of the English investigation should be other than well founded. But the place of English in a general comparative project should be kept in mind in any evaluation of the measures which were developed.

In 1965 IEA inaugurated a cross-national study of achievement in Six Subjects—Science, Reading Comprehension, Literature, Civics Education, French as a Foreign Language and English as Foreign Language. It had embarked upon a study of Mathematics (Husén, ed., 1967) some time earlier, and the results were known before the Six Subject Survey got under way. Over 20 countries have been engaged in the total IEA project, though not all of them have participated in every study. The countries participating in the English study are Belgium (French Region), Chile, Federal Republic of Germany, Finland, Hungary, Israel, Italy, the Netherlands, Sweden and Thailand. The aim of the project is to identify factors which are thought to be closely associated with scholastic achievement. Among those which have been selected for consideration some variables characterize the systems of education (the size of schools, for example), some reflect the social and economic background, others the personal characteristics of students and some have had to do with the characteristics of teachers.

By taking account of differences in the organization of education as well as in the economic foundations of the educational systems, and relating those *input* differences to differences in the achievement of the students in the different countries, the *output* variables, it may be possible to arrive at some conclusions about the relative importance of educational and social considerations in formulating educational policy. Comparative studies which take advantage of information about the variability of both "input" and "output" variables and seek to determine their inter-relationships are of immense importance, but they necessitate inquiries in several disparate countries as well as in the several subjects which represent the broad spectrum of formal education. Foreign languages constitute an important area of the curriculum of secondary schools in most countries, and English is among the most studied of such foreign languages.

THE ENGLISH LANGUAGE ABROAD

The English language may be studied on any one of three socio-historical levels. First, it is the traditional language of countries like England, the United States and Australia, as well as of parts of Canada. Second, it is an ex-colonial language in other countries where the indigenous languages have remained strong, as is the case in India and some African nations. Here it continues to be used, but in partnership with the indigenous languages, and plays an important part in fundamental education in those countries. Third, it is one of the major "languages of wider communication" (Ferguson, 1966) and, as such, plays an increasingly vital role in higher education and in the instruction of those students in secondary schools who propose to enter the professions, especially those in science and technology. Because English is studied in the three socio-historical settings described above, as well as for some other reasons, the place of English in education is complex and more bewildering in the variety of its interrelationships with other areas of the curriculum than most other languages at present, or of the "common languages" of past civilizations such as Aramaic, Greek or Latin. English has also a greater extent of geographical distribution than most other modern languages. It is spoken as a mother tongue on four continents, and it is difficult even to hazard a guess at the ever increasing numbers who speak it as their second language. It has been suggested that English is the first language of over 250 million people, of whom 60 % live in the United States, over 20 % in the United Kingdom, with the remaining 20 % spread among Canada, Australia, New Zealand, South Africa and other former British and United States dependencies. Estimates of those for whom English is an auxiliary language vary between 50 and 150 million people. It is probable, therefore, that the language is spoken habitually as a first or auxiliary language by between 400 and 500 million people—over one seventh of the population of the world. This does not take into account those who have learned English as a foreign language.

However, the variety of relationships that English enters into with the other languages spoken and taught in the various countries cannot be expressed by any numerical statement. Even where English is the national language it may not be the mother tongue of a substantial minority of the population. In some parts of the world English competes with the languages spoken by immigrant groups and coexists with other indigenous languages—for example, with the Celtic languages in the United Kingdom, with the Amerindian languages in the United States, and with French in Canada. There are other countries where English is the mother tongue of only a very insignificant proportion of the population, and where it is not even an auxiliary language. If it is a part of the curriculum in such countries, it is strictly as a foreign language. However, even among these countries there are important differences. In some, where English is not spoken habitually by the native population, it is taught and used in the education of very large numbers of children from the time they enter school. This is true of some African countries. In others, such as Hungary and the USSR, English is taught and used to teach other subjects in the special foreign language schools. Some of the countries where English is taught as a foreign language share common historical and cultural associations with English-speaking countries; others do not. The former tends to be the case in Western European countries like the Federal Republic of Germany; but in Eastern Europe, parts of Asia and Asia Minor, the traditions and even the scripts are generally vastly different from those of English.

A great deal depends on the purposes for which English is acquired as well as upon the social and cultural affinities of those countries. In Thailand, for instance, as in Germany, English is the first foreign language. In Iran well over 90 % of pupils in secondary schools are taught English. In the USSR English is the first foreign language, in the sense that it is taught to more than half the school population who are taught a foreign language. In most Eastern European countries English is the first foreign language after Russian, which is obligatory for all students. In France at the end of the 1960's nearly 75 % of the school students studied English as the first foreign language, compared with 20 % who studied German and 5 % who studied languages like Spanish, Italian and Russian.

Even in those countries where English plays an important role there may be profound differences in attitude towards the language. In some—Sweden, for instance—the intention is to teach the language so as to enable the students who have acquired it not only to communicate by means of it but to enter as fully as possible into the spirit of the civilization, the culture as well as the literature associated with the language. In other countries the aim may not be so high. English may be taught essentially as an instrument of communication in everyday affairs or for the purposes of industry, science and commerce. Still other countries, for instance the USSR and its associated states, teach the language partly in order to compete with if not to neutralize the social, political and economic influences of English in developing countries.

Other differences arise from the fact that in many countries where English is taught as a foreign language a *second Language* is already taught to members of different linguistic minority groups. In some countries, such as Belgium, Luxembourg and Switzerland, the second languages are native to the country. Elsewhere the second language, as is the case with Russian in Hungary, is foreign to the country. In other countries a non-indigenous language, such as French in former French colonial territories, is not only the first foreign language to be taught but is also a frequently employed medium of instruction. It is regarded very much as a national language and is the mother tongue of large numbers of native born African students.

English is taught as a foreign language for different purposes, and there are different individual motives for learning it. Many students who, sooner or later will help to constitute an identifiable highly educated group will require a knowledge of English for the professions of law, medicine and the sciences. Others will wish to become technicians or to hold other positions, in which case they may be satisfied with a "working knowledge" of English. These are instrumental uses of English. However, it is doubtful whether any language, no matter how utilitarian the aims of the student, can be completely divorced from its associated literature, its intellectual milieu, and the social context in which it has been formed. The person who has learned English as a foreign language is unlikely to remain completely immune from the influence of that tradition and culture. This being so, it is doubtful whether testing "achievement in English" measures what a student receives from his instruction in that language unless it takes account of these cultural or non-instrumental values. Nevertheless, rightly or wrongly, "achievement" in its more restricted connotation is the basis of more general competence and the only aim of many students. The present study has been based on such assumptions.

English is taught as a foreign language to almost all students during basic schooling in some countries, such as the Netherlands and Sweden. Comparisons between such countries are therefore of particular interest.

THE RATIONALE FOR THE INVESTIGATION
OF ENGLISH AS A FOREIGN LANGUAGE

Though the study of English is an important feature of the curriculum in many countries it is not usually the most important. In some cases the teaching of a foreign language, including English, may be reserved for a minority. Why then, it may be asked, after the initial study of Mathematics was English selected by IEA to be among the first of the subjects to be investigated? The inclusion of a subject within the humanities adjusts the balance of IEA interest after Mathematics (Husén, 1967) and Science (Comber and Keeves, 1973). Also, the social fact of a world-wide "communications explosion," which is not without its influence on the teaching of most other subjects, suggests that a cross-national investigation of one of the most important aspects of that phenomenon, namely the teaching of a "language of wider communication" would be rewarding and perhaps necessary. We have noted some aspects of the place of English in the contemporary world and, if we add to these considerations the changes which have occurred in the teaching of English, such as the tendency to provide both more extensive and more intensive courses in the subject, the introduction of the language at progressively earlier ages, as well as the establishment of special schools where the foreign language is used as a teaching language—if we take all these into account, a cogent case for an international investigation of English can be established.

Furthermore, the changes which have been introduced into the actual teaching of a foreign language have hitherto been influenced less by advances in our understanding of the operation of social factors than by developments in psychology and linguistics. It is true that the study of the influence of the home, social class, the school and its neighborhood, as well as the broad national background—for instance the level of economic development, social mobility and linguistic homogeneity or heterogeneity—are usually taken into account in thinking about the general provision of education or changes in the curriculum regarded as a single unit (the macrostructure). But these considerations have received less attention in the investigation of the teaching of individual subjects (the microstructures), and least of all in studying the teaching of foreign languages, compared, for example, with the teaching of science. At the same time the teaching of foreign languages is governed less and less by the traditions of philology or even by "humanistic" values. Instead there is increasing evidence that specifically practical objectives related to the need to enrich social interaction and improve face-to-face communication are given greater weight in preparing syllabuses and articulating the aims of language teaching. This tendency has been reinforced by the general movement to make foreign languages available not only to a selected and élitist minority but to an increasing proportion of the school population, to the extent that in some countries English as a foreign language stands in almost the same position as science or mathematics. Such changes have meant a shift in the relative importance of the different categories of educational variables, whether pedagogic, linguistic, psychological or social. But as yet we know too little about the operation and the interrelationship of variables other than the psychological or linguistic. One of the advantages of studying the place of a foreign language cross-nationally is that the social factors are extremely varied and the interaction of the social factors differs from country to country, and the extent as well as the nature of their relevance to English also varies.

There is another advantage to including English as a foreign language (or any other foreign language) in a series of comparative studies once attention has already been given to mathematics. In several ways the two subject areas may be regarded as standing at opposite ends of a scale, whether we consider them as symbolic systems or as elements within the normal school curriculum. Mathematics and English are both symbolic systems, but the one (Mathematics) is highly formalized, self-consistent and universal, while the other (English) is a *natural* and historically determined system and therefore not entirely "well ordered", in spite of Chomsky's claim (1961, 1965), nor are the characteristics of any one language universal. Students in some countries may find it more difficult to obtain high scores in mathematics than students in other countries. But the differences are not attributable to the existence of different national systems of mathematics which influence the learning of mathematics. There is very little that is French about the mathematical processes which are taught in France, any more than there is a German characteristic of the learning of mathematics in Germany. Whereas the learning of English is influenced differently by French and German. There are some factors which influence the learning of a foreign language similarly, namely, differences in ability and motivation, differences in the provision made for the subject in school, etc. But whereas the student of a foreign language has an additional "linguistic variable" to contend with, namely, the influence of the native language, the student of mathematics does not have to overcome the difficulty of an addititional *national mathematics* variable. Unlike mathematics, English is not the same thing to all students everywhere, nor is what is said in English interpreted by students in the same way everywhere, nor understood by them identically and uniformly everywhere, as are the formulae which constitute the language of mathematics. The foreign language is to some degree acquired and interpreted in terms which have been impressed on and are uniquely characteristic of the native language. Mathematics is not taught even partly through a veil of national mathematical presuppositions or preconceptions. On the other hand, the sounds of English are heard somewhat differently, the meanings of English words are interpreted somewhat differently, and the structure of the language is apprehended somewhat differently according to the native language of the learner of the foreign language.

Furthermore, the universality of mathematics is recognized by its inclusion, like the mother tongue, from the earliest age and at almost all levels of schooling. A foreign language is usually an optional subject. More often than not it is included in the curriculum much later than such subjects as mathematics, literature and reading, or even science. Schools where a foreign language is introduced in the first grade are so much the exception in the large majority of countries that they tend to be regarded and administered as special schools. For these reasons the inclusion of English offered an interesting and valuable comparison with the IEA studies of Mathematics and Science.

23

WHAT IS A FOREIGN LANGUAGE?

Those who were concerned with developing this investigation of English began with the belief that, in spite of the increasing influence of films, radio, television and newspapers, a foreign language depends for its acquisition on actual classroom instruction far more than do most other subjects of the curriculum. Almost by definition a foreign language has little background support in the immediate neighborhood of the school or in the students' homes. A good deal of the mother tongue, elementary mathematics and the observation of natural phenomena (which is the introduction to science) may be observed and practiced before the child goes to school, in the case of normal children. Formal classroom instruction thereafter in those subjects is powerfully reinforced by their outside-of-school activities and by the quality of the environment. This is not the case with a foreign language. Naturally, there are differences between countries in this respect: some have closer contacts with English-speaking countries or are more exposed to mass communication in English and so may be said to enjoy an English "presence" more than other countries do.

The English language may not be native to a particular country and yet may not be "foreign" to it either. A history of colonial government or military occupation may have resulted in the language having a considerable support among the population as well as in playing a considerable role in everyday life. Though it would be wrong to make a categorical distinction between a foreign and a second language, it remains true that in acquiring a foreign language the student cannot rely on non-institutional forces which, however, can be relied on to advance the learning of the second language. Except in rare cases the foreign language is learned in school or not at all. The confusion about the necessity for a high degree of formality in teaching a foreign language arises from a failure to make explicit this distinction between a foreign and a second language. In the latter case the value of such formality is subordinate to the operation of informal environmental factors, while in the case of a foreign language there are few environmental factors available to influence learning.

Of course, even if we arbitrarily exclude the recognized classical languages, such as Latin and Greek, it is difficult in practice to draw the line between a first, a second and a foreign language. Not all languages acquired subsequently to the first or the mother tongue constitute a uniform set. Languages learned in mass bilingual situations (like French in the Flemish area of Belgium, or French and English in Quebec) are not to be identified with the French taught in England or the English taught in France, where the two languages lack such strong demographic support. French is not a foreign language to a Flemish-speaking child any more than it is to English-speaking children in Montreal or Quebec. A second language is ordinarily acquired under the stress of immediate environmental requirements; the same pressures, whatever the motivation of the student, do not exist for acquiring a foreign language.

The distinction is not without significance for the researcher and test administrator, or indeed for the teacher. For instance, the same psychological factors operate differently in the two kinds of language acquisition. Both a favorable attitude as well as positive motivation facilitate the acquisition of the second and the foreign language; but in learning the former, attitude is the more important since motivation is provided by the strength of the immediate influence of the ethnic group whose language is involved (Spolsky, 1969). Personal attitude towards the foreign language, because the relevant ethnic group is by definition remote, does not weigh so heavily as do more abstract considerations normally subsumed under the heading of motives (Pimsleur, 1964).

Since it is acquired relatively early in life a second language is more deeply embedded than a foreign language can be in the fundamental processes of child development. In teaching the second language, therefore, it is necessary to give adequate weight to what is known of the function of language in the development of concepts and social attitudes. A second language is often learned during the development of the basic conceptualizing processes, while the fundamental concepts themselves are being formed. The foreign language, on the other hand, is usually introduced when the processes have been firmly established and concepts have reached a considerable degree of maturity. These facts are reflected in differences between the objectives set for learning a second and a foreign language. Since it begins earlier and is part of the general social background, the learning of a second language is envisaged as necessary to the student's social integration and to the fulfillment of the aims of a society not only in education but in health, for example, and citizenship. On the other hand, the teaching of a foreign language usually stresses individual attributes, such aims as "broadening the child's horizons." From a developmental standpoint learning a foreign language is an enrichment rather than a fulfillment of personal qualities.

There are equally significant differences between the two types of language in the more limited area of language learning. To a considerable extent the lexicon of the second language is acquired by the association of new words with their concrete or situational references. In teaching the foreign language it may be advantageous to act on the same principle, but beyond the most elementary stages it is usually difficult if not impossible to do so consistently or with the same frequency. While the student of a second language *may* find it necessary to use various translation strategies, it is very rarely the case that a foreign language is learned without some associative transfer or translation taking place, no matter how much the teacher may seek to avoid the use of such processes. The student's universe of meaning has already taken shape and he cannot avoid making comparisons in the process of learning a foreign language. Finally, whereas in teaching a foreign language it is often thought necessary to emphasize explicitly and consciously to the student the primacy of speech, and to delay his introduction to reading and writing, the child acquiring a second language does not need to be reminded of that primacy since he tends to depend far more upon the influence of normal speech situations than on school instruction.

More important than any of the considerations we have advanced so far in seeking to distinguish between second and foreign language learning is the question of the linguistic norm the teacher and the student have to observe. Communities which use a second language tend to create their own norms for that language, however well standardized and widely used the language may be. The English spoken in most parts of Wales or Ireland is recognizably local, with more than stylistic differences to distinguish them from *standard* English. Although the best Canadian schools teach Metropolitan French, the French of Canada diverges markedly from Parisian, and even well-educated French Canadians are easily recognized, especially by native speakers of French elsewhere. In India a variant of English is spoken which may be unintelligible to users of other varieties of English who have not experienced the typically Indian contexts in which the particular idiom is used. Several variants of English may be found in parts of Africa previously ruled by Englishmen, and nearly all of these lack certain of the phonological contrasts which are present in virtually every native dialect of North America or British English. Students who are acquiring a second language are exposed to it in the form in which it is spoken locally. They slip back and forth between their mother tongue and the second language almost unconsciously, and this influences both languages markedly. The foreign language is not similarly affected. Whatever the obstacle which the structure of the first language presents to the student of the foreign language, his intention is always to speak the latter in the standard form and, where it is a "language of wider communication," to speak it in its universal standard form. Although it may be a pity that he does not learn both British and American variants, a Swedish child learning English is usually aware of both sets of norms. On the other hand, the Welsh or Irish or African child is aware first of all of the local variant of English, which has its own easily recognizable norms. If he goes on to learn the "universal standard" English, he does so in school. The teacher of a foreign language, for instance in Sweden, is not troubled by alternative norms to the same extent. Once he has decided on his norms, then so far as he is concerned, the norms are prescribed and stable and no conflict arises. The teacher of the second language is faced with a dual set of norms, one of them local and the other identical with that adopted by the teacher of that language as a mother tongue.

This investigation is concerned with English as a Foreign Language, and the form of English which the National Centers were unanimous in requesting should be adopted as the model is British English. It may be assumed therefore that all countries participating in this study adhere to the same norms in teaching English. This would not be the case if the investigation were also concerned with English as a second language, though there are prominent linguists and teachers who argue that it should be so (Prator, 1968). The present study is only a beginning. It cannot be complete until a comparison is established between the operation of the key variables in second language situations as well. It is only then that we shall be able to ascertain how decisive the social as opposed to the pedagogic considerations are in the teaching of a foreign language.

TESTING PURPOSES

With the intensification of interest in having foreign language learning begin at a comparatively early age and within a mass system of education, as opposed to a highly selective elitist system, as well as the appearance of vastly improved techniques and materials, it is only to be expected that there should also be a corresponding acceleration of interest in testing as well as in the principles which ought to govern testing. Furthermore, the expansion of the provision for testing students from several countries on the same items or batteries of tests, as in the *Test of English as a Foreign Language* (TOEFL), has meant that the importance of cross-national testing is also increasing. These considerations have influenced the thinking behind the present study, and it is hoped that it will make some contribution not only to understanding the place of English in several systems of education but also to refining the theory of language testing.

From the standpoint of members of the English Committee, one of the main advantages of cooperating in the more comprehensive IEA project was the possibility of pursuing testing objectives beyond those of immediate relevance to the total project, and of obtaining data which can be analyzed after the particular demands of that project have been satisfied. To clarify this, we need to explain what the International English Committee conceived to be the general as well as more specific objectives of foreign language testing, looked at in the context of cross-national and comparative studies. One way of looking at these objectives is to identify the groups or institutions that may be suitable or prospective recipients of the information to be elicited from the results of the tests. These may be students, teachers, administrators of local or statewide educational systems, counsellors or placement officers, school and college principals as well as research organizations. Educational publishers concerned with the preparation of improved course books and other materials will also be sensitive to the findings. Each will be looking for different things in the present study, and though it is impossible or at least unlikely that each will be satisfied to the same degree, it is hoped that most of them will find something relevant to their needs, because the tests and other instruments are specific in their intention and precise in direction. At the same time, the items belong to many different categories and necessitate the use of several testing techniques.

There is an observable hierarchy in the list of possible recipients or beneficiaries. For instance, while some information useful to the teacher may be relevant also to a research institute or an administrator, it is not equally apparent that everything which interests one will be of significance to the others. This consideration implies that a report of the testing results should be as specific as possible with respect to what and who is being tested, and allow as well for the possibility of data being interpreted at the highest level of generality. For instance, there is considerable interest at the moment in the possibility of identifying universals of language (Greenberg, 1963). If such an interest is productive, there is no reason why we should not be equally interested in the possible existence of universals of other forms of cultural and social behavior. Just as it may be possible that all languages possess common characteristics so it may also be the case that social systems reflect common universal traits, and that selected variables may operate identically across nations. Thus, the data of this study could be of interest at a high level of generality to social philosophers and sociologists as well as to those who are interested in the specifics of foreign language pedagogy.

Achievement testing has at least two major purposes, and the results of the present study may be used to satisfy both. First, testing serves as a yardstick to be applied at periodic intervals to satisfy teachers and administrators about the rate of progress of a particular set of students or about the comparative standing of two or more such groups. In some cases the groups may be selected according to identical criteria; or various selection criteria may be used to constitute different groups. For example, distinct groups may be selected on the basis of exposure to different methods and materials or varying amounts or distribution of instructional time. Secondly, achievement testing can be used as an aspect of teaching; teaching may be modified and possibly improved in the light of the results of specific tests. If these tests are sufficiently precise and directed to clearly specified areas of linguistic performance the teacher can, if he wishes, refine his classroom techniques to meet the difficulties revealed by the test performance of his students.

As a result of this study a considerable amount of information is available about the kinds of errors which students of English have committed, the relative importance of those errors, and the possibility that some errors may be restricted to only one linguistic community while others may be restricted to other language groups. It is equally possible to repeat at well-defined intervals the administration of the tests designed for this study so as to compare the performance of similar groups of students in the same country and across several countries. Only by using such a series of comparative studies will it be possible to form an adequate picture of the standard of English performance and the rate of progress of any particular group of students as well as the possible effect of changes in the English curriculum.

In looking at language testing it is important to note the problem of distinguishing between actual and potential achievement. Teachers and course designers alike might find it of interest to compare these two zones of achievement, since it would be useful in deciding the kind of language program suitable for a particular type of student and especially helpful in the assignment of students to different levels or methods of instruction according to their aptitude and revealed potential. Some countries are dubious about the value of tests of actual achievement, and Vygotsky (1934), in making his distinction between the two zones of intelligence (potential and actual), reinforced their reluctance. Aptitude testing has done relatively little to enable us to measure potential with confidence. Yet it may be possible that a selection of students drawn from very different social environments and exposed to a great variety of different influences, or to the same influences operating at very different levels of impact, can be compared in such a way that information, norms, can be made available about what may reasonably or realistically be expected from specified groups—for example, groups based on age, sex, place of residence (urban/rural), or length of exposure to English. Admittedly such a procedure may do little, if anything, to help a teacher handle a particular child whose actual performance is influenced by a larger number of variables than any one study can identify and measure; however, the information could enable the teacher to come to a more realistic judgement about what is reasonable to expect of students with characteristics similar to those of students in the norm groups.

Diagnostic language testing, one of the purposes of testing kept in mind for this study, has been covered to some extent in the references to the analysis of errors. There is no theoretical objection to the use of such an analysis to predict the probability of specific errors occurring in the learning of a particular language among students with specified native languages, something that "contrastive studies" claim to be able to do. There are types of error which arise from individual idiosyncrasy, of course, but those which are due to general linguistic and intellectual processes are more fundamental and more important for the teacher to be able to recognize. An attempt is made in a later chapter to categorize these general sources of error. However, the discussion is limited to meet the needs of the present report. Future researchers might help teachers and course designers to profit considerably by providing a more detailed analysis and discussion than is possible or called for here.

Tests can be devised to help teachers and researchers identify the ways in which students acquire languages, the areas of language usage among bilinguals, and the degree of dominance exercised by one language over another in the context of societal bilingualism or of foreign language acquisition. However, these objectives are not proposed for the present investigation. Nevertheless, the present study might help to elucidate the argument in favor of the distinction between a foreign and a second language, a distinction which may become crucial in several countries which have ambitious foreign language programs. Although they eventually decided not to participate in the present investigation, countries like the United States, England and Wales, and Australia have significant minorities with English as their second language. In the light of the present report they may wish to reconsider the possibility of undertaking joint or separate studies.

A further purpose of testing is the evaluation of the efficiency of a school system in so far as it concerns language teaching. Such an evaluation may be restricted to one country, in which case, if it is to serve any useful purpose, it would need to be a longitudinal or cross-sectional investigation. Or the evaluation may be instituted as a cross-sectional study in several countries, several school systems or several schools within any one country. If, as in the present study, achievement in language is related to a representative selection of important variables, such an evaluation could be of use, practically and theoretically, to administrators as well as researchers. Since the types of language courses in various countries are often markedly different in scope and organization, a comparative evaluation of this kind can also be employed to measure the success of cources in achieving specified goals. A major contribution of the English study to the total IEA investigation is that it helps to identify, measure and determine the relationships among significant social, linguistic and pedagogic variables.

This chapter has attempted to set out the considerations explicit in the thinking which guided the present investigation. The development of the tests, the strategy of testing and to a considerable extent the contents of the report need to be viewed in the light of these preconceptions.

REFERENCES

Chomsky, N. *Syntactic Structures*. The Hague: Mouton, 1957.

Chomsky, N. *Aspects of the Theory of Syntax*. Cambridge, Mass: MIT Press, 1965.

Comber, L. C. and Keeves, J. P. *Science Education in Nineteen Countries. An Empirical Study*. Stockholm: Almqvist & Wiksell, and New York: John Wiley, 1973.

Ferguson, C. "National Sociolinguistic Profile Formulas" in William Bright (Ed.) *Sociolinguistics*. The Hague: Mouton, 1966.

Greenberg, T. H. (Ed.) *Universals of Language*. Cambridge, Mass.: MIT Press: 1963.

Husén, T. (Ed.) *International Study of Achievement in Mathematics: A Comparison of Twelve Countries. Vols. I and II*. Stockholm: Almqvist & Wiksell and New York: John Wiley, 1967.

Lewis, E. G. *Linquistics and Second Language Pedagogy: A Theoretical Study*. The Hague: Mouton, 1974.

Pimsleur, P. *Underachievement in Foreign Languages*. IRAL 53, 1964.

Prator, C. H. "The British Heresy in TESL" in Fishman, J. A. (Ed.) *Language Problems of Developing Nations*. London: Wiley, 1968.

Spolsky, B. *Attitudinal Aspects of Second Language Learning*. (Mimeograph) University of New Mexico, 1969.

Vygotsky, L. S. *Myslenie i rech*. Moscow, 1934. (*Thought and Language* 1962, MIT Press, Cambridge, Mass.)

Chapter 2

Conduct of the Study and Development of the Instruments

The investigation of English as a Foreign Language was organized on three levels: that of IEA International, the National Centers with their English Committees in each case, together with the International English Committee. The present study is the product of the cooperation of the National Centers, the technical officers of IEA, especially T.N. Postlethwaite who guided the English Committee during the developmental stages and his successor, Roy W. Phillipps. The International English Committee consisted of teachers of English and research writers in linguistics. They represented all levels of education, primary, secondary, teacher training and university. The principal author, E. Glyn Lewis, served as Chairman, the other members being Ian Dunlop (Sweden), Esther Heitner (Israel), P. Morette (France), Agnes Niyekawa-Howard (United States), Rauno Piirtola (Finland) and Cliff H. Prator (United States). The main function of the Committee was to prepare cognitive and non-cognitive instruments as well as to advise other members of IEA who were concerned with more general aspects of the investigation on what might be feasible and required in order to integrate the English study fully with the Six Subject Survey. Without the National Centers a great deal would have been left undone or done less effectively. They supplied information when requested to do so as well as examples of syllabuses, course books and test items, especially passages for use in testing reading comprehension.

The International Committee met for the first time in November 1966 at the UNESCO Institute for Education in Hamburg. It considered the hypotheses to be tested and the variables about which information would be required. It also decided on the general specifications for the tests and set out a *pro forma* which the National Centers were invited to use in indicating their teaching objectives and their relative importance (Tables 2.1 and 2.2). In October 1967 the International Committee met again to consider the observations of the National Centers. In the meantime some members of the Committee prepared a provisional set of tests and questionnaires. These were considered by the Committee and their conclusions were referred again to the National Centers. The French and English Committees cooperated closely in these developments. In November 1968 the International Committee met for the third time to consider the results of the pretesting of the provisional instruments, which had occurred during the Spring of that year. The tests were again modified in the light of the pilot testing, score distributions and item analysis data which had been assembled by the Technical Officers. In October 1969 the Committee met for the fourth time to review the results of the second pretesting of instruments revised during the third meeting and during sesssions in which one or two members of the Committee met with the Technical Officers. Each pretesting program involved approximately 2 000 students drawn from several countries. The 1969 revised tests and other measures were submitted to the National Centers and were then approved by the Council of IEA at the beginning of 1970. Most of the tests as they were published consisted of some original items, some supplied by National Centers and modified by members of the Committee, and some obtained from released sources in research organizations and institutes. In some of the multiple choice items the behavior of the offered alternative answers varied from country to country. Where these differences did not appear to affect the validity of the item it was not considered to be a serious disadvantage (and probably was inevitable in any case). The tests for the two target populations, it was decided, should conform to the same basic pattern.

The tests, questionnaires, and manuals of guidance on the administration and scoring of the tests (where this was not undertaken centrally) were published and distributed to the National Centers in 1971. Where it was necessary the National Centers translated into the native language test-item instructions to students, as well as instructions to administrators. They processed the taped recordings necessary for the listening tests. The National Centers organized the conduct of the investigation in their own schools. The period between 1971 and 1973 was devoted to scoring the tests and collating the data produced by other measures. This was undertaken partly at Teachers College Columbia University and partly at IEA International at the University of Stockholm. The Speaking and Writing Tests were scored and reported upon at the National Foundation for Educational Research in England and Wales (London) under the direction of Dr Clare Burstall (cf. chapter 5, part 1).

THE DEVELOPMENT OF TEST SPECIFICATIONS

Determination of the Comprehensiveness of Tests

Two questions were considered concerning the nature of the proposed tests. First, how far they would seek to encompass the different aspects of the language such as phonology, grammar, vocabulary, and so on. Second, whether they would be selected so as to assess competence in all the skills—Listening, Reading, Speaking and Writing—or only some of them, and if so which. These two considerations became the coordinates of a frame within which the tests were to be constructed. The National Centers were invited to make their observations and the *pro forma* in Table 2.2 was circulated to them. The resultant decisions affecting test development are indicated below.

Phonology. The Listening and Speaking tests would assess the student's acquaintance with the sound system of English including segmental units such as vowels and consonants, together with their relationships and distributional patterns as well as intonation. Phonological elements would be tested not in isolation but as parts of meaningful stimuli. In accordance with the views expressed by all the Centers, the model to be used would be British rather than American English.

Writing. Students would be tested for their ability to understand the Roman script and English orthography. In addition to reading tests, exercises in dictation would be given. The understanding of different kinds of prose, complex and abstract styles, as well as the ability to produce free composition would be tested.

Grammar. Students would be tested for their ability to understand and use grammatical signalling devices, such as inflectional affixes, word order and functional operatives in simple and complex contexts. No specified selection or grading of structures was contemplated.

Vocabulary. The range of the student's vocabulary, both active and passive, would be tested in context. For the same reason that no

35

specified system of selecting and grading structures was contemplated, the selection of the vocabulary would be undertaken in consultation with the National Centers.

Literature and Culture. The desirability of testing knowledge about the English language, English literature and its related culture and history would be determined by the consensus of the participants. However, whether knowledge of English literature were tested or not, it was proposed to obtain information about such questions as attitude to English, and student aims for learning the language by means of questionnaires.

Consideration of Teaching Objectives

To ascertain what the National Centers thought of the above decisions for specifications as well as to obtain information about the relative importance of possible objectives for English teaching, a *pro forma* was issued. Table 2.2 shows the *pro forma* completed by one country. When issued, the *pro forma* had only Column 1 filled in. Column 1 indicates the objectives. Each country responded only in Columns 3 and 5 using a declining three point scale to indicate how important each of these major and subordinate objectives were considered in their country. Columns 2 and 4 give the rank ordering of the objectives as reflected by an approximate consensus among all countries. A declining scale from one to six has been used for the major objectives and a similar scale from (a) to (g) for the subordinate objectives.

The areas where disagreement was most apparent among the countries was that of developing favorable attitudes. There was hardly any difference in the responses regarding the two Populations separately, except that for Population IV as compared to Population II some countries gave greater prominence to reading passages of different levels of abstraction and less prominence to reading short passages intensively. Further, some countries gave greater prominence in Population IV to free composition, reproduction and summarizing and the recording of oral conversation. All these changes in emphasis were taken to represent an anticipation in the National Centers that the level of ability in English would be higher in Population IV than in II. (For definitions of Populations, see page 52.)

Following a consideration of the statements of behavioral objectives, the tests were devised to assess ability to *use* the language without any attempt to measure *knowledge* of it. Since several countries did not agree that it was any part of the English teacher's task to create favorable attitudes, whether towards the language, the people or the literature, and since it was argued that such attitudes emerge as by-products of satisfactory teaching rather than as a direct consequence of specific attention to attitude formation, it was decided to rely entirely on questionnaires to elicit information about attitudes. Nevertheless, it was interesting to note how far disagreement about the appropriateness of creating attitudes can extend. Countries which place a considerable stress on the value of English in the curriculum and may create special schools for the purpose of ensuring high standards in the language, may be indifferent to the importance of encouraging a favorable attitude towards *English* (as distinct from *learning English*) as a factor in producing higher achievement.

Contribution of Pretesting

National Centers supplied well over 1 500 items and 30 passages of prose of widely ranging interest and difficulty. The great majority of these materials served to show the importance which was attached to Reading Comprehension as a measure of achievement in English even in those countries where reading was not regarded as the main teaching objective. During the process of collating material into the tests it became clear that the items submitted varied so much in quality and the numbers contributed by different countries varied so greatly, to say nothing of differences between countries in type-preference, that the possibility of constructing the ultimate test on a representative basis had to be abandoned. Nevertheless, the pretesting and the discussions of the rationale of the tests meant that each National Center was able to safeguard the interests of its own students and ensure that the tests were appropriate to the kind of courses they had followed.

Before the pretesting and in order to identify difficulties of interpretation and ambiguities in the tests and instructions, some of these tests were administered to a small sample of Welsh-speaking children for whom English was a second language. Further, National Centers were asked to note possibilities of general "culture or social bias" in the tests or illustrations. The original intention to have "back translation" of instruction, to insure uniformity of interpretation, was abandoned because of the time the process would take and the difficulties of organizing it. Pretesting took place in each of the participating countries. Approximately 150 students took part in the pretesting program in each country and every country sampled tests of Reading, Listening, Speaking and Writing.

The pretesting data which were available to the English Committee for the individual items included indices of the difficulty and power to discriminate between good and poor students. In some instances incorrect responses (distractors) were selected more frequently than correct responses by students who otherwise achieved high levels of success on the tests. Such items were discarded. Other items were rejected because no information was supplied in the test analysis, or because they were either too easy (having over 90 % correct response), or too difficult (below 20 % correct response), or because they were reviewed adversely by the National Centers. Nevertheless, the Committee did retain some items which were open to slight criticism, provided they could be improved, according to whether they were required to maintain a balance between types of tests reflecting important aspects of English or important behavioral objectives. These retained items were not pretested further. The operation of a too rigorous criterion of acceptability of items would have resulted in vocabulary tests, for instance, having a preponderant weight in the total battery. The Committee wished to provide not simply an accumulation of test items brought together for this single purpose, but a single balanced instrument as well organized as possible. In such a test, the control of different aspects of English, including vocabulary, grammatical structures and the sound system, together with the different skills required to handle these aspects, such as Listening, Speaking, Reading and Writing, would need to be related in some coherent fashion.

CONCERNS RELATED TO DEVELOPMENT OF TESTS

Theoretical Problems

Some General Differences among Participating Countries. The considerable differences known to exist between the countries in respect of the place of English affected the development of the tests and questionnaires. For instance, it was envisaged initially that the English study would embrace such countries as the United States, Australia and Britain as well as the ten already listed. In these three countries English is taught to a few students as a foreign language, to many more as a second language and to the great majority as the mother tongue. Had these countries participated an additional major factor would have affected the test design. For instance, it would have been possible and perhaps necessary to test children well below 14 years of age; and the range of test difficulty for the two existing target populations would have had to be extended well beyond its present limits. The fact that in the ten countries which continued to participate English is taught as a foreign rather than as a second language reduced but did not eliminate the complexity of the situation. In some countries English is used to teach some other subject(s) if only to a slight degree. Only some of the ten countries share historical associations with the English-speaking world, so that differences in motivation for acquiring English may be reflected in the types of courses the students pursue. Such differences are associated with the fact that in some cases English is the first foreign language offered to students, in other cases it is the second, while in one or two countries English is a required subject for all students. In some countries where English is taught to the majority of secondary students there may be a second indigenous national language which they are expected to acquire. The age at which English is introduced, the amount of time allotted to the subject each week as well as the type of training undertaken by teachers of English also differ greatly from country to country. If the tests of achievement were to be even minimally appropriate in such varying contexts they would need to be as simple as possible. They had to be true tests, aimed at as wide a range of achievement as the varying environmental circumstances of English pedagogy would necessitate, and refer to only the basic competencies.

Differences in Native Languages. The most critical problems arose from the fact that learning English presents different problems, or the same problems in different dimensions, to speakers of different native languages. The problem of transfer from the act of using the mother tongue to learning another language is central. It is not simply upon his ability to acquire a new skill, new knowledge or a new understanding of existing knowledge that a student is assessed, as might be the case with other subjects; he is assessed for his success, also, in overcoming deeply ingrained habits represented by his possession of the native language. The student of a foreign language is not asked to compete in a race on the flat so much as in a steeplechase where, moreover, the obstacles vary in height and difficulty for each student according to the distance of his native tongue from English. There can be no doubting the fact that the characteristics of one language influence the ease or difficulty with which a subsequent language is learned. Linguists differ in their assessment of the nature and value of the techniques of contrastive analysis which are associated with the prevalence of linguistic interference, and it is possible to adopt one of two strategies of testing according to the weight one attaches to the relevance of the phenomenon.

It can be argued that errors of learning arise from so many sources that it would be wrong to build a system of testing on the existence of one source, however influential. Over-generalization, ignorance of rule restrictions, incomplete application of rules and false hypotheses concerning the language to be learned are all sources of error, and there is little evidence to suggest that they are less important than the influence of the first language. One testing strategy, therefore, is to assume that the only linguistic variables of which the test needs to take cognizance are those which characterize the target language and to ignore all extrinsic sources of error. This alternative is based on the assumption that so far as English is concerned all students start from scratch and are faced with exactly the same linguistic obstacles. It is also based on the belief that any possible influence exerted by the native languages will, overall, be neutralized by the comprehensiveness of the test items and by the probability that positive and negative interference will tend to cancel each other if a sufficiently large number of items are used.

The case for a second, or alternative, strategy was pressed by several of the National Centers, which maintained that the discriminating power of a test is measured simply and precisely according to its selection of items which reflect aspects of English which contrast with or are lacking in the native tongue. The tests, they felt, need to be point-specific in relation to the contrasting aspects of the two languages, English and the mother tongue, where they diverge and only to those aspects. The acquisition of a foreign language is conceived, then, as the mastery of features which are unlike those of the mother tongue. One necessary deduction from this argument is that a uniform set of tests to be applied internationally cannot be equally valid in all countries, and that only tests which have been validated for each separate language community are permissible.

One National Center maintained that on the phonological level the tests for its students should concentrate on such consonant sounds as the sound /ð/ in "breathe" and /r/ in "ring," together with such vowel sounds as /ʌ/ in "cup" and /ə/ in "ago," which do not occur in their native tongue. Other differences such as in the syllabic structure of the two languages resulting in the pronunciation of class as /kəlɑːs/ and of practice as /pəræktis/, as well as other English consonant clusters, would need to be specified in the tests. Since neither gender, which has a place in the English language, nor the rule concerning sequence of tenses is a feature of the particular language of that Center it was suggested that these aspects of English should occupy a prominent place in the tests. Another National Center identified differences in orthography as the main problems of its students, its own orthography being largely phonemic and regular. Such instances could be multiplied from the very full and valuable observations contributed by the National Centers.

Apart from the extreme difficulty of producing within our terms of reference an international test along these lines—a purely pragmatic consideration—there are several theoretical justifications for the Committee's choice of the first testing-strategy mentioned above. In the first place, to adopt a system of contrastive testing places a premium on the contribution which contrastive analysis may make to teaching or the preparation of materials, and there is no unanimity among equally knowledgeable teachers and linguists that such a contribution deserves to be so distinguished. Even if contrastive analysis did merit the distinction, some countries participating in the study do not give it great prominence, and the present study is concerned with the situation as it is—not as theoretically it should be. Then again, if the errors in these tests are to provide objective data for future analysis the corpus should not be distorted artificially by the adoption of one principle for selecting items. It can very well be argued that contrastive testing is only one component of general error analysis. For these reasons the Committee came to the view, on practical and theoretical grounds, that it would be wrong to give precedence to testing only for purposes of contrastive analysis.

Differences in Student Exposure to English. Another consideration weighed by the Committee was the fact that although students in any one population would be within the same limited age range, they would not all have studied the language for the same or even comparable lengths of time. In testing the Mother Tongue, Mathematics and to a lesser extent Science, one is justified in assuming that within the participating countries age tends to reflect the length of the student's exposure to the subject, and that the level of his psychological and conceptual development tends to coincide with the stage at which the student is pursuing the subject. This cannot be assumed in the case of a foreign language because there may be a difference of four or more years of exposure among students of the same age. Since one of the objects of the testing was to measure the effect which different lengths of exposure might have on the achievement of students of the same

41

age, it was not possible to design tests which took this discrepancy into account. At the same time, tests which might be difficult for students with only two years of English might be too easy for others of the same age with longer periods of study behind them. This accounts for the fact that the tests the Committee decided upon having an extremely wide range of difficulty.

Differences in Cultural Background. Even when all students being tested have the same mother tongue, misconstructions of the test items or misunderstanding of the instructions are more than likely. In such cases, however, these misunderstandings tend generally to conform to a set pattern and can be remedied or taken into account in the final assessment. Students from different countries and possessing different educational backgrounds come to the same tests with different presuppositions, which may affect the results, however unbiased the test items may be. The Committee had two problems to consider: how to provide a more than normally adequate context for the items, without at the same time specifying the response, and how to avoid, as much as possible, any culture bias in the items and the accompanying illustrations. Culture bias in tests will continue for a long time to be a contentious issue. It is unlikely that all researchers, teachers and test designers will be equally satisfied whatever test strategy is adopted. One method is to relate the nonlinguistic content of the tests to the English-speaking cultural setting, in this case British, choosing illustrations and voices and so on which would reflect British characteristics unequivocally. The assumptions underlying this alternative are that most countries adopt the procedure in their course books and display materials, and that one of the objects of teaching the language may be to inculcate an understanding, however critical, of the "English way of life." This is not a valid assumption for the present study, however, because some of the participating countries are concerned almost exclusively with English as a "language of wider communication," a vehicular language, and little with English as the key to a national culture or way of life.

The second alternative, and the one adopted by the Committee, is to relate the nonlinguistic content to the lowest common denominator of culture traits—a kind of "basic culture content" common to all countries, and with which it is reasonable to expect that most students are familiar, irrespective of their national culture or native language. There are disadvantages in adopting this alternative: first, the test items may appear to be contrived and mechanical; and second, the students of some countries are not being tested over the entire range of their achievement in English which includes, for them, an understanding of more than the phonology, the grammar and the vocabulary of English.

One of the most difficult questions arising from national differences among students involves attitude to the idea of testing achievement at all. It is acknowledged that students possess different levels of motivation according to their different cultural backgrounds and interests, the economic orientation and the level of industrial development of their countries as well as possible historical association of their country with England or the United States. However, a country may not be economically advanced, and yet, because of its realization of the importance of English in promoting such development, it may accord the teaching of the language as important a place in its curriculum as the most advanced countries do. Economic factors help to motivate students to learn English. Furthermore, scores on identical tests may reflect not only the linguistic attainment of students, or the level of their educational motivation, but also the degree of competitiveness which may be acceptable to a particular country. The present study is fortunate in that most of the participating countries belong to a fairly homogeneous group as far as economic development is concerned, so that they tend to look at achievement through the same spectacles. But this is not as true within a country as it is of the countries taken as a group. In Israel, for instance, students are drawn from a large number of immigrant groups coming from very diverse European, African and Asian countries. Thailand is composed of several indigenous minorities whose attitudes differ towards education and other aspects of society.

Different Attitudes to Testing Techniques. The IEA countries adopted different attitudes towards the use of certain types of tests and varied in their experience of using certain types of testing equipment. The educational traditions of some countries, the training of their teachers and the attitude of administrators have produced certain restrictions on the use of particular testing techniques. For instance, the attitude to objective testing and to the use of multiple choice items in language tests has not been favorable in some countries, partly because of the fear that humanistic aspects of teaching and the freedom of the individual teachers to pursue their own methods of teaching might be endangered by the effect which the adoption of objective techniques might have. While France was represented on the English Committee this was expressed strongly. Sweden, while not objecting to multiple choice tests in principle, was dubious about the possible adverse consequences that the use of incorrect alternatives among the responses might have on the learning of English. Other countries that did not object to multiple choice items wished to include dictation and translation also, because these were the staple of their testing systems. In addition to the question of testing techniques, some countries questioned the justification of testing aspects of English which they were not accustomed to include in their test repertoires. This was particularly the case with intonation.

Problems in Selecting the Vocabulary and Grammatical Structures. In selecting the features of the language to be included in cross-national tests, those concerned with testing English as a Foreign Language are not in the same position as those concerned with, for instance, French. There is not the same assurance that the principles on which English vocabulary or grammatical structures are selected will be equally acceptable in all countries since there are no agreed criteria of selection. There is not the same centralized agency for the promotion of English abroad as there is for French. Furthermore, there are at least two major diffusion centers, Britain and the United States, each exemplifying different English-language norms. There is considerable disparity in the choice of vocabulary and grammatical structures after the most elementary levels of English foreign language courses. This became apparent during the analysis of the contents of course books supplied to the Committee by the National Centers. The *a priori* adoption of any one criterion of selection would favor some countries and disadvantage others. For this reason the Committee decided to adopt an empirical approach. The observations of the National Centers on the linguistic content of the items were invited at each stage, and the selection was modified in the light of criticism received, so that the vocabulary and grammatical structures which are included reflect a consensus.

Decision to Categorize Items. Eventually it was necessary to decide whether to categorize types of items or to design a large number of items distinguishable mainly or only in terms of difficulty. Eventually the English tests were developed so as to first identify items according to two categories; one focused on aspects of English, tenses for instance, or number or voice, while the other focused on levels of the English language, namely vocabulary, grammar and phonological features. In addition, the items were categorized according to two test techniques; one was intended and designed as far as possible to identify a specific feature (point specific), for instance the specific features of grammar; the other required a more general acquaintance with the English language (global), for instance, the comprehension of sentences or longer passages where the success of the students depended on the equal understanding of several aspects of English. The two ways in which items were categorized are not mutually exclusive. Although items which are meant specifically to assess control of identifiable grammatical features are excluded from the group meant to test control of vocabulary, items in both these groups can be classified as either a global or point specific type test item. It was recognized all along that the categories established for these tests could not be absolute—all tests made use of vocabulary obviously, but the tests are designed in such a way that when vocabulary is being tested the grammatical component of the item is minimized, and that when the grammatical feature is being tested the vocabulary component is made so simple as not to constitute a significant test variable in that item. Similarly an item which is directed specifically at the understanding of a tense form, for instance, needs to be placed in a sentence the whole of which would need to be understood. However, although a point specific test item is to some small degree also a test of general understanding of English, there is a marked difference between such items and those where the whole point of the item is to assess the ability to understand the purport of what is said or written, as in a reading comprehension item.

Practical Problems

Testing Time Needed. The international nature of the testing program, particularly the diversity of languages represented by the ten participants, the very large number of schools and students involved, and the fact that many schools would be testing more than one subject, made it necessary to produce tests that could be administered easily and would take up as little time as was consonant with the requirements of validity and reliability. These considerations were reinforced by the expectations, which were borne out in fact, that the processing of such a large amount of data would not be easy. So far as concerns the timing of the tests, all four sets—Reading, Listening, Speaking and Writing—were divided into sections according to the major categories of items. As a result of the two pre-testing exercises these sections were allocated sufficient time to enable the great majority of students to complete the test. The use of multiple-choice testing as the principal testing method was necessitated by the requirements already discussed, even though several participants were anxious to avoid the method, for several different reasons. Differences in experience in handling such tests may have contributed to some of the between-country differences in scores. Unlike the effect of other variables the effect of this could not be taken into account in the present program, but it should be in the minds of all those who will be interested in interpreting the results.

Use of Tape Recorder. The Listening and Speaking tests involved the use of tape recorders. Apart from the fact that some of the ten countries could deploy only a very few of these among the schools drawn into the sample, many teachers, even if they were accustomed to using them in teaching, felt they might do less than justice to their students in adopting tapes for testing. It was more difficult to handle the Speaking test than the Listening test, and it was decided for these reasons, among others, that the Speaking test (like the Listening and Writing test) should be an optional part of the total testing program. All the non-objective items were scored centrally.

Problem of Oral testing. Many of the students taking part in the IEA study had never been exposed to oral testing. The English Committee decided, in order to minimize the disadvantages from which students might suffer, that students should be given ample opportunity to work through untimed practice items with their teachers, who would be encouraged to prompt them as might be necessary during the practice period. All test instructions were given in the native language.

Clarity of Pictorial Materials. It is difficult to provide unambiguous pictorial material, and the experience of the English Committee verified this. The original material had to be discarded because of frequent misinterpretation. Finally, very simple black and white sketches were used to avoid ambiguities and yet measure what was intended. Pictorial material connected with free composition was less difficult to devise than that which was needed for testing grammatical structures.

Timing between Items. Some difficulty was experienced in the timing of pauses between elements in the stimulus questions. If the pauses were made too short, able students attempting a complex and possibly long response would not be able to complete their answer. If the pauses were made too long, students might become confused and attempt to elaborate a correct, though possibly short response.

Scoring Free-Response Materials. Possibly the greatest difficulty arises from the scoring of open ended and free composition responses. Because of the possibly subjective scoring problems which arise in such cases it was decided to employ a small team of experienced native speakers of English for all free-response items. As a check on the stability of scoring standards, each member of the team was given periodically a random sample of tapes and scoring scripts scored by other members of the team, as well as a random sample of material that he himself had scored previously. Observations on the practical difficulties arising from the Speaking and Writing tests are commented on by Dr Clare Burstall in Chapter 5.

Finally, questions arose concerning the handling of the noncognitive aspects of the inquiry. Theoretically, direct observational techniques would have had many advantages but these were ruled out for practical and economical reasons. It would have been an advantage as well to identify particular groups of students with particular teachers, but again the scale of the investigation as well as the simultaneous testing of several subjects in the same schools, involving a sampling of teachers which cut across subjects, made this impractical also. Once it was decided to use questionnaires the problem of what to include was what concerned the English Committee most, since the form and scoring of the questionnaires were handled by the technical officers. One of these content problems focused on the investigation of methods of teaching English, which the Committee regarded as central variables. Although there are several items in more than one questionnaire which concern aspects of method there is no single instrument devoted to that aspect of the inquiry. The Committee was dissuaded from preparing such an instrument by the advice it received from those who had been involved in the Mathematics Study.

FORMULATING HYPOTHESES

Like most investigations of this nature and complexity, the English study was initially conceived and developed within a framework of "informed hunches" or intuitions which had been generally approved by the experience of teachers and linguists and modified by the conclusions derived from previous research on language learning. These intuitions gradually crystalized into hypotheses, but it should be stressed that the relative importance attached to hypotheses was influenced by the overall aims of IEA. The opinions of teachers and linguists founded on experience can in some cases be expressed as relations to be expected among the measures in the study. If these relations actually occur they strengthen the evidence supporting the opinions. If they do not occur, then their absence weakens the support, unless there is reason to think that their failure to appear may be a consequence either of the sample being too small or the measures being too inaccurate. This being the case, we should not be too ready to stress the power of the conclusions arrived at in this study. Nevertheless the assumption to which we have referred is fundamental to all others. The status of the other hypotheses, whether specific to English or of a more general nature, are subordinate to this major assumption.

The English Committee was interested in the achievement predictions based on the consideration of three main categories of variables. The first set of variables concerned individual students and their differences. Included here are such things as student attitude towards schooling and learning English and toward the related culture; student expectation of further education and the uses to which English might be put in furtherance of the expectation; factors related to the socioeconomic level of the student's home, community and country; parental attitudes towards education and towards English; the linguistic environment of the student's home and neighborhood; the point of time at which the student begins learning English; the intensity of the student's instructional program in English; the type of school program which the student followed; the opportunities available for participation in English activities.

A second major category concerns the school. Here are included such variables as the type of school, its composition as to the sex of students and the types of programs provided; the location of the school and the amount of support in the way of inspection and advice which was made available; the type of teacher employed, e.g., specialist or non-specialist; the student–teacher ratio.

Finally, the English Committee was interested in predictions concerning the relationship of teacher characteristics and student achievement. Here the variables are related to classroom practice, e.g., grouping for instruction; use of the mother tongue in teaching English; the emphasis given to various aspects of language instruction such as teaching grammar; the early or later introduction of reading and writing; the relative importance attached to encouraging fluency or correctness in speech and writing; the nature of the teacher's training and the length of experience; the availability of opportunities for direct contact with English-speaking countries.

In addition to being interested in determining which variables contributed most towards predicting achievement, the Committee were interested in some purely linguistic and psychological considerations. For instance, it was hoped that an analysis of errors in Reading, Listening, Speaking and Writing English would provide information concerning how students learned English and the most frequent hazards they encountered.

In order to validate these predictions and to obtain a comprehensive picture of the status of English in the systems of education of the ten countries, the Committee outlined the kind of information which it thought relevant and necessary, in addition to the data concerning levels of achievement. The outline of this information is set out below:

I. Information Concerning National Characteristics
  A. General
    1. Coverage of educational system
      a. Age of beginning school
      b. Percentage of each age group attending school
      c. Expenditure on education
      d. Degree of industrialization and economic development
    2. Organization of curriculum
      a. Subjects taught
      b. System of options including that affecting the choice of English
      c. Degree of centralized control of syllabuses and courses
      d. Degree of centralized control of teachers
    3. Types of assistance to schools
      a. Nature of consultancy or inspection support
      b. Neighborhood support for education—museums, etc.

  B. Linguistic Background
    1. Languages spoken in the country and size of language groups
    2. Social factors affecting the teaching of English
      a. Types of English contact—media, tourism and trade
      b. English in professional life and industry
      c. English in higher education

3. General aims for English in the country
   a. As a vehicular language
   b. As an academic pursuit
   c. As a key to understanding English culture
   d. For administrative reasons
4. Proportion of students learning English at each stage of schooling, and proportion of those who take English as a first/second foreign language

II. Information Concerning School Characteristics
   A. Types of school
      1. According to program
      2. According to sex composition

   B. Method of recruitment to school, or school selection
      1. Public/private
      2. Denominational/state
      3. Neighborhood school or not

   C. Location of school—urban/rural

   D. Size of school

   E. Size of class on average

   F. Number of staff

   G. Composition of class—whether mixed ability or homogeneous

   H. Organization of curriculum
      1. Number of languages offered
      2. Proportion of students taking English
      3. Whether English is optional or obligatory at any stage
      4. Length of English course in years

   I. Extra curricular activities affecting English—e.g., English Society

III. Information Concerning Teacher Characteristics
   A. Teacher training
      1. Proportion of time given to language teaching method as part of course
      2. Inservice training of teachers of English—courses and conferences

   B. Individual teacher characteristics
      1. Age
      2. Sex

3. Qualifications and experience
4. Intensity of teaching task in English
   a. Number of classes
   b. Proportion of time given to English teaching
5. Attitude
   a. Towards English
   b. Towards aspects of English method
   c. Towards behavioral objectives, e.g., relative importance of reading and speaking English
   d. Towards time devoted to classroom preparation and correction of English homework
6. Membership in English teacher's association, attendance at inservice sessions, visits to English speaking countries, etc.

IV. Information Concerning Student Characteristics
   A. Age and Sex

   B. Home background
      1. Socioeconomic status of parents
      2. Attitude of parents towards English and towards education
      3. Home support for English, e.g., English books, parental help in English homework, etc.

   C. Attitude
      1. Towards career possibilities
      2. Towards schooling
      3. Towards English language and English culture
      4. Towards various aspects of English, e.g., reading as compared with speaking

   D. Aspirations for use of English in profession or for general purposes, etc.

   E. Age of first exposure to English, outside school contact with English, e.g., visits to English-speaking countries

   F. Amount of time devoted to English in school and in doing homework

V. Information Concerning Native Languages—Observations on possible differences between English and the national languages as they are found to affect the learning of English

51

SAMPLING FRAMEWORK AND TARGET POPULATIONS

Total Sample

The English Committee, conforming to the wishes of the IEA overall planners, was originally interested in three age groups: 10-year-old, 14-year-old and preuniversity grade students. The intention to test the first group was abandoned because the number of 10-year-old students who had been taught English for at least 18 months was not large enough to ensure a satisfactory sample. A sample of the students in the remaining two groups was tested. Because the success of the present study depended on the samples chosen being a good estimate of the total population, and because most countries have a policy of promoting students according to age, it was decided to draw samples from specified age groups. However, the use of the age sample posed some problems for those countries where promotion was determined by achievement, because students of the same age might be found in different grades. Further, it was also necessary to test and question in the preuniversity group those who had studied English for at least two years at any point in their school careers, including those who specialized in the subject as well as those who were not at present pursuing English courses or, if they were, did not propose to specialize. Therefore, although age was the criterion for sample selection, the sampling procedures were by no means simple. Certain adjustments were necessary for obtaining an adequate, representative sample in each country.

The target populations were, first, *Population II*, consisting of all students aged 14.0 to 14.11 currently studying English in full-time schooling but excluding mentally handicapped or disturbed children. This population was decided upon because it was the last point in the school systems of most countries where 100% of the age group remained in school. The second target population, *Population IV*, consisted of all students in the preuniversity grades in full-time schooling who were either specializing in English or who had studied it previously for at least two years. In addition to these two groups, Finland, Hungary, Sweden and Thailand included an optional group, *Population III*, which consisted of students in full-time schooling at a major terminal point in the school system between the Population II and Population IV level. The composition of Population III differed from country to country. Sweden, for instance, included in

Population III students who were in Grade 9, reserving for Population II those who were in Grades 7 and 8. This report does not discuss the study of the results of testing Population III, partly because the composition of the group was not consistent across countries, but also because too few countries included them in their investigation. The cognitive tests administered to Population III were identical with those for Population II, although supplementary national options were included in some countries.

The sampling procedures were complicated by the lack of initial information about which schools contained students taking English as a Foreign Language. Consequently it was suggested that the first step should be to draw stratified samples of schools by the same procedure as was used for the Science study, but large enough to leave a sample of reasonable size after the selected schools subsequently found not to contain such students had been discarded. If the sampling design kept a constant overall sampling fraction, as for the Science study, every student taking English would have the same chance of appearing in the sample. Each National Center prepared its own sampling plan, which was checked by the International Sampling Referee, (see Peaker, 1975), before it was finalized and the schools approached. The plan was designed according to the advice set out in IEA Bulletins and discussed at the meetings of the National Technical Officers. Thus although a plan for each sample was sent to the IEA sampling referee for approval, the responsibility for the quality of the sample and the data in the main analysis rested with each National Center. To a limited degree it was possible to correct for the shortfall of the students in any one stratum of a sample by computing sample weights proportional to the number of students in the stratum and employing those stratum weights in the calculation of the population statistics. To cover cases in which circumstances prevented a school from taking part in the survey, a second sample of schools was prepared, from which a replacement would be found to match any school which could not participate. The complication in English arises from the fact that the subject, unlike Mathematics and to some extent Science, is optional. Not all schools offer it and not all students choose to take it.

In Italy 30 % of the students who took a foreign language at all did not study English, while in some countries the lack of precise information about the place of foreign languages in the schools made the design process somewhat hazardous, involving the preparation of double samples in some cases. This occurred in Belgium, partly because of the difficulty of ascertaining whether the school taught English, and, when it did, of determining whether a student studied English as a first or second foreign language. In Finland further investigations were required because it was necessary to know whether students drawn in the sample followed the longer or shorter English course. In Hungary schools were differentiated not only according to whether they were academic or vocational but also as to the type of course offered since one of several different intensities of English could be given. These courses varied according to the curricular emphasis of the schools, some focusing on specialized instruction in Mathematics and Science, others focusing on the arts such as music, others on Russian, and others again on specialized instruction in English. These differences arose from the optional status of English.

Modifications had to be introduced into the sample pattern because of the lack of social or linguistic homogeneity in particular countries. Although most of the participants are homogeneous and possess largely uniform school systems, as in Sweden, at least one of the participants, Belgium, has two distinct language areas with two largely independent school systems in which different foreign language policies are pursued. In the French part, English is the second foreign language in Catholic schools and the first foreign language in the remainder. Even in a more homogeneous country there may be a complex pattern of separate systems administered by regional governments which are largely autonomous so far as the administration of research and the collection of information are concerned. This is the case in Germany which has 11 Länder. Some countries have school systems which are differentiated according to religious affiliation—Catholic, Protestant or nondenominational—which is the case in Belgium and the Netherlands. In Belgium the language policy varies with the affiliation of the school. In Israel there is a category of schools which is identified by the national origins and, to a large extent, therefore, by the language background of the students, namely the Arabic schools.

Finally, the sampling procedure had to be modified in some countries for less specifically educational considerations. In Thailand the design had to take into account the fact that 16 of the 71 districts could not be included because of their inaccessibility in times of military stress. In other countries changes occurred in the organization of the school systems during the time of the investigation so that students who would normally have been expected to attend one school were transferred to another. In Germany schools which had previously recruited students in Grades 1–9 were reorganized to allow for the creation of *Grundschule* with Grades 1–4, and *Hauptschule* with Grades 5–9. In Hungary the grade where English was taught, not the age of students or even the grade they normally attended, was defined as the sampling unit, instead of the school. In Hungary, too, the distinction normally used between urban and rural schools had to be modified, because, there, urban schools were defined as those in the Capital and the County Centers, while the rural schools were defined as all others, whether they were located in urban or rural areas.

A list of students belonging to the defined population was obtained from each school approached and the National Centers prepared for each school a set of materials, tests and questionnaires to be given to each student, specified by name and number, who had been drawn in the sample to be tested. It was perhaps inevitable that a few schools found it impossible to participate in the survey and withdrew at the last moment, and that some students, drawn in the samples, were absent from school on the days testing occurred. Furthermore, students sometimes failed to record a response to important items in the battery of tests or in the questionnaires, while school principals sometimes failed to reply to a School Questionnaire. There were schools, also, in which no teacher answered a Teacher Questionnaire. In such cases students and schools had to be omitted from some of the stages of the data analysis. However, the extent of the response from students, schools and teachers was very gratifying. Table 2.3 shows the number of students, teachers and schools included in the sample of each country.

Subsample Characteristics

Not all countries administered all five cognitive measures, and for various reasons—financial and administrative feasibility in particular—subsamples were selected in those countries giving the Listening, Writing and Speaking measures. Where subsampling took place, the subsample was a part of the total sample of a given population per country, and the attempt was to achieve a genuine random sample to match that of the total sample concerned.

In order to ascertain whether or not this goal of subsampling was achieved, each subsample was compared to the total sample of which it was a part on selected variables. These variables included Father's Occupation, Father's Education, Mother's Education, Type of Program, Sex, Grade beginning English, Years studied English, as well as mean scores on Reading, the Interest in English Scale, the English

Activities Scale, and the Utility of English Scale. Because the data would be quite voluminous, and not very meaningful regarding comparisons of the sample characteristics in particular, tables are not shown for this subsample-total sample comparison. However, the results indicate that with respect to the selected variables each subsample generally appears to be a close match to the total sample from which it was derived. The few instances where a subsample might be considered different from its parent sample occurred only with respect to one of the variables used for comparison. Table 2.4 gives the countries and sample size for each test that was given to a subsample.

REFERENCE

Peaker, G. F. *An Empirical Study of Education in Twenty-One Countries: A Technical Report.* Stockholm: Almqvist & Wiksell, and New York: John Wiley, 1975.

Table 2.1. *Specifications*

Level of Integration	Kind of Channel	Decoding	Encoding
Level 1	Auditory-vocal	Identification and discrimination of sounds	Pronunciation, intonation and stress
	Visual-kinesthetic	Identification and discrimination of letters	Spelling, punctuation and capitalization
Level 2	Auditory-vocal	Recognition of words; words and sentence patterns	Active vocabulary; production of grammatical units
	Visual-kinesthetic		
Level 3	Auditory-vocal	Auditory comprehension	Speaking
	Visual-kinesthetic	Reading comprehension	Writing

Table 2.2. *Behavioral Objectives for English*

1 Objective	2	3 Population II			4	5 Population IV		
		A	B	C		A	B	C
Listening	2	×			2	×		
Understanding spoken English in general	a	×			a	×		
Understanding different varieties of English	c			×	c			×
Understanding different registers: formal and conversational	b			×	b		×	
Speaking	3	×			3	×		
Speaking English generally	a	×			a	×		
Speaking different varieties	c			×	c			×
Speaking different registers	b			×	b		×	
Reading	1	×			1	×		
Reading for information at various levels: news items or science	a	×			a	×		
Reading at different levels of abstraction	c		×		b	×		

Table 2.2. (*Cont.*)

1 Objective	2 Population II	A	B	C	4 Population IV	A	B	C
Reading for pleasure e.g., literature at various levels of formality	e			×	e		×	
Reading quickly	d			×	d		×	
Reading short extracts intensively	b	×			c	×		
Writing	4		×		4	×		
Simple sentences	a				g		×	
Informal writing recording a conversation	f			×	d	×		
Formal writings e.g., a business letter	d		×		e	×		
Reproducing and summarizing	e			×	b	×		
Free composition e.g., description, narrative and exposition	c		×		a	×		
Frequent practice in writing	g			×	f		×	
Writing to instil accuracy	b	×			c			×
Knowledge about English	6			×	6		×	
History of the language	d			×	d			×
English literature	a		×		a		×	
English history	b			×	b			×
Acquaintance with the English way of life	c			×	c		×	
Developing favorable attitudes	5			×	5		×	
To the English language	a		×		a	×		
To English-speaking peoples	b			×	b		×	
To English culture and institutions	c		×		c		×	
Status of English in the curriculum								
As an academic study			×				×	
As a practical study		×				×		

Note: Columns 3 and 5 indicate the importance of the objectives on a three point declining scale (A–C) for a sample country.

Columns 2 and 4 indicate the international rank order of the objectives—major objectives 1–6 and subordinate objectives (a)–(g).

Table 2.3. *Country by Population Participation—Numbers of Students, Teachers and Schools Included*

	Belgium (Fr.)	Chile	Federal Rep. of Germany	Finland	Hungary	Israel	Italy	Netherlands	Sweden	Thailand
Population II										
Schools	42	–	47	71	–	44	62	91	97	40
Teachers	105	–	248	187	–	70	126	146	492	310
Students	725	–	1 110	2 164	–	1 096	809	2 098	2 454	1 957
Population IV										
Schools	54	80	59	73	46	20	18	52	81	15
Teachers	174	265	360	299	118	52	37	64	403	142
Students	1 485	2 314	1 379	2 369	1 063	614	329	1 568	1 767	936

Note: This table contains unweighted numbers: that is, the numbers refer to the actual numbers of cases occurring in the sample.

Dashes (–) indicate that no sample was represented.

Table 2.4. *Size of Subsamples*

Test Administered to a Subsample	Country and Population with Subsample		Number in Subsample	Number Total Sample
Listening	Chile	IV	231	2 314
Writing 1, 2, 3	Chile	IV	182	2 314
Writing 4	Chile	IV	157	2 314
	Finland	II	605	2 164
		IV	997	2 369
	Hungary	IV	565	1 063
	Italy	II	582	809
Speaking	Belgium	II	162	725
		IV	192	1 485
	Finland	II	200	2 164
		IV	279	2 369
	Hungary	IV	118	1 063
	Italy	II	70	809
		IV	28	329
	Sweden	II	218	2 454
		IV	204	1 767

Chapter 3

Description and Psychometric Properties of the Reading and Listening Tests and the Non-Cognitive Instruments

DESCRIPTION OF THE TESTS

Population II Reading and Listening Tests

Listening. The Listening Tests took 30 minutes to complete and had a maximum possible score of 36. There were two sections comprising a total of 24 items together with a Dictation. The first section consisted of 12 items testing the ability to discriminate sounds: students were required to listen to tape recordings of a series of three words (e.g., wall, ball and fall) while looking at pictorial representations of one of the words (e.g., a wall) in the test booklet. Essentially, they had to discriminate between either initial or final consonants or median vowels by choosing the word appropriate to the picture. The maximum score was 12. The second section, 12 items with a maximum score of 12, tested comprehension of spoken sentences. Students listened to a sentence or short paragraph and then selected from three sentences printed in their own language in the test booklet the alternative they thought gave the correct interpretation of the taped sentence. This section tended to be more difficult than the first section. The third section, Dictation, with a maximum score of 12, consisted of a passage of simple prose of about 110 words. It was scored as follows: faulty punctuation was ignored, but each incorrect word, even when it might represent more than one error, counted as one. Omissions and faulty inclusions were scored as errors. Up to 8 errors produced a score of 12, and each subsequent set of up to 8 errors meant a loss of one on the score scale of 0 through 12, so that between 97 and 112 errors produced a zero score.

Reading. Reading was the key area of the investigation and the test took one hour to complete. The test consisted of six sections comprising a total of 60 multiple-choice items. Except for those which are based on comprehension of short sentences or longer texts, the reading items are "point specific" rather than "global" in form. The first section contained six items in which students selected one from among five choices as the antonym to a specified word in a simple sentence. This section proved to be the least difficult part of the Reading test. The second section consisting of eight items tested the ability to recognize the pronunciation of written words. One stimulus word followed by five possible responses constituted an item. The student was required to identify the one word which contained a matching vowel or consonant to that underscored in the stimulus. The item proved to be of moderate difficulty. The third section was comprised of ten items and tested the ability to produce a correct grammatical structure by selecting from three alternatives the one which satisfactorily completed a stimulus sentence. Those items which involved the use of prepositions or prepositional adverbs of duration proved to be difficult especially in Belgium, Israel and Thailand. The fourth section was concerned with the definition of specified words included in very short simple sentences. These vocabulary items were considerably more difficult than those of the first section. The maximum score was six. The next two sections were Reading Comprehension tests. The first consisted of 14 fairly simple sentences for which three possible interpretations were offered. The second section contained four passages of continuous prose on each of which four questions were provided with four possible answers being offered for each question. The maximum scores in the fifth and sixth sections were 14 and 16 respectively.

Population IV Reading and Listening Tests

Listening. The four sections of this test totaled 36 multiple-choice items for which 30 minutes were allowed. Students responded on paper. The first section was identical with the first section of the Listening Test for Population II. As expected, these items were less difficult for Population IV except in Israel where Population IV students found the Listening test difficult. The second section, with a maximum score of eight, consisted of eight taped multiple-choice items assessing the ability to recognize differences in meaning carried by differences in intonation. This section proved less difficult than the pretesting had indicated. The three sentences in each item contained the same words in the same order but spoken with different intonations. Students were asked in their own language to note which sentences contained

61

intonation or stress which changed the meaning to a simple question, a question requiring the answer "yes" or "no" or emphasizing the time of an action. Sometimes only one sentence, at other times two or all three sentences or none conveyed the specified intention, and students were asked to identify which sentences if any, did so. In the third section, which consisted of eight multiple-choice items with a maximum score of eight, students were asked to listen to a sentence or short paragraph in English and to select from the printed alternatives the correct inference to be drawn from the stimulus. This section proved to be more difficult in Belgium, Hungary and Israel than elsewhere. The maximum score of the next section was also eight. It differed from the third section only in that it required the student to listen to passages of conversation in which male and female voices were used.

Reading. The five sections consisting of 60 multiple-choice items were allotted 60 minutes. Each of the first three sections consisted of eight items. The first assessed ability to identify words in which the stress pattern was the same by having students pair words. These items were generally difficult, especially in Chile and Thailand, one of the reasons being the problem of distinguishing simple from compound word stress. Furthermore, it is possible that students might have found it less difficult to reproduce the correct stress than to recognize and compare different or identical stress patterns. The second section assessed the ability to relate a given adjective to the one inappropriate noun in a series of five nouns, so as to produce a satisfactory collocation. Although the pretesting gave no indication of more than average difficulty, this section proved to be difficult for the majority of students. This may have been because the students were required to come to a negative conclusion and because the items necessitated a good measure of sensitivity to idiomatic usage. The items tended to have low within-country discrimination but seemed to discriminate satisfactorily between countries. The third section, which was less difficult than any of the others, required the completion of sentences by selecting in some instances the correct form of a verb, in others the correct order of words, and in others the use or omission of the article. The fourth section had 11 items designed to test comprehension of fairly simple sentences. The correct response in some instances was a choice of paraphrases and in others of correct inferences. Others involved the substitution of direct for indirect speech. The fifth section contained five continuous passages of prose which were graded very steeply in terms of difficulty. Each passage was followed by five or six questions to each of which four alternative responses were provided. Some questions were on details, such as the meaning of single words, while others required an interpretation of the narrative, description or argument. Such a set of questions tested not simply a command of the English language but also more general intellectual behaviors underlying but independent of knowledge of a particular language. The last four items relating to a complex prose text were very difficult.

Reading and Listening Tests in Summary

A brief summary of the tests for both Populations II and IV is given in Table 3.1.

Anchor Items

Sixteen items in the Reading test and 12 items in the Listening test were common to both populations. Table 3.3 supplies the Means and Standard Deviations of the Reading and Listening anchor items. Information is thus available concerning the behavior of the anchor items across the two populations. However, it is to be noted that the anchor items do not provide a representative sample of the total test and for this reason cannot be used to compute a "measure of growth" in English Reading and Listening. As expected, these items appeared to be easier for Population IV than for Population II, particularly the Reading items.

Classifications of Items in the Reading and Listening Tests

The English tests were organized so as to ensure the possibility of obtaining scores for groups of items as well as total Reading and Listening scores. The total Listening, Reading, Speaking and Writing tests were each set out in different sections aiming to measure different aspects of English achievement. In addition, independently of the sections to which they belonged, items might be mainly vocabulary or mainly structural items. Furthermore the same items might also test specific aspects of English (like the formation of plurals from singulars of verbs) or they might be global items and require an understanding of several aspects of English (like Reading Comprehension items). The section in Chapter 2 discussing the decision to categorize items provided the rationale for the two ways of organizing items into categories. Table 3.4 shows how the items were classified, first as vocabulary or structure items and then as analytical (point specific) or global items. Further analysis is possible to compare performance between the two halves of each dichotomy, however, since the items are the same in each system it is not possible to compare performance between the two systems, or parts of the two systems, e.g., analytical items with vocabulary items. Note should be made that it was recognized that the distinctions which lie at the base of the two halves of either system cannot be categorical and absolute.

Special Cognitive Measures as National Options

In Sweden a special Listening Comprehension test was administered to a subsample of a Population IV sample in secondary schools, (the *gymnasia*). It was designed to test understanding of different "registers" and accents, different levels of complexity and different speeds of speaking. Finland also prepared extra cognitive tests but these did not bear specifically on English.

QUESTIONNAIRES AND SCALES

For Student Data

Students replied to two sets of questions, one concerned with English specifically and the other of a more general character. Students were asked about the mother tongue of the parents, the language spoken in the home (whether it was the native language of the country and if not whether the language was English) and the number of books in the home. The students were also asked about the subjects they studied and their attitudes towards them. English was included among these subjects. Among the questions which were specific to English the following appeared to be important: to what extent English was used in learning other subjects, the attitude of parents towards English, the extent to which parents had studied English, the extent of the student's own knowledge of English prior to formal instruction. Other questions referred to the time spent in learning English and possible contacts with English outside school. The student's own perception of his ability in English and the difficulty he experienced in learning the language were probed. Finally three scales were designed. One focused on student interest in English as well as the nature of that interest. Another measured student activities in English outside school, for instance in reading and correspondence. The third was to serve as an indicator of the student's intentions with respect to the use to which he might put English later in life; that is, it considered his general aims for English, whether these were utilitarian or broadly cultural for instance.

For Teacher Data

In the general questionnaire for teachers information was requested about the level of their formal education, the extent of their general teaching experience and of their interest in teaching as a profession, the degree to which they specialized and their reliance on centrally produced syllabuses, texts and method guidelines, as well as standardized tests. Among the questions which referred to the teaching of English the following kinds of questions were included: about the teacher's native tongue, the extent of his exposure to English (visits to English-speaking countries, etc.), the teacher's self-perception of ability in English, the degree to which he specialized in English and the range and number of English classes he taught. Finally inquiries were made about aspects of teaching method, the use of materials for teaching, the approach adopted to grammar, the point at which reading was introduced, and the reliance on imitation or formal "rule" instruction.

For School Data

Questions concerning schools were addressed to the school principal and were of two kinds, those of a general nature and those concerned with English specifically. Among the former type of questions were those which related to the availability of ancillary services like libraries and a foreign language society, the proportion of the school budget earmarked for foreign languages, and the employment of ancillary staff like foreign language assistants. The questions specifically concerning English included those that focused on the organization of English, grades in which English was introduced, differentiation of instruction according to student ability, the use of English in non-English classes, the selection of English students, the amount of time the school allowed for English at various stages, and the number of native speakers of English on the staff.

National Questionnaire

As a part of the total IEA Six Subject Survey, a questionnaire was completed by each National Center in which information was requested about the educational, social and economic as well as linguistic background of the country. From the standpoint of the English study, it is important to note that several countries listed as one of the recent innovations in education a greater emphasis on an audio/visual or audio/oral approach to language instruction. The social and economic conditions of the countries, the level of economic development, and the degree to which development depended on foreign and especially English trade were considerations which might affect the motivation for English and the extent to which English was involved in the school curriculum. Further, since the degree of linguistic complexity in any country might affect the age of introduction, the selection of students and the intensity of the English course, of import to the English study were questions about the linguistic background of each country, the number of minority groups and their languages and whether these were taught, the official language and the extent to which there were regional differences in the use of that language. Also of interest were questions about the circulation of foreign language (especially English) newspapers, periodicals and films.

National Options

In Finland, where the linguistic background of a school may be more complex than in most countries, the National Center included questions that were in addition to the set of international questions in order to probe in greater detail whether the Finnish or Swedish language predominated in each locality. Other questions were mainly interested in investigating in considerable detail the attitudes of students and teachers towards language testing and the effects of types of tests on teaching. Sweden also included additional questions addressed to students and teachers concerning classroom approaches to English teaching, such as the use of different types of textbooks, the use of the mother tongue in teaching, and the value of translation. Hungary probed the differences between special English programs and general programs in their approaches to English classroom practice, especially the use of phonetic transcription and television. In Israel, the additional questions reflected the considerable diversity of linguistic experience of students, a large number of whom were immigrants from very different linguistic communities. Both students and teachers were asked about their countries of origin and the date of their arrival.

VALIDITY AND RELIABILITY OF THE COGNITIVE TESTS AND THE DESCRIPTIVE MEASURES

The validity of the measures was ensured, so far as possible, by the consultations which were conducted with National Centers at all stages. The steps taken when constructing the items aimed at achieving content validity. There is reason, therefore, to be confident that effective measures were produced; but until it is possible to compare the performance of students on the present tests with their performance on others, such as external school examinations in English, statistical evidence of the validity of the cognitive tests cannot be provided. Another qualification must be recorded: the usefulness of the measures may have been affected by the need to translate some of the instructions as well as the responses in two instances. There is also the question of the reliabilities of the subscores, since there were very few items in each category or group.

Reliability data are reported for total scores and subscores in English Reading and Listening as well as for the affective measures (scales). However, in some instances, though a country might have participated in testing a particular aspect of English, the sample of students for some parts of the test (Listening, for instance) was so small or the number who completed the test was so unrepresentative of the total sample that a computation of reliability became pointless. Because of the nature of the major portions of the Speaking and Writing tests, it was not possible to produce reliabilities such as those for Reading and Listening for these measures.

Estimates of the reliabilities using the Kuder-Richardson Formula 20 (Kuder and Richardson, 1937; Lord and Novick, 1968) were obtained for each population tested in each country for the Reading and Listening tests. These are presented in Tables 3.5 through 3.8. This estimate of reliability is based on the internal consistency of all the items in the total test or subsection of the test as indicated by the heading of the column in which the various reliabilities appear. The subscores for these tests involve fewer items and the reliabilities were therefore expected to be lower, which is generally the case. The estimated reliabilities for the affective measures were calculated by using the Coefficient α (Cronbach, 1951). Separate coefficients were calculated for each test and for each country. The reliabilities for the affective measures are given in Table 3.9.

Generally speaking, the achievement tests in Reading and to a lesser extent in Listening (in those countries where the conditions of testing justified the computation of reliabilities) proved to be relatively reliable measures when taken in each case as one complete test. Since they are based on fewer items and thus have relatively low reliabilities, the scores for the subtests need to be interpreted with caution. Generally speaking, too, the descriptive measures tend to be less reliable than the cognitive measures.

Since the measures in language skills are used mainly for group comparisons, moderate or low reliabilities of sub-tests do not pose the same limitations as they do when the measures are used at the individual level.

Listening

Although they participated in the Listening test, the Federal Republic of Germany, the Netherlands and Thailand had such low reliability levels and the number of students taking the test or completing a sufficiently representative number of items was so small that those countries have been omitted from discussion in this report. It is also probable that the levels of reliability of the Listening test in other countries were affected by the difficulties of administering the tests. Given this fact that the test was difficult to administer, the range of reliability levels across countries is wide for both populations. As was the case with Reading, the Listening Comprehension section tended to have higher reliabilities than other sections for both populations. The reliabilities of the section concerned with Discrimination of Sounds (same test used for both populations) tended to be at the same level for both populations. As indicated earlier, the reliabilities of the subtests were invariably lower than those for the total Listening test in both populations.

Reading

The reliabilities for the total test are relatively high for both populations but higher for Population II than for Population IV. There generally are only small differences between countries, especially for Population II. The subtests almost invariably have lower reliability coefficients than the total test, and this is true of all countries. The section with the highest reliability levels is Section VI, for Population II, and Section V for Population IV, both sections dealing with comprehension of longer passages. The next highest level of reliability for Population II is for Section V, Comprehension of Short Sentences. It is to be expected that the countries with the lowest or highest reliabilities on the subtests tend to have corresponding low or high reliabilities on the total test also. The least reliable of the subtests for Population II are Section III, Recognition of Structures, and for Population IV the least reliable appears to be Section II, Collocations. There is a marked uniformity between countries with respect to which subtests are most or least reliable.

Table 3.10 presents reliabilities for the Reading test according the two ways of classifying the items which were discussed earlier. Perhaps future researchers will be able to take a more detailed look at the Reading test and do analyses based on different categorization of items.

The items which are included in the two categories, A and B, cut across the subsections already discussed above. Because Column A and Column B represent two ways of classifying the *same* 60 items in the Reading test caution is needed when comparing the reliabilities in Column A with those in Column B for either population. Since in some cases the items are few, reliabilities tend to be lower. Perhaps if there were more items the reliabilities might also be higher. For example, if for Population IV there were more than 16 Vocabulary items in the Reading test, the reliabilities for this category might be higher. The several categories tend to have lower reliabilities in Population IV than in Population II, quite expected since the reliabilities for the total Reading test are lower for Population IV than for Population II (See Tables 3.7 and 3.8). In general for both Populations the Global category tends to have higher reliabilities than the Analytical category. A comparison of the Vocabulary with the Structure category shows the Structure category as having a higher reliability, this perhaps because there are more items in that category.[1]

Descriptive Measures

Five descriptive measures were included in the study but because of low reliabilities the School Environment scale has been disregarded. The Like School Scale, which was not specific to the English study, had moderately acceptable reliabilities in most countries for both populations, the reliabilities tending to be close across countries. The three measures which affect English directly, with the exception of the Utility of English Scale, also tend to have moderate levels of reliability. The Utility of English Scale has high reliabilities for Population IV. Countries do differ in the reliability of the different scales, and, taking all three English scales into account, the reliabilities tend to be higher in Belgium, Finland and Italy for Population II. For Population IV, however, there appears to be little difference between countries when the reliabilities are considered for each scale separately.

---

[1] "Structure" is here conceived in a wider sense than just "grammatical structures".

TEST DIFFICULTY

The distribution of scores for the Reading and Listening tests reflects the inherent characteristics of the tests to measure a wide range of ability. The nature of the IEA study, drawing as it did on samples of students from countries differing considerably in their organization of English in the curriculum at every stage and including in the samples of students those who varied in their home background, their exposure to English outside school as well as in experience of English in school, made it inevitable that the test results would have wide distribution of scores. At the same time that the tests served their purpose satisfactorily in distributing the scores, each test appeared to have a spread of level of difficulty which was appropriate to the population being tested.

Some observations on the comparative difficulty of sections and items have been offered earlier. Another way of assessing the difficulty of the items is to examine the proportion of students who omitted responding to particular items (although they continued the test beyond those items) or who did not finish the test. Population II differed from Population IV in that the former had comparatively low overall percentages of students who omitted items, thus the Population II tests appear to be less difficult than the Population IV tests.

With regard to the Reading test there was a tendency for Population IV students to omit responding to a particular group of items, Section 2 (Collocations), especially in Belgium, Chile, Hungary and Israel. Table 3.11 gives the percentage of students in both populations who failed to respond to the items in the last sections of the Reading test. The failures to complete the test, as recorded in the table, may be due to a time factor operating in conjunction with the difficulty of earlier sections as much as they may be due to the difficulties presented by these last sections themselves. That the last sections of the Reading test may have been very difficult is supported by the fact that the point at which most students did not finish the test occurred earlier in some cases, after Item 47 in the case of Israel and Italy.

Since the Listening test was paced, due to administration by tape recorder, all students should have been able to finish the test. However, the administration of the test by tape recorder may have made it more difficult for students where there were mechanical problems involved with the recorder, sound quality, etc.

ITEM ANALYSIS AND DIAGNOSIS OF ERROR

The analysis of error is an important aspect of teaching since it can promote an effective diagnosis of difficulty. While the individual teacher may be faced with considerable differences in student performance arising from idiosyncratic behavior, the theoretician of foreign language pedagogy is mainly interested in general types of error, like those which may be common to a large proportion of, if not all, students from a particular country. Evidence of different national bias towards characteristic errors would strongly support the contention that the native language influences the learning of a subsequent language fundamentally, while the lack of a consistent national tendency, though it would not disprove the existence of such a native language influence, would tend to indicate the operation of more powerful factors. There exists some evidence in favor of this latter argument in the data of this study. Perhaps through use of the item analyses from the IEA Data Bank in Stockholm and elsewhere future researchers will be able to make a more complete diagnosis of student error and elucidate the influence, if any, of the mother tongue on achievements in English.

Student Error Due to Test Design

Student errors arose from several sources, one of which was a degree of failure in the preparation of the tests themselves. This failure may be due to a formal or design weakness, where for instance one of the distractors, though strictly speaking not a correct answer, does not sufficiently differentiate itself from the correct response to constitute a fair test to the average student. For example, for Population II Item 39 of the Reading Test read:

Jack said he did want to come.
- (A) I don't think I shall come.
- (B) I really would like to come.
- (C) I think I shall come.

The students were asked to select the option that meant the same thing as the stimulus material. The correct response is B which takes account of the emphatic nature of the original statement—*"did* want". But quite considerable numbers in many countries selected the more neutral statement C which, though correct so far as it goes, does not convey the intended meaning. This failure in design is equally apparent in Item 33 of the Population IV Reading test:

I thought I had seen the car and the girl driving it yesterday.

(A) I thought I had seen the car and its driver before.

(B) I saw the car before I saw the girl.

(C) I thought I had seen a girl driving a car.

The correct response is A, which conveys the definiteness of the original statement—"*the* car" and "*the* girl," rather than the more open and indefinite statement C which was selected by large numbers of students. Except in Sweden where the proportion of students selecting C was 33 % compared with 65 % for the correct response, the percentage choosing the distractor C was over 50 % in the Netherlands and nearly 75 % in Belgium, Hungary and Thailand. The distractor C is obviously too close to the designated response so that it constituted an unfair test to the average or even slightly above average student. However, both of the above items may serve to discriminate for the above average student, those who did very well on the test as a whole. For this reason, they still have a place in the test.

The over-all design of the test, though not affecting the performance of students unduly, may have favored some students. This may have happened where similar test items were placed in close proximity, this being one of the disadvantages of designing the complete test in homogeneous sections. In these cases there may have been a "practice effect" since the performance on the second of the two closely related items may have been better than if the first item were not there. For instance, each of the following pairs tested one aspect of English in each case—Listening, Population II, Items 13 and 15, 14 and 18, 16 and 20, 17 and 19. In all countries the percentages of students passing the second of the items in each pair are almost always higher than the percentages passing on the first.

These are formal or design features which may have tended to distort the percentages passing particular items, but there are also substantive characteristics which may have tended to do so. This is particularly the case where the selection of items or of certain features of individual items may have proved more difficult than had been suggested by the results of pretesting. Reference has been made already to Items 1 through 8 of the Population IV Reading test where the students were asked not so much to produce or reproduce correct stress patterns but to analyze them and to institute comparisons. The complexity of this exercise proved too much for otherwise good students, and the percentages passing in all countries are lower by far on this set of items than they are in other Sections.

The same is true of Section II of the Population IV Reading test,

Items 9–16, where the students were required to match an adjective to one of five nouns. In spite of the favorable results of the pretest this section proved exceedingly difficult and the items were not attempted by higher percentages than was the case with other items or sections. The undoubted difficulty of these items arose from their excessive sophistication.

Student Error Due to Native Language Interference

Other student errors are due neither to failure in the design of the test nor to the inherent difficulties which the English language poses to all students alike. Difficulties are imposed upon the students by the characteristics of the languages the students already know, their native language. It is apparent from the analysis of some items that this tendency exists, and that some countries have found some items more difficult and others less difficult because the national language has either tended to handicap or facilitate the acquisition of those aspects of English. This may be so for students in Chile where items 17–24 of the Population IV Reading test are concerned, since it is evident that students in that country have a greater problem in handling the infinitive construction than do students in other countries, and this may arise from the fact that Spanish does not use this construction to the extent or in the same way that English does. But it is not a difficulty the Chilean students share with speakers of other Romance languages, for instance those in French Belgium and Italy, where the same lack of congruity with English exists. A national tendency is also observable in Finland with respect to the use of prepositional adverbs of duration, the basis for Item 20 in the Population II Reading test. It is the Listening test, however, that exemplifies this tendency towards possible distortion by the native language most clearly. The focusing of the question by the location of a rising intonation, characteristic of English, is not prevalent in Spanish and it is significant that Population IV students in Chile found the Listening test Item 14, with just such a characteristic, very difficult. The difficulty they also found in distinguishing between "sheep" and "cheap" or "yet" and "jet" may not be unassociated with the influence of Spanish on their approach to the sounds of English.

National Centers will be better able to estimate the validity of the "interference" argument and its strength in their individual cases by their own detailed analysis of the incidence of distractors, and especially of the choice of "popular distractors." But from an admittedly inadequate survey across countries belonging to many language groups, markedly different from each other and from English, the evidence for the argument does not appear to be convincing. The same popular distractors tend to be selected by students speaking very different languages far more often than they are differentiated by them. Sometimes not only is a popular distractor not common to speakers of the same language in different countries but it tends to be popular across speakers of very different languages.

The fact that on the present set of tests a positive or negative distortion deriving from the national languages cannot be confirmed does not imply that such an influence may not be substantiated in other tests, since it may well be that in selecting the present test items the designers by chance avoided items which clearly disadvantaged or advantaged one country more than another. Another reason may be that the teaching of English in the several countries has been directed to take account of the problem of native language interference and has safeguarded itself very successfully against such an influence. If this is the case, since few of the countries in the present investigation have based their teaching on contrastive analysis techniques, it may be argued that there is little point in extending the practice since they have succeeded very well without recourse to it.

Other Sources of Student Error

Whatever the justification for these arguments may be, pro and con, there are certainly more powerful causes of student error than native language interference. In the first place, students tend to be misled by irrelevancies. For instance for Item 8, in the Population II Reading test, students were required to match "island" with "like," since the initial vowel of the former is included in the latter. But students in all countries tended to match "milk" with "like" possibly because of the irrelevant fact that the two words share the two consonantal sounds [l] and [k] and because they are both monosyllables. In this sense the error arises from the students' search for a regularity in the item stimulus and response though the regularity is not required for a correct answer. This also occurs in Item 10 of the same test where "whole" is the correct response to "over." High percentages selected "one" as the correct response to "over," presumably because the initial vowel is repeated in its written form and catches the student's eye immediately as the obvious regular feature.

Inattentive reading, or failure to take account of the context of the item is a powerful factor in producing student error. Thus in Item 50 of the Population IV Reading test an attentive reading of the passage will direct the student to the choice of response B, "There are good harbours sheltered from the sea," as the reason for there being so many amateur sailors in England. However, high percentages of students in many countries chose A, "There are so many sailing boats," though this is the consequence rather than the cause of the existence of so many sailors. It is even more apparent in Item 29 in the Reading test for Population II where the failure to read attentively is a clear cause of failure. Students were asked to select one of three alternatives to questions about the meaning of "thirsty." The correct response is C, which reads "I wanted something to drink." Large numbers chose A, "I wanted to sleep," presumably because the stem includes a reference to being "thirsty at night."

This cause of failure is related to another; namely the tendency to ignore the semantic content of either stem or response and to select a response which echoed a formal but semantically inappropriate feature of the stem. For instance, for Item 25 in the Population II Reading test the student is asked to select the correct response "go out of" as the meaning of "He plans to leave the house." But many students selected response A, "live in," possibly because of the similarity of "leave" and "live," rather than be guided by the deeper semantic similarity of the stem and correct response. Item 28 brought out the same tendency, for instead of selecting "bring back" as corresponding to "return the book" many chose "turn the pages," possibly because of the correspondence between "return" and "turn." The same inclination to be guided by the surface similarity or formal identity rather than by deeper semantic correspondence is exemplified by an analysis of the responses to other items in Population II. So far as what may be regarded as predominantly linguistic error enters into the analysis, it may be argued that the preference for the repetition of formal features as clues to the correct response rather than correspondence of meaning between stem and response is the most important single factor. This has very significant linguistic implications not unrelated to the distinction currently favored by some linguists between "deep" and "surface structures." It should be an interesting area for future development of research into error analysis.

There is one set of causes of student error which is strictly speaking not linguistic so much as a manifestation of more deep-seated inadequacies, namely those arising out of the operation of intellectual processes which, though they express themselves in language, are not exclusively or primarily linguistic. Beyond the first stages of foreign language learning it becomes progressively more difficult to measure linguistic competence in isolation from general intellectual ability. Other extra-linguistic capacities, like the ability to draw inferences, to come to correct or permissible conclusions and to elicit the relevant information are also involved. Thus the successful reading of passages for comprehension depends not only on an acquaintance with the foreign language but also on the ability to bring to bear cognitive forces which are basically independent of a particular language though expressible in it. This is certainly the case with the kinds of questions asked in the concluding items of the Population IV Reading test, where fairly advanced intellectual capacities are required as well as knowledge of vocabulary and of the structure of the English language. It is most apparent in Items 50 through 60 which are concerned with the understanding of a discourse on attitude to political thinking. But the same factor runs through the operation of nearly all the test items.

REFERENCES

Cronbach, L. J. "Coefficient Alpha and the Internal Structure of Tests." *Psychometrika,* 16, 1951, pp. 297–334.

Kuder, G. F. and Richardson, M. W. "The Theory of the Estimation of Test Reliability". *Psychometrika,* 2, 1937, pp. 151–160.

Lord, F. M. and Novick, M. R. *Statistical Theories of Mental Test Scores.* Reading, Mass.: Addison-Wesley, 1968.

Table 3.1. *Summary of Reading and Listening Tests*

Population II				Population IV			
Type of Test	Description of Items	No. of Items	Max. Score	Type of Test	Description of Items	No. of Items	Max. Score
Listening				Listening			
Section 1	Discrimination of sounds	12	12	Section 1	Discrimination of sounds	12	12
Section 2	Comprehension of sentences	12	12	Section 2	Intonation	8	8
Section 3	Dictation		12	Section 3	Listening comprehension	8	8
				Section 4	Listening comprehension	8	8
Reading				Reading			
Section 1	Recognition of antonyms	6	6	Section 1	Recognition of word stress	8	8
Section 2	Recognition of pronunciation	8	8	Section 2	Collocations	8	8
				Section 3	Grammatical structures	8	8
Section 3	Grammatical structures	10	10				
Section 4	Definition of the meaning of words	6	6	Section 4	Comprehension —short sentences	11	11
Section 5	Reading comprehension—short sentences	14	14	Section 5	Comprehension —continuous texts	25	25
Section 6	Reading comprehension—continuous texts	16	16	–	–	–	–

Table 3.2. *Anchor Items—Populations II and IV*

	Population II		Population IV	
Reading Comprehension	Sect. III	23	Sect. III	24
	Sect. V	34		26
		42		25
		44		27
		41		28
		40		29

Table 3.2. (Cont.)

		Population II		Population IV
		43		30
		45		36
		46		37
		47		38
		48		39
		39		32
	Sect. VI	57	Sect. V	40
		58		41
		59		42
		60		43

Total 16 Items

Listening, Section I: Items 1–12 in Population II and Population IV.

Table 3.3. *Means and S.D.'s for Anchor Items—Reading and Listening*

Country	Population	Reading Anchor Items		Listening Anchor Items	
		M	S.D.	*M*	S.D.
Belgium (Fr.)	2	6.1	2.7	7.5	2.2
	4	9.0	2.2	8.6	1.9
Chile	4	5.8	2.5	5.5	2.2
Fed. Rep. of Germany	2	7.6	2.9	–	–
	4	11.3	0.8	–	–
Finland	2	5.9	2.8	7.3	2.7
	4	10.9	1.2	9.6	1.6
Hungary	4	8.6	2.2	8.1	2.0
Israel	2	7.0	3.2	–	–
	4	9.5	2.3	–	–
Italy	2	5.2	3.1	7.3	2.2
	4	8.1	2.6	7.7	1.9
Netherlands	2	8.2	2.6	–	–
	4	11.3	0.9	–	–
Sweden	2	8.4	2.6	9.3	1.6
	4	11.0	1.3	10.0	1.3
Thailand	2	5.9	2.3	–	–
	4	8.9	2.0	–	–
No. of Items		16		12	

Table 3.4. *Categorization of Test Items*

Section	Items	Vocabulary	Structure	Analytical	Global
Population II					
	Listening				
I	1–12	×		×	
II	13–24		×	×	
III	Dictation		×		×
	Reading				
I	1–6	×		×	
II	7–14	×		×	
III	15–24		×	×	
IV	25–30	×		×	
V	31–44		×		×
VI	45–60		×		×
	Writing				
I	1–13	×		×	
II	14–23	×		×	
III	24–31	×		×	
IV	Composition				×
	Speaking				
I	1–10		×	×	
II	Oral Reading				×
III	Fluency				×
Population IV					
	Listening				
I	1–12	×		×	
II	13–20		×	×	
III	21–28		×	×	
IV	29–36		×	×	
	Reading				
I	1–8	×		×	
II	9–16	×		×	
III	17–24		×	×	
IV	25–35		×		×
V	36–60		×		×
	Writing				
I	1–13		×	×	
II	14–23		×	×	
III	24–31		×	×	
IV	Composition				×
	Speaking				
I	1–10		×	×	
II	Oral Reading				×
III	Fluency A				×
	B				×

Table 3.5. *Reliabilities for Listening Total Test and Subscores—Population II*

| Country | Total Test | Subscores in order of Sections | |
		I	II
Belgium (Fr.)	.93	.50	.64
Finland	.96	.44	.71
Italy	.83	.59	.77
Sweden	.95	.35	.64
Median Value	.94	.47	.67
Number of Items	24	12	12

Subscores

Section I: Discrimination of Sounds

Section II: Listening Comprehension

Section III: Dictation (No reliability available due to nature of test)

Table 3.6. *Reliabilities for Listening Total Test and Subscores—Population IV*

| Country | Total Test | Subscores in Order of Sections | | | |
		I	II	III	IV
Belgium (Fr.)	.76	.49	.55	.55	.53
Chile	.67	.42	.56	.27	.12
Finland	.71	.38	.51	.50	.52
Hungary	.75	.52	.45	.54	.54
Italy	.84	.50	.48	.55	.62
Sweden	.78	.32	.50	.46	.52
Median Value	.75	.45	.50	.52	.52
Number of Items	36	12	8	8	8

Subscores

Section I: Discrimination of Sounds

Section II: Intonation

Section III: Listening Comprehension

Section IV: Listening Comprehension (Conversation)

Table 3.7. *Reliabilities for Reading Total Test and Subscores—Population II*

Country	Total Test	Subscores in order of Sections					
		I	II	III	IV	V	VI
Belgium (Fr.)	.91	.50	.63	.45	.58	.78	.80
FRG	.93	.56	.67	.51	.62	.78	.82
Finland	.93	.64	.72	.57	.62	.77	.79
Israel	.95	.73	.69	.62	.74	.83	.88
Italy	.94	.71	.71	.68	.70	.80	.86
Netherlands	.94	.69	.73	.66	.71	.77	.83
Sweden	.93	.58	.66	.52	.66	.76	.80
Thailand	.87	.53	.52	.59	.59	.65	.70
Median Value	.93	.61	.68	.58	.64	.77	.80
Number of Items	60	6	8	10	6	14	16

Subscores
Section I: Recognition of Antonyms
Section II: Letter-Sound Correspondence
Section III: Recognition of Structural Features
Section IV: Vocabulary Recognition
Section V: Comprehension of Short Sentences
Section VI: Comprehension of Longer Passages

Table 3.8. *Reliabilities for Reading Total Test and Subscores—Population IV*

Country	Total Test	Subscores in order of Sections				
		I	II	III	IV	V
Belgium (Fr.)	.86	.40	.46	.41	.58	.82
Chile	.85	.41	.34	.29	.58	.81
FRG	.68	.49	.31	.27	.17	.57
Finland	.78	.51	.39	.33	.28	.72
Hungary	.85	.44	.52	.57	.51	.77
Israel	.91	.58	.59	.56	.66	.87
Italy	.90	.55	.59	.41	.61	.90
Netherlands	.69	.59	.24	.39	.14	.59
Sweden	.84	.66	.26	.46	.41	.79
Thailand	.76	.17	.17	.47	.46	.66
Median Value	.84	.50	.36	.41	.48	.78
Number of Items	60	8	8	8	11	25

Subscores
Section I: Recognition of Word Stress
Section II: Collocations
Section III: Recognition of Grammatical Structures
Section IV: Comprehension of Short Sentences
Section V: Comprehension of Longer Passages

Table 3.9. *Reliabilities (Coefficient) for the Affective Measures for Populations II a*

Country	Population II				Population IV		
	English Activities Outside School	Interest in English	Utility of English	Like School	English Activities Outside School	Interest in English	Utility of English
Belgium (Fr.)	.52	.70	.64	.70	.61	.70	.87
Chile	–	–	–	–	.63	.75	.90
FRG	.40	.64	.70	.71	.58	.57	.88
Finland	.52	.81	.72	.74	.51	.60	.84
Hungary	–	–	–	–	.60	.72	.86
Israel	.55	.62	.66	.60	.53	.61	.85
Italy	.53	.71	.70	.68	.58	.67	.89
Netherlands	.49	.63	.55	.62	.55	.60	,83
Sweden	.46	.68	.62	.61	.58	.60	.88
Thailand	.52	.56	.64	.60	.57	.63	.88
Median Value	.52	.66	.65	.65	.58	.62	.87
No. of Items	6	10	12	11	6	12	10

Table 3.10. *Comparisons of (A) Specific with Global Items and of (B) Vocabulary with Structure Items: Reliabilities (Kuder-Richardson 20) of the English Reading Subtests Pertaining to the Two Divisions (A and B) of the Total Test for Each Population in Each Country*

Country	Population II				Population IV			
	A		B		A		B	
	Analytical	Global	Vocabulary	Structure	Analytical	Global	Vocabulary	Structure
Belgium (Fr.)	.82	.87	.78	.90	.66	.84	.61	.85
Chile	–	–	–	–	.69	.89	.68	.88
FRG	.82	.88	.79	.90	.54	.57	.48	.61
Finland	.87	.88	.85	.91	.58	.70	.54	.72
Hungary	–	–	–	–	.67	.80	.56	.84
Israel	.89	.92	.86	.94	.76	.89	.66	.90
Italy	.89	.90	.87	.93	.61	.91	.55	.90
Netherlands	.89	.89	.87	.92	.57	.58	.49	.62
Sweden	.82	.85	.79	.89	.65	.72	.61	.74
Thailand	.83	.81	.77	.87	.44	.73	.23	.77
Median Value	.85	.88	.82	.91	.63	.77	.56	.81
Number of Items	30	30	20	40	24	36	16	44

le 3.11. *Percentage of Students Not Reaching the Last Items in the Final Section of the ding Test*

ntry	Population II Sum of Wts	Item No. 57	58	59	60	Population IV Sum of Wts	Item No. 55	56	57	58	59	60
gium (Fr.)	687	11.7	12.9	13.3	15.1	1 440	11.2	14.3	17.1	19.7	21.5	24.5
e	–	–	–	–	–	2 117	34.6	39.0	42.2	43.8	45.2	48.8
;	1 074	5.8	6.2	8.2	8.7	1 374	1.1	2.1	3.2	4.0	5.3	7.5
and	2 100	3.7	4.2	4.6	5.3	2 310	6.1	8.4	9.4	10.6	12.1	13.4
gary	–	–	–	–	–	1 062	13.7	16.7	17.8	18.5	18.8	19.7
el	1 065	11.9	12.6	14.6	14.9	604	24.8	27.9	28.8	30.0	30.8	32.4
	791	17.6	18.0	19.1	20.3	324	32.6	36.8	38.4	38.4	39.5	40.8
erlands	2 090	1.6	1.7	1.8	2.1	1 560	1.6	2.6	2.7	2.8	3.3	4.2
den	2 322	1.1	1.3	1.5	1.7	1 626	2.1	3.1	3.3	3.6	4.4	5.4
iland	1 951	4.7	5.1	5.5	5.8	937	7.8	8.2	8.3	8.5	9.6	9.2

Chapter 4

Some Aspects of Student Performance in Reading and Listening

The means which are reported in this Chapter cannot be used to make simple or unadjusted comparisons between the different countries because the proportion of the relevant populations taking English varied considerably. Nor is it possible to make unadjusted comparisons between the performance of the same sample of students on different tests because the number of items in the tests may also be different. Nevertheless, overall comparisons between countries and comparisons on different tests within countries are important aspects of the present investigation. Converting the means on all tests into standardized scores would make the interpretation of the data more straight-forward and the reporting more economical. However, such a procedure would not eliminate the problem of sample size but simply mask its relevance. Furthermore, the apparently uniform frame of reference which standardized scores are intended to ensure might, in this instance, induce the idea that students from different countries were being placed on a simple and uniform scale of achievement. This would be contrary to the major assumption of the study, namely that differences in achievement are of interest in so far as they reflect the operation of a large number of different variables. Achievement scores are best regarded not simply as the end product of the tests but as possible indices of the relative importance of differences in the characteristics of the students and the influences to which they may be subjected. For these and other reasons it was decided in the English study to rely on less economical methods of comparison based mainly on the use of the median value across countries as a point of referrence.[1]

READING—TOTAL AND SUBTESTS

Tables 4.1 and 4.2 give the means and standard deviations for the Total Reading test and the sectional subtests. Figures 4.1, 4.2 and 4.3

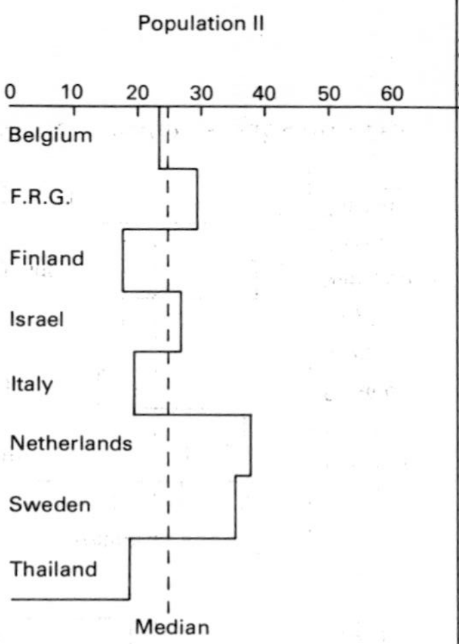

Figure 4.1. Total Reading Means.

[a] All students in Populations II and IV have not necessarily pursued English classes for the given number of years. These are the maximum possible. See also Tables 6.8, 8.7 and 8.8 for detailed analysis.

Population IV

Country	% of Age group in school	% Studying English	Range in years of Engl. study[a]
Belgium	33	87.1	6
Chile	16	97.6	9
F.R.G.	30	79.6	9
Finland	21	88.4	10
Hungary	28	35.6	5
Israel		92.8	8
Italy	16	67.7	8
Netherlands	13	98.2	7
Sweden	45	91.3	9
Thailand	10	93.6	9

Population II

Country	% of Age group in school	% Enrolled in English	Range in years of Engl. study[a]
Belgium	90	72.5	3
F.R.G.	94	89.0	5
Finland	99	75.8	7
Israel		74.4	5
Italy	55	55.4	4
Netherlands	98	97.3	3
Sweden	99	94.1	6
Thailand	90	97.6	5

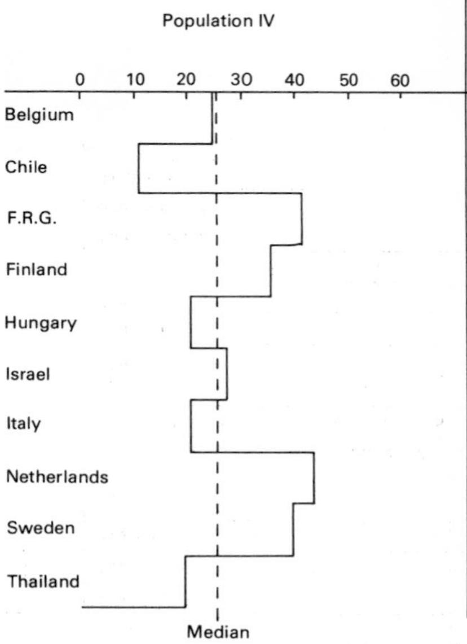

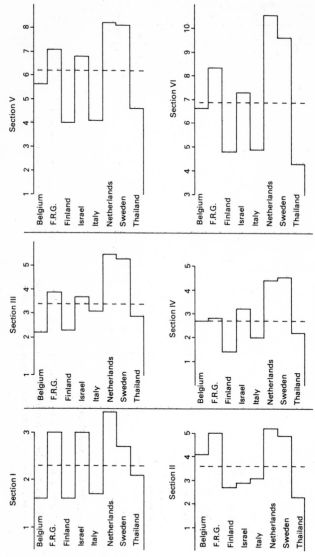

Figure 4.2. Reading – Subscore Means—Population II.

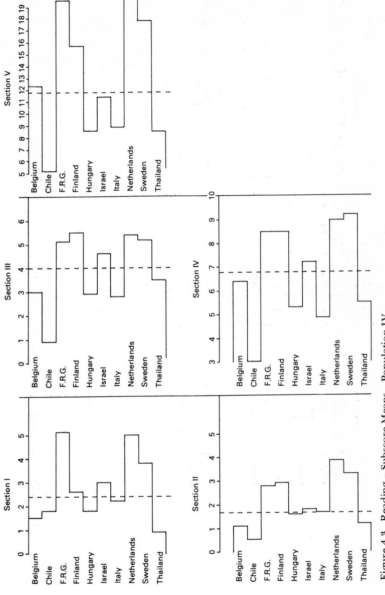

Figure 4.3. Reading – Subscore Means—Population IV.

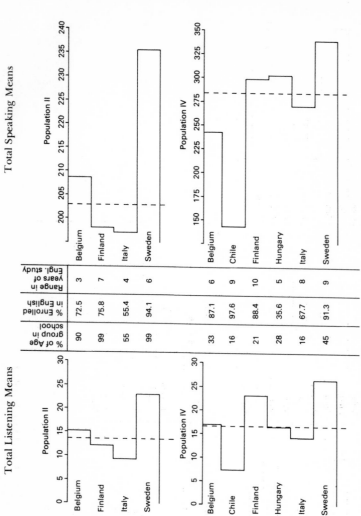

Figure 4.4. Total Listening and Speaking Means.

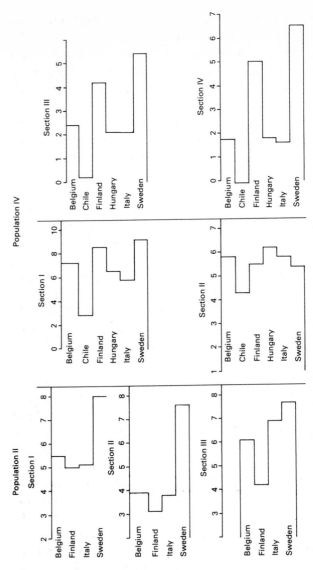

Figure 4.5. Listening – Subscore Means.

pictorially show the means in relation to the median value for the total test and the subtests. Figure 4.1 adds further information about the percentage of the relevant age group attending school, the proportion of the age group studying English and the maximum length of the English course available to each population in each country. This information needs to be taken into account in comparing the levels of achievement in different countries. It should also be noted that the sections of the tests for each population do not normally correspond, so that no comparison can be instituted between performances of the two populations on the individual subtests.

The mean levels of performance on the Total Reading test range widely between countries in both populations, and the range of differences tends to be slightly greater for Population IV than for Population II. This may be attributable to some extent to the fact that the ages of Population IV students, the length of the English courses they have followed and the level at which they study English, whether as a first or second foreign language for instance, are more varied than is the case with Population II. The Netherlands and Sweden in both populations and Federal Republic of Germany and Finland in Population IV tend to compare most favorably with other countries on Total Reading. The performance of the countries which tested both Populations tend to stand in the same relationship to each other in the two populations apart from Finland where the performance of Population IV compares more favorably with the performance of other countries than does the performance of Population II.

As with the Total Reading test the range in the level of performance is greater on the subtests in Population IV than in Population II and probably for the same reasons. The relative position of some of the countries on some subtests is better than on the Total Reading test. For instance, whereas Israel approximates the median value on the Total Reading test as well as on most of the subtests it tends to be well above the median in Section I for Population II. Belgium tends to be below the median value on Total Reading and most of the subtests, but its relative position is higher on Section II for Population II and on Section V for Population IV. For Population IV Chile tends to compare with other countries most favorably on its performance in Section I, whereas in Finland Section I is where the students compare least favorably with those of other countries. The Population IV samples in all countries generally tend to perform most satisfactorily in Section I and least satisfactorily in Section IV. For the same population, Section V reveals the greatest between-country variability

90

and Section II the least. For Population II, Section I has the greatest and Section II the least between-country variability. These differences reflect in all probability variations in type of English courses adopted by the different countries, or national differences in emphasis on aspects of the English courses.

LISTENING—TOTAL AND SUBTESTS

Tables 4.3 and 4.4 present the means and standard deviations for the total Listening test and subtests. Figures 4.4 and 4.5 pictorially show the means in relation to the median value, and Figure 4.4 gives added information about the sample in order to avoid inappropriate interpretations.

The levels of achievement in both populations differ considerably between countries, Sweden being the country which tends to compare most favorably with others in each case. The relative positions of the countries on the Total Listening test correspond closely to their relative positions on the subscores. As was the case with Reading, the Listening performance of Population IV in Finland compares more favorably with other countries than does the performance of Population II. Of the countries which tested only Population IV, Chile tends to compare with other countries relatively less favorably than does Hungary which approaches the median value on Total Listening subtests.

The greatest and least range of differences between countries in Population II are recorded for Sections II and I respectively, and for Sections IV and II respectively in Population IV. As was the case with Reading some countries compare with other countries more favorably on some of the subtests than they do overall. For instance, for Population IV both Sweden and Finland are below the median value in Section II whereas on Total Listening they tend to compare favorably with other countries. In Hungary the opposite is the case; compared with the performance of other countries, the performance on Section II is more satisfactory than is the performance on Total Listening. For Population II, Belgium tends to compare most favorably with other countries on Section II and for Population IV, Finland compares most favorably on Section IV. As in Reading it may be that differences between countries on the subtests reflect national strengths and weaknesses or variations of emphasis on particular aspects of the English courses.

91

BETWEEN-COUNTRY COMPARISON OF PERFORMANCE IN THE FOUR SKILLS—READING, LISTENING, WRITING AND SPEAKING

For Populations II and IV, the performances of the different countries tend to hold a consistent relationship with each other in regard to the aspects of English they tested. For instance the Swedish students tended to compare most favorably with all countries on all four tests (Total Test and Subtests), except for Writing 4 in Population II and in Writing 1, 2, 3 in Population IV. Of the countries participating in all four tests Swedish students tended to achieve the highest levels of success. Belgian students in Population II and Finnish students in Population IV tended to achieve levels of success second only to Sweden. Chile, on the other hand tends to be less well placed than most countries for Population IV. For Population II Italy and Finland tend to share the intermediate position on all tests, and Italy tends to be below the median value on all tests for Population IV.

BETWEEN-COUNTRY COMPARISON OF AFFECTIVE MEASURES

Table 4.5 presents the means and standard deviations for the three English-specific affective measures: the English Activities Scale, the Interest in English Scale, and the Utility of English Scale.

Between-country variations in the means for these scales are generally slight in both populations. This is especially the case with the English Activities Scale. However, there are some interesting differences. Thailand has the highest mean for all countries on the Utility of English Scale for Population II and, together with Hungary, is relatively well placed in Population IV. Israel compares most favorably with other countries on the English Activities Scale for both populations, and Belgium and Sweden on the Interest in English Scale for Population II. Finland, which is the least well placed country on the Interest in English Scale for Population II, is among the best placed for Population IV. Finland is also better placed comparatively on the cognitive tests for Population IV than for Population II. Whether the higher level of interest in the Finnish Population IV is the result or the cause of higher levels of achievement in comparison with other countries is an interesting speculation which could be taken further in research. The switch of relative performance on the scales between the two populations is not exceptional, though the general tendency is for both populations of the same country to behave almost identically in comparison with other countries on each of the three scales.

Intercorrelations of Cognitive
and Affective Measures

It has always been agreed that achievement in English, as in other subjects, is influenced by the operation of such affective factors as are referred to in the three scales included in this study. Tables 4.6 through 4.23 present the intercorrelations for the cognitive and affective measures together with the number of students responding to each measure. Caution should be exercised in interpreting these correlation coefficients since the reliabilities of some measures (Speaking, Writing 1,2 and 3, and Writing 4) were not computed and are, in any case, likely to vary considerably, just as do these reliabilities that have been computed (cf. Chapter 3). Further, some correlations are based on data obtained from a subsample (e.g., Speaking and Writing 4) which may or may not have influenced the size of the correlation coefficients.

Inconsistency from country to country as well as between populations in the same country tends to be the main characteristic, even though corrections for attenuation are made where reliabilities have been computed. Such between-country and between-population differences may be attributable to the nature of the abilities tested, the tests used, the skills and motivation or attitudes of the students being tested, curricular emphases, or other factors that affect test results. Against this background of between-country and between-population differences, two general tendencies may be observed: the affective measures tend to have from low to moderate positive correlations among themselves, and the cognitive measures tend to show from moderate to high positive correlations among themselves, the cognitive measures not being as highly correlated with the affective measures as among themselves. There are cases, however, where the correlations between some of the cognitive and some affective measures are higher than the cognitive measures intercorrelations. For example, in Finland and Sweden at the Population IV level English activities outside of school may be a little more highly related to achievement in Speaking than is achievement in writing essays.

Reading in Relationship to the Affective Measures
and Other Cognitive Measures

Reading appears to correlate more highly with the cognitive than with the affective measures. If we take a general view of the countries[2] that participated in all four tests in both populations, it appears that

Reading tends to correlate highest with Writing 1, 2 and 3, but not with Writing 4. Regarding the correlations for other measures with Reading, generally the pattern varies for each country and between the two populations.

The correlations of the Total Reading test score with scores on its subtests (Tables 4.24 and 4.25) tend to be relatively high, higher than the intercorrelations among the subtests.

Further research may prove useful in defining the exact nature of these aspects of reading ability and the extent to which they make their own specific contribution to overall reading ability at each stage of development.

Listening as Related to the Affective
Measures and Other Cognitive Measures

The general tendency is for Listening to correlate at a lower level with the affective measures and other cognitive measures than Reading does. Furthermore, as in the case of Reading, the correlations for Listening with the affective measures are lower than those for Listening with the other cognitive measures. If we view all the countries and both populations, of all the correlations of Listening with other cognitive measures those with Reading are the highest. This tends to be the case in Belgium (Fr.), Finland and Sweden at both population levels, and in Italy and Hungary for Population IV. Further, the trend is for Listening to correlate lowest with Writing 4.

As would be expected the correlations for the total Listening test and its subtests tend to be relatively high (Tables 4.26 and 4.27). However, as in Reading, the correlations between subtests themselves are not so high as those with the Total Listening test.

For Listening, as for Reading, the subtests may be measuring different aspects of ability, but further research is needed to confirm this suggestion. It should also be emphasized that, for reasons that have been indicated earlier, the interpretation of these correlation coefficients must be handled with caution because the reliabilities of subtests are often low and vary widely.

INTERCORRELATIONS OF THE AFFECTIVE MEASURES

One of the most consistent tendencies so far noted is that the correlations for the affective measures with the cognitive tests are, generally speaking, not as high as are those between the cognitive measures themselves. The affective scales tend, however, to have from low to moderate correlations among themselves, although the Utility of English scale and the Interest in English scale correlate at a higher level with each other than either does with the English Activities Outside School scale or any of the cognitive measures. This is true across all countries and both populations, even when the correlations are corrected, because of the rather widely varied reliabilities of the three measures. This is not unexpected, since the extent and nature of a student's interest may be influenced by the view he has formed of the usefulness of English to him personally as well as to society generally. On the other hand, even if a student is interested and has formed a positive view of the personal and societal usefulness of English, he may not find it easy to participate in English-speaking activities outside school because the facilities for these exchanges may not exist in his locality or community. The fact that the correlations for the English Activities scale tend to be higher for Population IV than for Population II may imply that, whether these facilities exist or not, a higher level of competence in English and of experience of the language in school may be required if the student is to take advantage of the facilities that do exist. As the students continue with their English course to the pre-university level (Population IV) they appear to be in a better position to exploit the opportunities to participate in English-speaking activities because the activities become more meaningful.

In any case although the affective measures tend to be related to each other fairly closely the differences between them may indicate that each is measuring different aspects of the students' attitude towards English.

CORRELATIONS OF EXPLANATORY VARIABLES WITH READING AND LISTENING

Achievement in Reading and Listening as related to explanatory variables was examined for both populations in nearly all countries. However, in the Federal Republic of Germany, Israel, the Netherlands and Thailand the Listening test was not administered. The variables were organized in four sets (Tables 4.28 through 4.43). The first of these groups consists of Student Background variables (Tables 4.28–4.31). The second set of student variables concern their personal characteristics (Tables 4.32–4.35). Of the two remaining sets of variables, one (Tables 4.36–4.39), focuses on variables which reflect characteristics of the teachers and the fourth set (Tables 4.40–4.43) has to do with school organization for the teaching of English and actual classroom practice, such as the teaching of grammar and class grouping.

Levels of significance of the correlations are not specified because the main intention of the investigators is to draw inferences from the general patterns of results across countries rather than to deal with particular results in any one country. It is anticipated that the National Centers in the several countries will report the data for their own countries and it will be more appropriate for them to make explicit the strengths and weaknesses of the teaching of English in their own schools, as well as the levels of confidence that can be placed on the results.

Where a relationship varies from country to country, it is possible that the effect of the variable on achievement will be different in different countries and where both positive and negative correlations exist for the same variable it may be that the variable will have not simply different, but very opposite effects on achievement. However, when the correlation coefficients are quite small, as they frequently are in the present study, a more plausible explanation may be that the variations represent chance fluctuations around a zero "true" value. For this reason it is wise to be cautious in interpreting the results. General trends are discussed and some explanations are offered, though, where the correlations are very low the possibility of exceptions occurring to any generalization must be quite high.

Student Background Variables

It is the degree of inconsistency from country to country and between populations which is the most immediate impression emerging from a study of Tables 4.26 and 4.28 in which some variables have both positive and negative correlations for different countries and for different populations. The closest relationship appears to exist between word knowledge of the mother tongue and each of the criterion variables, Reading and Listening. Since the correlation of this variable with the achievement variables is generally moderate to high and consistently positive, it would seem that "word knowledge" of the mother tongue could serve as a predictor of achievement in a foreign language.

The English activities outside school variable is also of interest. This is a composite scale based on consideration of such activities as

96

Reading English newspapers and magazines, Listening to radio programs in English, Looking at television programs and films in English, Writing to English-speaking correspondents and Visiting an English-speaking country. This variable tends to have a low to moderate consistently positive correlation with achievement.

In general the other background variables tend to have low levels of correlation with the criterion variables. This may be an effect of the testing instruments, but it may also be that some of the variables such as Time spent in an English-speaking country may be more closely related to aspects of achievement in English other than Reading or Listening, such as "Speaking English," which were not investigated because of a lack of time. This is an area for further research.

In several countries favorable parental attitude towards the learning of English by their children, as perceived by those children, has a negative relationship to achievement, although the correlation coefficients are very low in general. It may be, therefore, that the variations represent only chance fluctuations around a near zero "true" value. For this reason, and in view of the fact that there is evidence from some countries, like the United States, which tends to suggest that there is a positive relationship between parental attitude and achievement, considerable caution should be exercised in interpreting the data. It is an area where more research is required. An attempt should be made to discover under what circumstances a favorable parental attitude has a negative relationship to achievement and how far negative relations may be neutralized by schooling.

Student Attitude, Aspiration and
Self-Perception Variables

With few exceptions the variables dealing with student aspirations regarding the ability to use English and student self-perception of their present ability in using English have relatively moderate to high relationships with achievement in Reading and Listening in most countries. However, the moderate to high relationships are not invariably the case. For instance, in Italy and Belgium (Fr.) in Population II the correlations tend to be low. The range of differences among countries is smaller for Population IV than for Population II. This may be accounted for by the fact that Population IV students are a more highly selected set of students than those in Population II, since they are well beyond the terminal point of compulsory education and their continuance with English is a matter of personal choice. Consequently it is to be expected that Population IV students in every country aspire to be able to use English well and perceive themselves as being able to do so.

However, of note is the fact that the data for Hungary, testing Population IV only, appear to indicate for these variables a lower degree of relationship with achievement in Listening than Reading.

The relationships of the remaining variables of this group to achievement are not consistent between countries, and some variables have both negative and positive correlations for both populations. However, as might be expected, the variables Perceived difficulty of English, Perceived utility of English Scale and the Interest in English Scale generally tend to be related positively to achievement but with from low to moderate correlation coefficients. It would seem that the factors of Liking school, Perceiving the difficulty of English, Feeling that one is industrious in studying English, Having an interest in English and Viewing the language as useful, together with the Number of hours one does of homework in English tend to relate differently to achievement in the different countries. These between-country differences may arise from the effects of social-cultural factors on the form as well as the substance of the questions used to elicit information concerning these variables. Differences in school programs for English may also have a bearing on the correlations. There are undoubtedly fundamental individual and social-psychological considerations to be taken into account also.

Teacher Characteristics

The variables which constitute this set may be divided into three subgroups: (1) those which relate to the teacher's self-perception of competence in the four main aspects of skill in English; (2) variables such as Time spent in preparation or Time spent in marking papers, which represent aspects of the teacher's teaching practices; (3) certain factors which, for want of a better name, may be referred to as biological variables, namely Sex.

Correlations of achievement in Reading and Listening with these variables tend, generally speaking, to range from quite low to moderate and to be inconsistent from one country to another.

Although in some countries higher achievement is correlated with male teachers, the tendency on the whole is for greater achievement to be correlated with women teachers. Here again, because of the degree of inconsistency and the low correlations, any interpretation must be tentative.

The teachers' self-perception of ability in English, the time spent correcting papers and in preparing lessons have from low to moderate correlations with Reading and Listening in both populations but no consistent trend can be observed across countries. The main exceptions to the rather low correlations are to be noted at the Population II level in the Federal Republic of Germany, Finland and in the Netherlands. In these countries, a positive self-perception of ability in English on the part of the teacher, expenditure of a relatively large number of hours in preparation of lessons and in correcting papers all tend to correlate with student achievement in English.

School and Classroom Variables

This set of variables consists of those which have to do with the school's organization for the teaching of English, such as the hours of instruction, together with those variables concerned with method of teaching or extent to which certain approaches are adopted, like the use of teaching aids, as well as the extent to which teaching is influenced by such considerations as the requirements of the next grade or the demands of examinations. Inconsistency seems to be the trend for all these variables. The tables (4.40–4.43) give some indication of the relative strengths and directions of the relationships of these variables with Reading and Listening.

Hours of instruction tend to show a positive relationship to achievement for both populations, that is, the greater the number of hours the higher achievement tends to be.

The correlation coefficients for the years students have studied English tend to move from negative to positive as the number of years of study increases. In other words, for the students in the present samples one year of study does not produce high achievement whereas four or more years of study tend to do so. With few exceptions the data suggest that when English is introduced in early grades achievement is higher than when it is introduced in later grades. This is consistent with the finding that achievement is positively related to the number of years a person studies the subject, since, presumably, students beginning English at earlier grades will have studied the language longer by the age of 14 or 18 than those beginning later. What the data do not indicate is whether those starting in early grades learn English more effectively than those starting in later grades. This inference could only be made when age beginning

English is compared within groups of students having the same number of years of language training. Although this was not done in the present study, such a comparison might reveal the existence of an age level below which it is not practical to introduce formal instruction in a foreign language, an optimal point of entry, so to speak. Of course both beginning age and years of instruction will also interact with other variables in unique ways. Thus they need to be examined in concert with other variables, a task which is best handled by regression analysis, on which Chapter 9 will focus.

A consideration of the methods and classroom variables suggests that teachers tend to be pragmatic rather than dogmatic in their adherence to teaching methods. For instance, teachers were asked whether they adopted a method of teaching grammar rules including translation (a basically deductive approach) or encouraged the students to acquire a knowledge of the language (including the rules) from imitation and practical use of the language (a basically inductive approach) or whether they compromised and used both methods as the occasion demanded. It appears from the data that the eclectic (compromise) approach generally relates to higher achievement in Reading and Listening than the two mutually exclusive approaches, though this is not true of all countries and the correlation coefficients for both populations tend to be low. Using the mother tongue to teach English, another method variable, also tends to produce varied results between countries, between the two populations, as well as among the levels of study within a given population, beginning, intermediate and advanced. Several considerations may account for these between-country, between-population and between-stage differences. The most obvious is that teachers in some countries have been trained to use the mother tongue and those in other countries have not. Where the use of the mother tongue is part of the tradition of a country the teachers are likely to achieve better results by adopting than by not adopting the approach, irrespective of any scientific justification for the practice or the lack of it. Then again, some languages, like German, are closer to English so that the use of the mother tongue may facilitate positive transfer which may not be the case when Thai or Finnish is used. Different aims in teaching English, the choice of fluency or correctness for instance, may influence the advantage to be derived from using the mother tongue. These considerations should be studied at greater depth in actual classroom research and with languages that vary in distances from English.

The remainder of the variables related to classroom practice are generally characterized by low to moderate correlation coefficients, both negative and positive, with considerable variability between countries and between populations. These differences may reflect the varying national characteristics of English courses and especially differences in aim. For example, at the Population II level in Finland, to a higher degree than elsewhere, higher achievement levels tend to be related to the tendency to base instruction on the demands of an external examination. For Population II in the Federal Republic of Germany the use of small group instruction, contrary to the general tendency, has a relatively high negative correlation with achievement in Reading. The results in Finland and Germany may reflect a national characteristic of the approach to English teaching in each case. For that reason further information about the behavior of these method variables will, it is hoped, be provided in the forthcoming reports by the National Centers of the participating countries.

NOTES

[1] The main discussion of students' achievement in Writing and Speaking is reserved for Chapter 5 for three reasons. The samples of students drawn for the Writing and Speaking tests were a subsample of the population sample from each country. Only a few of the countries tested Writing and Speaking, which were optional tests. And finally, the scoring and the reporting of these tests were undertaken at the NFER (London).

[2] Although all tests were given in Chile no correlations were computed between Speaking and the other measures because fewer than 5 % responded to that measure.

Table 4.1. *Means and Standard Deviations for Reading Total Test and Subscores and Word Knowledge—Population II*

Country	Total Test		Subscores in Order of Section													Word Knowledge	
			I		II		III		IV		V		VI			
	Mean	S.D.	Mean	S.D.	Mean	S.D.	Mean	S.D.	Mean	S.D.	Mean	S.D.	Mean	S.D.	Mean	S.D.
Belgium (Fr.)	22.8	15.2	1.6	1.8	4.1	2.4	2.2	2.8	2.7	2.3	5.6	4.8	6.6	4.7	24.1	9.7
FRG	29.9	16.2	3.0	1.8	5.0	2.3	3.9	3.0	2.8	2.5	7.1	4.9	8.3	4.9	15.3	9.8
Finland	16.7	17.8	1.6	2.1	2.7	2.7	2.3	3.2	1.4	2.6	4.0	5.1	4.8	5.0	15.5	10.1
Israel	26.3	18.7	3.0	2.2	2.9	2.5	3.7	3.3	3.2	2.7	6.8	5.3	7.3	5.9	20.5	11.6
Italy	18.6	17.3	1.7	2.2	3.1	2.6	3.1	3.5	2.0	2.6	4.1	4.7	4.9	5.3	25.9	10.2
Netherlands	37.4	16.4	3.5	2.2	5.2	2.4	5.5	3.2	4.4	2.2	8.2	4.2	10.5	4.6	21.1	9.8
Sweden	35.0	14.9	2.7	2.0	4.9	2.4	5.3	2.7	4.5	2.0	8.1	4.3	9.6	4.5	13.5	8.2
Thailand	18.4	13.4	2.1	1.8	2.3	2.1	2.9	3.1	2.2	2.3	4.6	4.0	4.3	3.9	30.3	8.8
Median Value	24.5	16.3	2.4	2.1	3.6	2.4	3.4	3.1	2.7	2.4	6.2	4.7	6.9	4.8	20.8	9.8
Number of Items	60		6		8		10		6		14		16		40	

Subscores

Section I: Recognition of Antonyms
Section II: Letter-Sound Correspondence
Section III: Recognition of Structural Features
Section IV: Vocabulary Recognition
Section V: Comprehension of Short Sentences
Section VI: Comprehension of Longer Passages

Table 4.2. *Means and Standard Deviations for Reading Total Test and Subscores and Word Knowledge—Population IV*

| Country | Total Test | | Subscores in Order of Section | | | | | | | | | | Word Knowledge | |
| | | | I | | II | | III | | IV | | V | | | |
	Mean	S.D.	Mean	S.D.	Mean	S.D.	Mean	S.D.	Mean	S.D.	Mean	S.D.	Mean	S.D.
Belgium (Fr.)	24.2	10.8	1.5	2.0	1.1	1.8	3.0	2.5	6.4	2.8	12.3	5.7	30.7	7.9
Chile	10.6	9.8	1.6	2.0	0.7	1.5	0.9	2.2	2.9	3.0	4.9	5.2	20.9	9.5
FRG	41.2	6.1	5.1	1.8	2.8	1.7	5.1	1.8	8.7	1.5	19.5	3.0	24.0	7.0
Finland	35.6	8.3	2.6	2.3	2.9	2.0	5.5	1.9	8.7	1.7	15.9	4.5	14.8	6.9
Hungary	20.1	11.2	1.8	2.1	1.6	2.2	2.9	2.8	5.3	2.7	8.6	5.5	34.3	6.4
Israel	27.4	12.9	3.0	2.4	1.8	2.2	4.6	2.5	7.2	2.8	11.4	6.7	18.7	7.8
Italy	20.2	12.6	2.2	2.4	1.7	1.9	2.8	2.6	4.9	3.0	8.8	7.0	32.9	6.7
Netherlands	42.9	6.5	5.0	2.2	3.9	1.9	5.4	2.1	9.0	1.5	19.7	3.0	25.6	7.6
Sweden	39.5	9.0	3.8	2.6	3.3	1.7	5.2	2.2	9.2	1.8	17.8	4.5	25.1	7.4
Thailand	19.7	9.1	0.9	1.7	1.2	1.7	3.5	2.6	5.7	2.7	8.4	4.7	34.2	6.6
Median Value	25.8	9.4	2.4	2.1	1.7	1.8	4.0	2.3	6.8	2.7	11.8	4.9	25.3	7.2
Number of Items	60		8		8		8		11		25		40	

Subscores
Section I: Recognition of Word Stress
Section II: Collocations
Section III: Recognition of Grammatical Structures
Section IV: Comprehension of Short Sentences
Section V: Comprehension of Longer Passages

Table 4.3. *Means and Standard Deviations for Listening Total Test and Subscores—Population II*

Country	Total Test A		Total Test B		Subscores in Order of Sections					
					I		II		III[a]	
	Mean	S.D.	Mean	S.D.	Mean	S.D.	Mean	S.D.	Mean	S.D.
Belgium (Fr.)	15.4	8.4	9.4	5.7	5.5	3.1	3.9	3.7	6.1	3.7
Finland	12.1	9.9	8.1	6.2	5.0	3.1	3.1	4.1	4.2	4.3
Italy	9.1	6.8	8.9	6.4	5.1	3.2	3.8	4.1	6.9	3.7
Sweden	23.0	7.3	15.5	4.6	8.0	2.2	7.6	3.2	7.7	3.4
Median Value	13.7	7.8	9.1	5.9	5.3	3.1	3.8	3.9	6.5	3.7
Number of Items	[b]		24		12		12		[c]	

Total Test Scores
Total Test A: Contains information based on all three subsections.
Total Test B: Contains information based only on Subsections I and II, the two multiple-choice tests, and excluded Subsection III, the dictation test.

Subscores
Section I: Discrimination of Sounds
Section II: Listening Comprehension
Section III: Dictation

[a] This is based on raw score information. No correction for guessing has been made due to the nature of the test.
[b] Maximum score possible is based on the total number of items in Subsections I and II in addition to the score for Subsection III.
[c] Maximum score possible is 12 for the passage dictated.

Table 4.4. *Means and Standard Deviations for Listening Total Test and Subscores—Population IV*

	Total Test		I		II		III		IV	
Country	Mean	S.D.	Mean	S.D.	Mean	S.D.	Mean	S.D.	Mean	S.D.
Belgium (Fr.)	16.9	7.0	7.1	2.7	5.8	1.9	2.4	2.7	1.7	2.6
Chile	7.1	4.5	2.9	2.8	4.3	2.1	0.2	1.9	–0.2	1.8
Finland	23.2	6.1	8.4	2.3	5.5	2.0	4.2	2.4	5.0	2.3
Hungary	16.3	7.3	6.2	3.0	6.2	1.6	2.1	2.8	1.8	2.8
Italy	14.7	7.6	5.7	2.8	5.8	1.6	2.1	2.6	1.6	2.7
Sweden	26.2	5.4	9.2	1.9	5.4	1.9	5.4	2.1	6.5	1.8
Median Value	16.6	6.5	6.6	2.7	5.6	1.9	2.2	2.5	1.7	2.4
Number of Items	36		12		8		8		8	

Subscores in order of Sections

Subscores

Section I: Discrimination of Sounds
Section II: Intonation
Section III: Listening Comprehension
Section IV: Listening Comprehension (Conversation)

Table 4.5. *Means and Standard Deviations for the English-Specific Descriptive Measures for Each Population in Each Country*

	Population II						Population IV					
	English Activities		Interest in English		Utility of English		English Activities		Interest in English		Utility of English	
Country	Mean	S.D.	Mean	S.D.	Mean	S.D.	Mean	S.D.	Mean	S.D.	Mean	S.D.
Belgium (Fr.)	3.5	1.8	14.9	2.9	25.4	4.8	3.5	2.0	14.1	3.2	24.2	5.4
Chile	–	–	–	–	–	–	3.1	1.8	12.5	3.4	24.0	5.8
FRG	2.9	1.5	13.0	3.0	24.4	5.0	4.3	2.1	13.1	2.7	24.2	5.0
Finland	3.6	1.6	12.6	3.9	21.9	5.2	4.8	1.7	14.4	2.5	23.7	4.4
Hungary	–	–	–	–	–	–	4.1	2.0	14.1	3.1	27.1	5.2
Israel	4.6	2.0	13.8	2.9	24.0	5.0	5.0	2.0	13.1	2.9	23.7	4.9
Italy	2.5	1.6	13.1	3.2	27.1	5.5	2.7	1.8	12.9	3.3	25.6	6.0
Netherlands	3.6	1.5	13.8	2.7	21.1	4.5	4.9	1.9	14.1	2.5	21.8	4.6
Sweden	3.6	1.6	13.7	2.8	23.1	5.0	4.8	2.1	13.7	2.5	24.5	5.2
Thailand	3.2	1.5	14.1	2.4	26.8	4.4	3.2	1.5	13.9	2.7	26.4	4.9
Median Value	3.5	1.6	13.7	2.9	24.2	5.0	4.2	1.9	13.8	2.8	24.2	5.1
No. of Items	6		10		12		6		10		12	

Table 4.6. *Intercorrelations of Cognitive and Affective Measures for Population II and Number Responding to Each Measure—Belgium (Fr.)*

	1	2	3	4	5	6	7	8	Number Responding to Each Measure
1. English Reading	–	.66	.25	.20	.28	.49	.54	.84	687
2. English Listening		–	.25	.16	.24	.51	.37	.65	670
3. Perceived Utility of English			–	.28	.52	.15	.20	.23	677
4. English Activities outside school				–	.26	.22	.17	.19	678
5. Interest in English					–	.15	.18	.22	678
6. Total Speaking						–	.34	.49	162
7. Total Writing 4							–	.51	680
8. Total Writing 1, 2, 3								–	696

Note: Each correlation represents the relationship between two measures on the same individuals. Since the number responding to each measure varies, the entire sample was not always used to compute the correlations. However, for those measures showing a marked decrease in number responding as compared to the Reading Test, the sample represented is generally the result of the best possible subsampling of the total sample per country.

Table 4.7. *Intercorrelations of Cognitive and Affective Measures for Population IV and Number Responding to Each Measure—Belgium (Fr.)*

	1	2	3	4	5	6	7	8	Number Responding to Each Measure
1. English Reading	–	.64	.29	.28	.27	.62	.50	.75	1 439
2. English Listening		–	.24	.28	.23	.63	.40	.62	1 394
3. Perceived Utility of English			–	.36	.59	.20	.23	.26	1 392
4. English Activities outside school				–	.37	.26	.23	.26	1 395
5. Interest in English					–	.27	.25	.25	1 395
6. Total Speaking						–	.54	.59	192
7. Total Writing 4							–	.52	1 360
8. Total Writing 1, 2, 3								–	1 390

Note: Each correlation represents the relationship between two measures on the same individuals. Since the number responding to each measure varies, the entire sample was not always used to compute the correlations. However, for those measures showing a marked decrease in number responding as compared to the Reading Test, the sample represented is generally the result of the best possible subsampling of the total sample per country.

Table 4.8. *Intercorrelations of Cognitive and Affective Measures for Population IV and Number Responding to Each Measure—Chile*

	1	2	3	4	5	6	7	8	Number Responding to Each Measure
1. English Reading	—	.27	.11	.26	.27	×	.41	.45	2 117
2. English Listening		—	.04	.25	.10	×	.36	.37	231
3. Perceived Utility of English			—	.39	.61	×	×	.26	1 982
4. English Activities outside school				—	.44	×	×	.39	1 981
5. Interest in English					—	×	×	.36	1 986
6. Total Speaking						—	×	×	93
7. Total Writing 4							—	.72	157
8. Total Writing 1, 2, 3								—	182

Note: Each correlation represents the relationship between two measures on the same individuals. Since the number responding to each measure varies, the entire sample was not always used to compute the correlations. However, for those measures showing a marked decrease in number responding as compared to the Reading Test, the sample represented is generally the result of the best possible subsampling of the total sample per country. × is used to designate those cases where correlations were not computed because there were less than 5 % of the total sample responding on both measures considered as a pair.

Table 4.9. *Intercorrelations of Cognitive and Affective Measures for Population II and Number Responding to Each Measure—Federal Republic of Germany*

	1	2	3	4	Number Responding to Each Measure
1. English Reading	—	.20	.23	.49	1 074
2. Perceived Utility of English		—	.30	.58	1 108
3. English Activities outside school			—	.30	1 106
4. Interest in English				—	1 106

Note: Each correlation represents the relationship between two measures on the same individuals. Since the number responding to each measure varies, the entire sample was not always used to compute the correlations. However, for those measures showing a marked decrease in number responding as compared to the Reading Test, the sample represented is generally the result of the best possible subsampling of the total sample per country.

Table 4.10. *Intercorrelations of Cognitive and Affective Measures for Population IV and Number Responding to Each Measure—Federal Republic of Germany*

	1	2	3	4	Number Responding to Each Measure
1. English Reading	–	.23	.15	.27	1 373
2. Perceived Utility of English		–	.39	.59	1 371
3. English Activities outside school			–	.36	1 371
4. Interest in English				–	1 372

Note: Each correlation represents the relationship between two measures on the same individuals. Since the number responding to each measure varies, the entire sample was not always used to compute the correlations. However, for those measures showing a marked decrease in number responding as compared to the Reading Test, the sample represented is generally the result of the best possible subsampling of the total sample per country.

Table 4.11. *Intercorrelations of Cognitive and Affective Measures for Population II and Number Responding to Each Measure—Finland*

	1	2	3	4	5	6	7	8	Number Responding to Each Measure
1. English Reading	–	.86	.32	.44	.48	.82	.71	.92	2 100
2. English Listening		–	.31	.44	.46	.80	.65	.86	2 118
3. Perceived Utility of English			–	.41	.66	.24	.25	.32	2 115
4. English Activities outside school				–	.45	.53	.34	.42	2 116
5. Interest in English					–	.44	.32	.47	2 116
6. Total Speaking						–	.67	.79	200
7. Total Writing 4							–	.74	605
8. Total Writing 1, 2, 3								–	2 087

Note: Each correlation represents the relationship between two measures on the same individuals. Since the number responding to each measure varies, the entire sample was not always used to compute the correlations. However, for those measures showing a marked decrease in number responding as compared to the Reading Test, the sample represented is generally the result of the best possible subsampling of the total sample per country.

Table 4.12. *Intercorrelations of Cognitive and Affective Measures for Population IV and Number Responding to Each Measure—Finland*

	1	2	3	4	5	6	7	8	Number Responding to Each Measure
English Reading	—	.63	.27	.32	.33	.60	.38	.62	2 310
English Listening		—	.23	.35	.27	.53	.33	.51	2 296
Perceived Utility of English			—	.38	.54	.26	.18	.21	2 301
English Activities outside school				—	.33	.48	.27	.27	2 303
Interest in English					—	.24	.20	.29	2 303
Total Speaking						—	.37	.50	279
Total Writing 4							—	.33	997
Total Writing 1, 2, 3								—	2 238

Note: Each correlation represents the relationship between two measures on the same individuals. [Si]ne the number responding to each measure varies, the entire sample was not always used [to] compute the correlations. However, for those measures showing a marked decrease in [n]umber responding as compared to the Reading Test, the sample represented is generally [th]e result of the best possible subsampling of the total sample per country.

Table 4.13. *Intercorrelations of Cognitive and Affective Measures for Population IV and Number Responding to Each Measure—Hungary*

	1	2	3	4	5	6	7	8	Number Responding to Each Measure
1. English Reading	—	.45	.24	.30	.29	.68	.47	.69	1 062
2. English Listening		—	-.06	.05	.00	.44	.18	.39	1 062
3. Perceived Utility of English			—	.48	.63	.46	.37	.24	1 062
4. English Activities outside school				—	.52	.64	.40	.31	1 059
5. Interest in English					—	.53	.51	.35	1 060
6. Total Speaking						—	.78	.62	118
7. Total Writing 4							—	.54	565
8. Total Writing 1, 2, 3								—	1 062

Note: Each correlation represents the relationship between two measures on the same individuals. Since the number responding to each measure varies, the entire sample was not always used to compute the correlations. However, for those measures showing a marked decrease in number responding as compared to the Reading Test, the sample represented is generally the result of the best possible subsampling of the total sample per country.

Table 4.14. *Intercorrelations of Cognitive and Affective Measures for Population II and Number Responding to Each Measure—Israel*

	1	2	3	4	Number Responding to Each Measure
1. English Reading	–	.02	.24	.28	1 064
2. Perceived Utility of English		–	.30	.42	986
3. English Activities outside school			–	.33	995
4. Interest in English				–	1 001

Note: Each correlation represents the relationship between two measures on the same individuals. Since the number responding to each measure varies, the entire sample was not always used to compute the correlations. However, for those measures showing a marked decrease in number responding as compared to the Reading Test, the sample represented is generally the result of the best possible subsampling of the total sample per country.

Table 4.15. *Intercorrelations of Cognitive and Affective Measures for Population IV and Number Responding to Each Measure—Israel*

	1	2	3	4	Number Responding to Each Measure
1. English Reading	–	.17	.22	.27	603
2. Perceived Utility of English		–	.30	.52	586
3. English Activities outside school			–	.34	592
4. Interest in English				–	592

Note: Each correlation represents the relationship between two measures on the same individuals. Since the number responding to each measure varies, the entire sample was not always used to compute the correlations. However, for those measures showing a marked decrease in number responding as compared to the Reading Test, the sample represented is generally the result of the best possible subsampling of the total sample per country.

Table 4.16. *Intercorrelations of Cognitive and Affective Measures for Population II and Number Responding to Each Measure—Italy*

	1	2	3	4	5	6	7	8	Number Responding to Each Measure
1. English Reading	–	.48	.13	.05	.22	.63	.60	.68	790
2. English Listening		–	.04	.07	–.04	.63	.32	.52	694
3. Perceived Utility of English			–	.22	.55	.15	.10	.21	768
4. English Activities outside school				–	.21	.10	–.01	.08	770
5. Interest in English					–	.01	.31	.18	770
6. Total Speaking						–	.44	.80	70
7. Total Writing 4							–	.57	582
8. Total Writing 1, 2, 3								–	731

Note: Each correlation represents the relationship between two measures on the same individuals. Since the number responding to each measure varies, the entire sample was not always used to compute the correlations. However, for those measures showing a marked decrease in number responding as compared to the Reading Test, the sample represented is generally the result of the best possible subsampling of the total sample per country.

Table 4.17. *Intercorrelations of Cognitive and Affective Measures for Population IV and Number Responding to Each Measure—Italy*

	1	2	3	4	5	6	7	8	Number Responding to Each Measure
1. English Reading	–	.65	.28	.18	.31	.71	.62	.70	323
2. English Listening		–	.08	.14	.21	.50	.47	.61	314
3. Perceived Utility of English			–	.31	.61	.55	.21	.14	316
4. English Activities outside school				–	.42	.37	.23	.11	317
5. Interest in English					–	.65	.31	.25	317
6. Total Speaking						–	.59	.58	28
7. Total Writing 4							–	.61	315
8. Total Writing 1, 2, 3								–	321

Note: Each correlation represents the relationship between two measures on the same individuals. Since the number responding to each measure varies, the entire sample was not always used to compute the correlations. However, for those measures showing a marked decrease in number responding as compared to the Reading Test, the sample represented is generally the result of the best possible subsampling of the total sample per country.

Table 4.18. *Intercorrelations of Cognitive and Affective Measures for Population II and Number Responding to Each Measure—Netherlands*

	1	2	3	4	Number Responding to Each Measure
1. English Reading	–	.06	.13	.38	2 089
2. Perceived Utility of English		–	.27	.41	2 075
3. English Activities outside school			–	.31	2 075
4. Interest in English				–	2 075

Note: Each correlation represents the relationship between two measures on the same individuals. Since the number responding to each measure varies, the entire sample was not always used to compute the correlations. However, for those measures showing a marked decrease in number responding as compared to the Reading Test, the sample represented is generally the result of the best possible subsampling of the total sample per country.

Table 4.19. *Intercorrelations of Cognitive and Affective Measures for Population IV and Number Responding to Each Measure—Netherlands*

	1	2	3	4	Number Responding to Each Measure
1. English Reading	–	.13	.13	.26	1 560
2. Perceived Utility of English		–	.28	.51	1 550
3. English Activities outside school			–	.34	1 551
4. Interest in English				–	1 551

Note: Each correlation represents the relationship between two measures on the same individuals. Since the number responding to each measure varies, the entire sample was not always used to compute the correlations. However, for those measures showing a marked decrease in number responding as compared to the Reading Test, the sample represented is generally the result of the best possible subsampling of the total sample per country.

Table 4.20. *Intercorrelations of Cognitive and Affective Measures for Population II and Number Responding to Each Measure—Sweden*

	1	2	3	4	5	6	7	8	Number Responding to Each Measure
1. English Reading	–	.80	.25	.20	.49	.69	.57	.81	2 331
2. English Listening		–	.21	.21	.45	.66	.55	.78	2 277
3. Perceived Utility of English			–	.35	.52	.31	.21	.22	2 168
4. English Activities outside school				–	.29	.24	.21	.21	2 168
5. Interest in English					–	.49	.36	.46	2 171
6. Total Speaking						–	.44	.66	218
7. Total Writing 4							–	.61	2 009
8. Total Writing 1, 2, 3								–	2 279

Note: Each correlation represents the relationship between two measures on the same individuals. Since the number responding to each measure varies, the entire sample was not always used to compute the correlations. However, for those measures showing a marked decrease in number responding as compared to the Reading Test, the sample represented is generally the result of the best possible subsampling of the total sample per country.

Table 4.21. *Intercorrelations of Cognitive and Affective Measures for Population IV and Number Responding to Each Measure—Sweden*

	1	2	3	4	5	6	7	8	Number Responding to Each Measure
1. English Reading	–	.62	.19	.29	.18	.43	.41	.64	1 619
2. English Listening		–	.12	.28	.14	.41	.34	.51	1 588
3. Perceived Utility of English			–	.38	.55	.27	.21	.16	1 436
4. English Activities outside school				–	.37	.41	.33	.27	1 447
5. Interest in English					–	.26	.16	.15	1 447
6. Total Speaking						–	.24	.30	204
7. Total Writing 4							–	.47	1 489
8. Total Writing 1, 2, 3								–	1 526

Note: Each correlation represents the relationship between two measures on the same individuals. Since the number responding to each measure varies, the entire sample was not always used to compute the correlations. However, for those measures showing a marked decrease in number responding as compared to the Reading Test, the sample represented is generally the result of the best possible subsampling of the total sample per country.

Table 4.22. *Intercorrelations of Cognitive and Affective Measures for Population II and Number Responding to Each Measure—Thailand*

	1	2	3	4	Number Responding to Each Measure
1. English Reading	–	.16	.06	.33	1 951
2. Perceived Utility of English		–	.26	.47	1 945
3. English Activities outside school			–	.27	1 950
4. Interest in English				–	1 951

Note: Each correlation represents the relationship between two measures on the same individuals. Since the number responding to each measure varies, the entire sample was not always used to compute the correlations. However, for those measures showing a marked decrease in number responding as compared to the Reading Test, the sample represented is generally the result of the best possible subsampling of the total sample per country.

Table 4.23. *Intercorrelations of Cognitive and Affective Measures for Population IV and Number responding to Each Measure—Thailand*

	1	2	3	4	Number Responding to Each Measure
1. English Reading	–	.21	.12	.36	937
2. Perceived Utility of English		–	.35	.57	936
3. English Activities outside school			–	.37	937
4. Interest in English				–	937

Note: Each correlation represents the relationship between two measures on the same individuals. Since the number responding to each measure varies, the entire sample was not always used to compute the correlations. However, for those measures showing a marked decrease in number responding as compared to the Reading Test, the sample represented is generally the result of the best possible subsampling of the total sample per country.

Table 4.24. *Intercorrelations for Reading Total Test and Subscores—Population II*

Country	Total Test with Subscores in Order of Sections						Between Subscores														
	I	II	III	IV	V	VI	I II	I III	I IV	I V	I VI	II III	II IV	II V	II VI	III IV	III V	III VI	IV V	IV VI	V VI
Belgium (Fr.)	.64	.77	.78	.76	.89	.86	.41	.44	.47	.51	.45	.53	.55	.65	.60	.52	.61	.59	.61	.57	.66
FRG	.72	.77	.79	.80	.90	.89	.55	.49	.51	.57	.60	.55	.56	.65	.60	.58	.64	.62	.67	.65	.72
Finland	.80	.84	.81	.81	.92	.91	.64	.59	.63	.69	.67	.62	.63	.72	.72	.60	.69	.66	.69	.69	.77
Israel	.77	.75	.81	.83	.92	.89	.57	.60	.62	.66	.62	.57	.56	.63	.58	.62	.70	.61	.75	.68	.76
Italy	.78	.78	.82	.81	.87	.88	.59	.58	.65	.63	.62	.57	.59	.64	.60	.63	.66	.63	.61	.65	.66
Netherlands	.83	.83	.85	.84	.91	.92	.66	.67	.66	.70	.71	.65	.65	.71	.72	.66	.70	.70	.72	.73	.78
Sweden	.75	.74	.77	.79	.89	.89	.52	.51	.54	.61	.61	.51	.53	.60	.57	.56	.59	.59	.67	.66	.73
Thailand	.72	.67	.78	.77	.83	.84	.43	.51	.53	.50	.55	.43	.46	.46	.48	.54	.55	.55	.56	.57	.59

Subscores

Section I: Recognition of Antonyms
Section II: Letter-Sound Correspondence
Section III: Recognition of Structural Features
Section IV: Vocabulary Recognition
Section V: Comprehension of Short Sentences
Section VI: Comprehension of Longer Passages

Table 4.25. *Intercorrelations for Reading Total Test and Subscores—Population IV*

Country	Total Test with Subscores in Order of Sections					Between Subscores									
	I	II	III	IV	V	I II	I III	I IV	I V	II III	II IV	II V	III IV	III V	IV V
Belgium (Fr.)	.56	.49	.65	.75	.89	.26	.30	.31	.33	.23	.22	.31	.38	.43	.58
Chile	.56	.43	.57	.75	.89	.25	.22	.32	.36	.19	.20	.27	.30	.35	.55
FRG	.51	.57	.59	.47	.78	.16	.19	.10	.20	.19	.16	.29	.14	.29	.22
Finland	.54	.61	.60	.54	.86	.20	.21	.16	.25	.25	.19	.41	.25	.37	.34
Hungary	.53	.50	.76	.74	.89	.18	.35	.29	.32	.23	.23	.33	.52	.57	.56
Israel	.59	.53	.72	.77	.90	.21	.37	.40	.40	.31	.30	.34	.57	.53	.59
Italy	.48	.57	.63	.77	.94	.09	.23	.24	.32	.30	.37	.49	.35	.48	.67
Netherlands	.57	.54	.63	.46	.74	.13	.25	.11	.20	.22	.12	.24	.17	.27	.24
Sweden	.65	.52	.67	.63	.85	.23	.37	.27	.35	.25	.23	.32	.36	.39	.45
Thailand	.38	.41	.68	.72	.86	.07	.15	.16	.18	.16	.18	.22	.39	.44	.49

Subscores

Section I: Recognition of Word Stress
Section II: Collocations
Section III: Recognition of Grammatical Structures
Section IV: Comprehension of Short Sentences
Section V: Comprehension of Longer Passages

Table 4.26. *Intercorrelations for Listening Total Test and Subscores—Population II*

Country	Total Test with Subscores in Order of Sections			Between Subscores		
	I	II	III	I–II	I–III	II–III
Belgium (Fr.)	.74	.82	.84	.40	.45	.54
Finland	.75	.89	.92	.48	.56	.76
Italy	.82	.89	*	.53	*	*
Sweden	.67	.85	.86	.41	.37	.60

Note: * is used to designate those cases where correlations were not computed because there were less than 5 % of the total sample responding on both measures considered as a pair.

Subscores
Section I: Discrimination of Sounds
Section II: Listening Comprehension
Section III: Dictation (no reliability was computed due to nature of test)

Table 4.27. *Intercorrelations for Listening Total Test and Subscores—Population IV*

Country	Total Test with Subscores in Order of Sections				Between Subscores					
	I	II	III	IV	I–II	I–III	I–IV	II–III	II–IV	III–IV
Belgium (Fr.)	.72	.50	.77	.78	.18	.38	.39	.22	.22	.52
Chile	.58	.53	.46	.49	−.01	−.05	−.07	.02	.14	.11
Finland	.66	.54	.75	.75	.14	.29	.32	.21	.21	.48
Hungary	.75	.47	.77	.78	.28	.38	.36	.14	.22	.52
Italy	.79	.51	.79	.82	.30	.41	.46	.23	.24	.58
Sweden	.54	.62	.73	.71	.17	.19	.24	.25	.24	.42

Subscores
Section I: Discrimination of Sounds
Section II: Intonation
Section III: Listening Comprehension
Section IV: Listening Comprehension (Conversation)

Table 4.28. *Correlation of Student Background Variables and Achievement in Reading, Population II*

	Bel-gium (Fr.)	FRG	Fin-land	Israel	Italy	Nether-lands	Sweden	Tha land
1. Word knowledge	.25	.65	.59	.57	.38	.63	.54	.3
2. Parent interest favorable	−.05	−.21	.28	−.09	.03	−.14	.09	.0
3. Time spent in English-speaking countries—up to one year	.12	.08	.00	.01	.02	−.04	.03	−.0
4. Time spent in English-speaking countries— over two years	.06	*	−.01	.14	.11	.01	.01	−.0
5. Exposure to English— (Often being exposed to English)	.15	.11	.17	.13	−.02	.07	.08	.0

Note: * is used to designate those cases where correlations were not computed because th were less than 5 % of the total sample responding on both measures as a pair.

Table 4.29. *Correlation of Student Background Variables and Achievement in Reading Population IV*

	Bel-gium (Fr.)	Chile	FRG	Fin-land	Hun-gary	Is-rael	Italy	Neth-er-lands	Swe-den	Th lar
1. Word knowledge	.29	.27	.43	.32	.20	.37	.37	.28	.54	.
2. Parent interest favorable	−.05	−.02	−.04	.11	−.10	.02	−.01	−.06	−.05	−.
3. Time spent in English-speaking countries—up to one year	−.08	.22	.03	.12	.09	.08	.17	.06	.15	−.
4. Time spent in English-speaking countries—over two years	.12	.08	−.02	.05	.11	.15	.00	.05	.07	*
5. Exposure to English—(Often being exposed to English)	.17	.19	.03	.14	.13	.10	.10	.08	.11	.

Note: * is used to designate those cases where correlations were not computed because t were less than 5 % of the total sample responding on both measures as a pair.

Table 4.30. *Correlation of Student Background Variables and Achievement in Listening—Population II*

	Belgium (Fr.)	Finland	Italy	Sweden
1. Word knowledge	.16	.56	.10	.50
2. Parent interest favorable	.01	.27	.04	−.08
3. Time spent in English-speaking countries—up to one year	.07	.01	.07	.03
4. Time spent in English-speaking countries—over two years	.08	−.02	.12	.03
5. Exposure to English— (Often being exposed to English)	.12	.17	.03	.17

Table 4.31. *Correlation of Student Background Variables and Achievement in Listening—Population IV*

	Belgium (Fr.)	Chile	Finland	Hungary	Italy	Sweden
1. Word knowledge	.22	.15	.24	.19	.36	.37
2. Parent interest favorable	−.11	.01	.11	−.04	.04	−.05
3. Time spent in English-speaking countries—up to one year	.11	.29	.16	.05	.18	.14
4. Time spent in English-speaking countries—over two years	.10	.00	.04	.10	−.03	.05
5. Exposure to English— (Often being exposed to English)	.18	.17	.17	.01	.10	.12

Table 4.32. *Correlations of Aspects of Student's Self Perception and Student's Aspirati to Be Able to Use English and Achievement in English Reading—Population II*

	Bel-gium (Fr.)	FRG	Fin-land	Israel	Italy	Nether-lands	Swe-den	Thai land
1. Like school	−.11	.16	.20	−.05	.11	.10	.22	.00
2. Aspiration to be able to speak	.21	.34	.51	.38	.06	.40	.52	.26
3. Aspiration to understand	.19	.39	.53	.32	.08	.37	.50	.28
4. Aspiration to read	.20	.34	.48	.33	.07	.32	.47	.32
5. Aspiration to write	.18	.32	.46	.23	.08	.26	.43	.29
6. Perceived ability to speak	.17	.26	.38	.31	.10	.26	.40	.12
7. Perceived ability to listen	.25	.33	.42	.38	.07	.35	.44	.24
8. Perceived ability to read	.16	.25	.32	.19	.11	.27	.37	.20
9. Perceived ability to write	.09	.22	.37	.21	.10	.29	.40	.22
10. Perceived diffi-culty of English	.17	.19	.14	.27	.07	.29	.34	.12
11. Perceived industry in studying Eng-lish	−.09	.10	.25	−.19	.03	−.10	.09	−.22
12. Hours of homework in English	.07	.25	.34	.07	.07	.12	−.02	.17

Correlations of Aspects of Student's Self Perception and Student's Aspiration Be Able to Use English and Achievement in English Reading—Population IV

	Belgium (Fr.)	Chile	FRG	Finland	Hungary	Israel	Italy	Netherlands	Sweden	Thailand
Like school	.06	−.16	.05	.02	.00	.00	.01	.05	.10	.01
Aspiration to be able to speak	.32	.28	.15	.35	.32	.29	.41	.21	.36	.24
Aspiration to understand	.31	.27	.13	.34	.30	.16	.29	.19	.34	.30
Aspiration to read	.30	.26	.18	.36	.28	.28	.32	.17	.36	.20
Aspiration to write	.30	.24	.16	.30	.27	.19	.28	.19	.35	.21
Perceived ability to speak	.39	.36	.24	.36	.29	.36	.43	.24	.36	.17
Perceived ability to listen	.37	.40	.25	.36	.28	.39	.43	.28	.31	.34
Perceived ability to read	.36	.33	.24	.34	.24	.33	.40	.28	.34	.14
Perceived ability to write	.32	.32	.24	.35	.32	.28	.37	.24	.38	.20
Perceived difficulty of English	.17	.27	.17	.24	.21	.22	.16	.32	.28	.24
Perceived industry in studying English	.07	−.13	.01	.11	.04	−.02	.08	−.18	−.06	−.30
Hours of homework in English	.13	.10	−.02	.02	.20	.11	.21	−.15	−.09	.15

Table 4.34. *Correlations of Aspects of Student's Self Perception and Student's Aspiration to Be Able to Use English and Achievement in English Listening—Population II*

	Belgium (Fr.)	Finland	Italy	Sweden
1. Like school	−.04	.20	−.01	.20
2. Aspiration to be able to speak	.14	.50	−.02	.46
3. Aspiration to understand	.18	.52	.06	.45
4. Aspiration to read	.09	.47	.03	.44
5. Aspiration to write	.08	.45	.06	.39
6. Perceived ability to speak	.17	.39	.07	.38
7. Perceived ability to listen	.23	.44	.11	.40
8. Perceived ability to read	.11	.33	.06	.38
9. Perceived ability to write	.09	.37	.13	.37
10. Perceived difficulty of English	.21	.14	.02	.33
11. Perceived industry in studying English	.08	.25	−.03	.08
12. Hours of homework in English	.07	.36	−.02	−.02

Table 4.35. *Correlations of Aspects of Student's Self Perception and Student's Aspiration to Be Able to Use English and Achievement in English Listening—Population IV*

	Belgium (Fr.)	Chile	Fin-land	Hun-gary	Italy	Swe-den
1. Like school	.04	.05	.01	.02	−.14	.09
2. Aspiration to be able to speak	.28	.21	.34	.11	.29	.31
3. Aspiration to understand	.26	.18	.32	.11	.17	.30
4. Aspiration to read	.23	.22	.29	.07	.23	.28
5. Aspiration to write	.22	.15	.24	.05	.24	.27
6. Perceived ability to speak	.38	.26	.37	.10	.25	.31
7. Perceived ability to listen	.40	.25	.39	.08	.27	.29
8. Perceived ability to read	.32	.11	.31	.02	.35	.27
9. Perceived ability to write	.31	.13	.31	.06	.34	.29
10. Perceived difficulty of English	.13	.12	.22	.04	.17	.25
11. Perceived industry in studying English	.07	−.11	.07	−.08	.04	−.10
12. Hours of homework in English	.15	.04	−.02	−.08	.10	−.09

Table 4.36. *Correlation of Teacher Characteristics and Achievement in English Reading Population II*

	Belgium (Fr.)	FRG	Fin-land	Is-rael	Italy	Nether-lands	Swe-den	Thai-land
Self-perceived skill in speaking	.11	.52	.40	−.14	.08	.44	.00	.14
Self-perceived skill in reading	.11	.53	.39	−.12	.12	.31	.02	.11
Self-perceived skill in writing	.07	.33	.40	.09	.12	.41	.00	.17
Self-perceived skill in pro-nunciation	.13	.38	.38	−.10	.01	.31	.00	.01
Hours weekly of lesson prep-aration	−.07	.19	.53	.14	.20	.17	−.01	−.04
Hours weekly of marking papers	.11	.45	.40	.17	.13	.27	.05	.05
Sex of teacher	.17	−.20	.43	.31	−.10	.19	.04	.06

Table 4.37. Correlation of Teacher Characteristics and Achievement in English Reading— Population IV

	Belgium (Fr.)	Chile	FRG	Finland	Hungary	Israel	Italy	Netherlands	Sweden	Thailand
Self-perceived skill in speaking	.07	.12	.04	.05	−.01	.11	.37	−.08	.08	−.23
Self-perceived skill in reading	.21	−.05	.15	.10	.17	−.04	.18	−	−.01	−.14
Self-perceived skill in writing	.07	.07	.01	.03	−.01	.19	.30	.07	.05	−.05
Self-perceived skill in pronunciation	.09	.13	.06	.06	.00	.08	−.24	.01	.16	.01
Hours weekly of lesson preparation	−.16	.19	.05	−.08	.09	−.13	.00	−.05	−.05	.50
Hours weekly of marking papers	.14	.13	.05	−.05	.25	.17	.00	−.14	.01	.04
Sex of teacher	.13	−.23	.05	.07	.13	.16	.27	−.02	−.01	.02

Table 4.38. Correlation of Teacher Characteristics and Achievement in English Listening—Population II

	Belgium (Fr.)	Finland	Italy	Sweden
Self-perceived skill in speaking	−.02	.41	.06	.02
Self-perceived skill in reading	.10	.37	.01	.03
Self-perceived skill in writing	−.01	.42	−.04	.04
Self-perceived skill in pronunciation	.00	.40	.17	−.01
Hours weekly of lesson preparation	.00	.53	.11	.03
Hours weekly of marking papers	.17	.40	.05	.04
Sex of teacher	.21	.41	−.01	.07

Table 4.39. *Correlation of Teacher Characteristics and Achievement in English Listening—Population IV*

	Belgium (Fr.)	Chile	Finland	Hungary	Italy	Sweden
Self-perceived skill in speaking	.03	.22	.11	−.11	.19	−.04
Self-perceived skill in reading	.15	.23	.15	.15	.36	−.07
Self-perceived skill in writing	.01	.06	.07	.06	.04	−.05
Self-perceived skill in pronunciation	.04	.06	.07	−.06	−.39	.07
Hours weekly of lesson preparation	−.11	−.12	−.07	.07	−.10	−.08
Hours weekly of marking papers	.12	−.17	−.05	.00	−.35	.00
Sex of teacher	.11	.09	.05	.25	.14	−.05

Table 4.40. *Correlations of School and Classroom Variables with Reading—Population* |

	Belgium (Fr.)	FRG	Finland	Israel	Italy	Netherlands	Sweden	Thailand
Hours of instruction in English	.06	.22	.60	.19	−.12	.23	−.17	.08
Grade beginning English	−.03	.04	−.24	−.17	−.22	.06	−.20	−.22
Method of teaching grammar—inductive	−.05		.03	−.20	−.01	−.02	−.01	−.01
Method of teaching grammar—deductive	.06	−.42	−.31	.16	.09	−.34	−.01	−.12
Method of teaching grammar—eclectic	−.06	.22	.42	.28	−.09	.27	−.01	.11
Use of mother tongue—Beginning	.01	.01	.36	.07	.02	−.08	.00	.06
Use of mother tongue—Intermediate	.09	.16	−.11	.19	−.12	−.17	−.01	−.06
Importance of student needs in determining approach	−.19	.15	−.14	−.02	.01	−.05	.02	−.04
Importance of exams in determining approach	−.17	−.18	.53	.07	−.10	−.19	.03	.15
Frequency of small group work	−.20	−.55	−.33	−.15	.12	.14	.02	.01
Importance of needs in next grade	−.23	−.45	.19	.12	.02	−.13	.03	.13
Use of A/V	−.27	−.17	.02	.04	.11	.12	−.05	−.02
Use of language auxiliary	−.24	.22	.30	.13	.20	.17	−.06	.01

Table 4.41. *Correlations of School and Classroom Variables with Reading—Population IV*

	Belgium (Fr.)	Chile	FRG	Finland	Hungary	Israel	Italy	Netherlands	Sweden	Thailand
Hours of instruction in English	.29	.27	.12	.14	.42	.35	.40	−.09	−.12	.02
Grade beginning English	−.20	−.32	.04	.33	−.11	−.21	−.35	.05	−.06	.23
Method of teaching grammar—inductive	−.09	.04		−.15	−.02	−.22	−.23	.08	−.08	−.04
Method of teaching grammar—deductive	.03	.03	.03	.00	−.08	−.13	−.29	.02	−.01	−.19
Method of teaching grammar—eclectic	.07	−.02	.03	.07	.03	.35	.37	.12	.04	.14
Use of mother tongue—Beginning	−.26	.03	.01	.10	−.08	−.31	.39	.11	−.03	−.12
Use of mother tongue—Intermediate	.08	−.18	.07	.05	−.22	.24	.43	.07	.05	.31
Use of mother tongue—Advanced	.02	−.12	.08	−.09	.19	−.11	.15	.06	.02	−.46
Importance of student needs in determining approach	−.10	.05	−.03	.00	−.04	.08	−.09	−.02	.00	.18
Importance of exams in determining approach	.00	−.11	.12	.03	−.09	−.01	−.29	−.07	.09	.00
Frequency of small group work	.07	.14	.00	−.03	−.09	.04	−.09	.02	−.10	.46
Importance of needs in next grade	.03	−.04	.06	−.01	.00	.10	.11	.03	.07	−.11
Use of A/V	−.09	.09	−.07	.12	.00	.22	−.23	−.02	.10	.42
Use of language auxiliary	−.13	.36	−.14	.06	.15	−.11	.37	.07	−.08	−.12

Table 4.42. *Correlations of School and Classroom Variables with Listening—Population II*

	Belgium (Fr.)	Finland	Italy	Sweden
Hours of instruction in English	.09	.55	−.02	−.14
Grade beginning English	.03	−.29	−.16	−.19
Method of teaching grammar—inductive	−.05	.02	.15	−.01
Method of teaching grammar—deductive	.05	−.27	−.04	−.03
Method of teaching grammar—eclectic	−.05	.38	−.06	.02
Use of mother tongue—beginning	.11	.36	.24	−.02
Use of mother tongue—intermediate	.02	−.09	.08	.00
Use of mother tongue—advanced	−.15	.55	−.20	.00
Importance of student needs in determining approach	−.21	−.14	.04	−.02
Importance of exams in determining approach	−.19	.53	.04	.04
Frequency of small group work	−.14	−.26	−.04	.01
Importance of needs in next grade	−.10	.20	.08	.06
Use of A/V	.02	.04	−.01	−.05
Use of language auxiliary	−.32	.24	.13	−.05

Table 4.43. *Correlations of School and Classroom Variables with Listening—Population IV*

	Belgium (Fr.)	Chile	Fin-land	Hun-gary	Italy	Swe-den
Hours of instruction in English	.34	.22	.09	.12	.37	−.06
Grade beginning English	−.21	−.10	−.28	−.04	−.27	−.11
Method of teaching grammar—inductive	−.09	.00	−.13	.01	−.40	−.08
Method of teaching grammar—deductive	.09	−.05	−.01	.10	−.25	−.00
Method of teaching grammar—eclectic	.01	.05	.08	.19	.49	.02
Use of mother tongue—beginning	−.25	.12	.09	−.04	.44	−.20
Use of mother tongue—intermediate	−.06	−.12	.09	−.16	.45	.06
Use of mother tongue—advanced	.01	−.03	−.07	.12	.11	.02
Importance of student needs in determining approach	.00	−.16	.05	−.11	−.24	−.04
Importance of exams in determining approach	.00	−.01	.03	−.27	−.11	.02
Frequency of small group work	.01	−.04	−.04	−.10	.04	−.10
Importance of needs in next grade	.07	−.06	−.02	−.06	−.15	.05
Use of A/V	−.01	.11	.13	.02	.19	−.04
Use of language auxiliary	−.07	.05	.09	.10	.42	.03

Chapter 5

Speaking and Writing Tests

Part 1: Description and Some Results[1]

TEST RATIONALE

The construction of tests to measure a student's ability to speak and write in a foreign language demands different procedures from those used to test his understanding of the language. For instance, the precise definition of test content is less crucial in the development of tests to measure *expressive skills* than it is in the construction of tests to measure *receptive skills*. These latter must present the student with a sample of language adequate to test his comprehension, whereas tests of expressive skills need only provide him with an appropriate framework within which to produce an oral or a written response. The main function of the items in Speaking and Writing tests is thus to stimulate the production of creative responses, rather than to provide both a stimulus and a selection of prepared responses. This element of creativity does, however, bring certain practical difficulties in its train. Tests which permit "free" or "guided" responses tend to be cumbersome to administer, particularly if they involve the tape-recording of responses, and invariably require specialist scoring. Further, unless a language laboratory with highly sophisticated equipment can be made available to the whole of the sample to be tested, tests of speaking skills must inevitably be administered on an individual basis. This is an expensive and time-consuming procedure that is difficult to control, especially on a cross-national basis. In the IEA study of English as a Foreign Language, the Speaking tests had to be administered in the normal school environment under the supervision of staff relatively unaccustomed to the task, using recording equipment of a fairly simple nature. Under such circumstances, it was of major concern to develop standard procedures for administration and scoring which would ensure that the eventual tests were as accident-proof as possible

[1] This part was written by Clare Burstall of the National Foundation for Educational Research in England and Wales.

and "equally unfair, if not equally fair, to all potential users" (Agard and Dunkel, 1948).

It will be recalled that the English Committee had taken the view that all the countries participating in the IEA study of English as a Foreign Language should use the same tests to measure achievement in English, and that these tests should be constructed with regard to selected features of the English language whose mastery at different stages in the learning process could be held to constitute a growing command of the language. Every effort was to be made during the construction of the tests to ensure that the language used was as authentic as possible and as "natural" as the constraints of the testing situation would allow. It was agreed that test items would, wherever possible, be in the form of "complete and natural utterances" (Johnson et al., 1963), avoiding the use of isolated lexical items or language elements out of context. It was recognized, however, that previous attempts to use completely natural material in the test situation had not met with a great deal of success. Both Spearritt (1962) and Wilkinson (1965) had been unable to produce reliable test materials when they attempted to use recordings of spontaneous speech. Wilkinson eventually analyzed a series of such recordings to establish the characteristic features of spoken language, and then "fabricated" passages of utterance. Most test constructors have tended to follow Wilkinson's example and to use material which represents a compromise between natural and artificial language: this was the procedure adopted in the IEA study.

There has been some controversy as to whether broad-ranging tests of "communication skills" should replace the testing of discrete linguistic features. Some authors (Plaister, 1967; Upshur, 1971; Palmer, 1972) have rejected the "discrete-point" approach to testing and have concentrated on the development of tests in which the subject is given a "communication task." For example, he may be required to describe to an examiner one of four pictures, in such a way that the examiner is able to guess correctly which picture is being described; he may have to elicit specific information from the examiner by engaging him in dialogue. It has been contended that such tests "are measuring factors not being measured in the traditional foreign language proficiency test battery" (Palmer, 1972). Most authors, however, have tended to produce tests of expressive skills which contain both "discrete-point" items and items designed to test the subject's general ability to communicate in the foreign language (Pimsleur, 1961; Andrade et al., 1961, 1963; Johnson et al., 1963). A similar approach was adopted in the IEA study, although it was agreed that, insofar as the measurement of speaking and writing skills was concerned, the major effort in test construction should be to provide stimuli which would elicit relatively "free" responses. In this, the view of the English Committee reflected the current trend of opinion (Godshalk et al., 1966; Palmer, 1972) that free-response material has a unique contribution to make in the assessment of expressive skills. It was recognized, however, that the greater the freedom of response, the more formidable would be the development of adequate scoring procedures. It was also accepted that, in the earlier stages of foreign-language learning, when only an elementary level of competence had been attained, the test items might need to be closely structured if they were to elicit an adequate response. It would clearly be pointless to give a student opportunities to demonstrate spontaneous fluency in a foreign language if he still had to struggle to produce a single, limited response to a familiar and well-defined stimulus. For this reason, in the IEA study of English as a Foreign Language, closely-structured types of items entailing only a limited range of response were invariably used in the earlier sections of the Speaking and Writing tests; the free-response material was reserved for the later sections of the tests.

Chomsky (1967) has made a useful distinction between linguistic competence—knowledge of "the system of rules that determine both the phonetic shape of the sentence and its intrinsic semantic content"—and actual performance, pointing out that the production of speech involves many "extralinguistic" factors. Nowhere is this more apparent than in the oral testing situation. Rand (1963) developed oral tests of English as a foreign language and found the reliability of his tests affected by "the nervousness which prevents some participants from performing to maximum capacity." Carroll (1967) also described how a student's performance on an oral test might depend not so much on his linguistic competence as on his general fluency and self-confidence in spontaneous speech, whether in his mother tongue or in a foreign language. Graham (1971) has similarly pointed out that, as well as sampling language proficiency, oral tests "freely sample also personality and dispositional variables," describing how "some children are habitually loquacious, resort readily to language and their output is correspondingly large in size and perhaps in diversity. Others, however, are laconic, unforthcoming and often fail to deploy their language capacities to anything like their full extent. The investigator has no way of distinguishing between reluctance and inability." Graham emphasizes the importance of incorporating a sufficient number of practice examples into any test of oral production, particularly when young children are involved, and argues that one of the main concerns of the test constructor should be to place the subject in a situation which will maximize his chances of producing a particular utterance, if it lies within his linguistic competence to do so. Dyson (1972), in a recent survey of oral testing procedures has also described how test performance may be affected by "nervousness or boldness in the presence of a stranger," adding: ". . . the candidate's performance and the examiner's reaction to it may be conditioned by the appearance, sex and age of candidate and examiner." Such observations receive support from the findings of Sarason, Patterson, and their associates, who reported that highly anxious children tend to show a marked decrease in verbal production in the test situation (Sarason et al., 1958; Patterson et al., 1960). Similarly, Cotler and Palmer (1971) found that test anxiety significantly affected the accuracy with which elementary school children read passages aloud.

Since many of the students taking part in the IEA study had never previously been exposed to oral testing, it was a matter of concern to the English Committee that their test performance should not be adversely affected by the unfamiliar situation. The need to alleviate potential test anxiety wherever possible was therefore one of the factors which shaped the development of the speaking tests used in the study. For instance, untimed practice examples were always provided at the beginning of each test and, within the test, before the introduction of any unfamiliar type of item. In the test instructions, provision was made for the students to work through the practice examples with their teacher, with as much prompting as was deemed necessary, until the teacher was satisfied that each student was thoroughly familiar with the test procedure. All test instructions were given in the student's mother tongue to avoid causing unnecessary anxiety or penalizing a student for failing to understand what he was required to do.

The disarray that can be caused if precautions such as these are not taken has been vividly described by Agard and Dunkel (1948) in their report of an early investigation into foreign-language learning in America. Agard and Dunkel had devised a listening comprehension test which was preceded by an announcement that the directions for the test would be given in the foreign language, to familiarize the students with the voice and manner of the native speaker. They describe in their report how this "warm-up" passage invariably had an effect exactly opposite to that desired. "Instead of relaxing and accustoming themselves to the speaker's voice, the students were more unnerved than before because they understood nothing of what was being said. This was of course merely because the vocabulary of directions was unfamiliar; but the psychological effect was bad as the students approached the first test item with the fearful conviction that they would continue to comprehend nothing." Agard and Dunkel came to the conclusion that the instructions for the test should have been given in the mother tongue and the test itself preceded by "a series of easy sample items of the same type as those making up the body of the test." This was the procedure adopted in the IEA study.

In the measurement of expressive skills, test reliability will be adversely affected if there are variations in the administration of the test materials or in the application of scoring procedures. No matter how careful the preparation of the test materials has been, the results obtained will be meaningless unless standard procedures for administration and scoring can be devised and implemented. There are few problems involved in the administration of Writing tests, but the administration of Speaking tests is fraught with difficulties of both a technical and a psychological nature. Partial standardization of administration can be achieved by the use of standardized test materials (by the use of a restricted range of pictorial material, for example, in conjunction with closely-structured questions), but poorly-maintained equipment, an acoustically inadequate room, or intrusive interventions on the part of the test administrator, can have disruptive effects of unknown extent. In order to combat this possibility, it is necessary to provide extremely clear and detailed instructions to accompany the test materials and to subject these to pilot-testing procedures as rigorous as those used in the trial runs of the test items themselves.

The other potential source of unreliability which affects both Speaking and Writing tests lies in the procedures used to score open-ended or free-response types of items. As Pimsleur (1961) has commented, with reference to the development of tests of speaking ability in French: "The effort to test speaking ability entirely objectively is doomed to fall short of complete success, for an evaluation of how well a person speaks French requires judgements on the part of a hearer. These are necessarily subjective." Pimsleur stresses the need for further research into methods of improving inter-rater reliability in the assessment of expressive skills. Most of the research in this area has concerned the reliability of scoring essays written in the subject's mother tongue, but the issues raised are germane also to the assessment of written and spoken fluency in a foreign language. Wiseman (1949) had drawn attention to the importance of the "self-consistency" of markers and pointed out that the consistency coefficient obtained from a simple mark-remark correlation was "the one single measure which is quite clearly a true consistency, and one which is closest allied to the normal concept of test reliability." Other workers (Morrison and Vernon, 1941; Finlayson, 1951; Vernon and Millican, 1954; Godshalk et al., 1966; Chaplen, 1971) have attempted to determine the optimum number of scorers and of samples of a given subject's written work necessary to ensure adequate reliability. There is general agreement that it is possible to score essay scripts with a high degree of reliability (the reliability coefficients quoted commonly exceed 0.90), provided that a closely-structured scoring scheme is employed and that potential scorers are carefully trained in its use. Chaplen (1971) concludes: "As is to be expected, a plurality of either essays or examiners results in a quite substantial reduction of error in marking, and a plurality of both essays and examiners results in a further considerable reduction." In the IEA study, it was agreed that a small team of native English speakers should be employed to score all the free-response material. As a check on the stability of scoring standards, each member of the team would periodically be given a random sample of tapes and scripts to score which had already been scored by another team member. Each would also periodically re-ceive a random sample of tapes and scripts to re-score which he had scored himself on a previous occasion. In this way it was hoped that a high level of scoring reliability would be maintained.

PILOT-TESTING

The problems peculiar to the administration of a given test are usually brought to light during its first full-scale pilot-tests, although their solution may not be reached until the draft test materials have undergone considerable revision. The purpose of pilot-testing is to try out the draft test materials on a sample of students as similar as possible in age and range of ability to those for whom the test is ultimately intended. This process serves to reveal defective or ambiguous items, highlight any problems of administration and scor-ing, and establish the potential range of performance on the test. That this is an essential process in the development of a test may be indicated by the amount of revision necessitated by the pilot-testing of the draft versions of the English Speaking and Writing tests. Pilot-testing was carried out in the summer of 1970 on necessarily limited but nevertheless cross-national samples of students. The countries taking part in the pilot-testing were Chile (Population IV), Finland (Population II) and Italy (Populations II and IV). The results of the pilot-testing clearly indicated that the draft test materials were defective in several respects. These results may be summarized as follows:

Test Instructions

The instructions given to the student were found to be seriously inadequate. For example, the items for the original version of the Structural Control section of the Speaking test were presented on magnetic tape. After each item had been spoken on the tape, there was a pause and then a signal tone, followed by a longer pause which varied in length from 12 to 25 seconds. The student was simply instructed to respond as soon as he had heard the item: he was not warned about the signal tone. Consequently, the majority of students responded, or attempted to respond, in the short pause immediately following the spoken item, before the signal tone sounded. Some students managed to complete their response during this time; others were interrupted by the signal tone and either faltered or totally abandoned their attempt to respond. Clearly, the function of the signal tone should have been made explicit in the test instructions.

Another source of confusion lay in certain written cues which had been provided in the student's test booklet. These were intended to guide the student and to help structure his responses but, in the event, proved extremely misleading. In the Structural Control section of the Speaking test booklet, for instance, incomplete printed responses were provided, with blank spaces left for the words which the student was supposed to supply. One of the items in this section consisted of the question: "Do they like milk?" A picture of students drinking milk was provided, with the caption: "Yes, they ..., but they don't like coffee." The students taking the test were given no instructions at all as to the function of the written cues. Some of them attempted initially to treat the cues as complete responses and to read them aloud instead of producing a response of their own. For example, the cue: "... this is a car?," intended to elicit the response: "Is this a car?," was simply read aloud as it stood. As the cues became more fragmentary, however, most students attempted to tailor their responses to the number of blank spaces provided, abandoning a correct response if it did not fit into the required number of spaces. For example, in answer to the question: "Do they like milk?," many students began to reply: "Yes, they like milk ...," then, realizing that they had one word too many, changed their response to: "Yes, they like, but they don't like coffee,"—a response which scored zero. The students had not been informed whether their responses should conform to the cues provided or whether they would be penalized if they failed to do so. In the event, many were misled into producing incorrect responses in their attempts to conform.

Pictorial Material

It is widely recognized that the creation of totally unambiguous pictorial material for use in foreign-language testing is an extremely exacting task. Rivers (1966) describes how a picture which is ambiguous in concept "may concentrate the attention on a misleading feature and arouse false associations": this is particularly true when young or unsophisticated students are concerned. Wright (1967) reports a tendency for younger students to assume that "any mark made by an artist in a representational drawing must be an attempt to depict something concrete." He also emphasizes the difficulty of reliably conveying an abstract notion to young students by pictorial means, describing how a picture of a boy sitting at a desk, reading from a book and, at the same time, writing, reliably suggested the concept of "working" to adults but was interpreted as "reading," "writing," "sitting," or even "crossing his legs" by younger students, who completely failed to form the more general concept intended by the artist. Plaister (1967) has suggested that, because of difficulties of this kind, representational drawings should not be used in foreign-language testing but should be replaced by diagrams, geometric figures, simple charts and graphs, and occasional stick figures. This procedure would, however, entail the disadvantage of introducing an uncontrollable source of variation in test performance, since students are known to vary widely in their ability to interpret diagrams, geometric figures, charts and graphs.

In the IEA study, simple black-and-white illustrations, drawn in somewhat "comic-strip" style, were used in the Speaking test booklets and, in their original versions, were found to have misleading and ambiguous features. For example, a picture of a boy drinking from a glass was provided, to elicit the response: "He is drinking." Many students noticed that, in the drawing, the liquid in the glass did not actually touch the boy's lips and therefore responded: "He is not drinking yet." Another picture, intended to convey the action of having fallen, was almost universally misinterpreted. The question asked in connection with this picture was "What has the man done?" It was almost impossible to tell from the picture precisely what the man had done, in that it showed only the outcome of an unpictured and unknown action. The most frequent response to this item was "I don't know what he's done." One puzzled student suggested: "Perhaps he's drunk!"

Similar difficulties of interpretation were raised by one of the pictures used in the Fluency section of the Speaking test. The picture was supposed to show two boys on ladders, painting a house. It was rather crudely drawn, however, and was variously interpreted as showing window-cleaners working, men building a house, workmen painting the walls, boys washing the walls, and so on. This inevitably gave rise to an unacceptably wide range of responses.

Timing and Length

When test material is presented on tape, the correct timing of the pauses intended for the student's responses is extremely important. If the pauses are too short, students attempting a correct but complex response will be unable to complete it. If the pauses are too long, uncertainty is created and students often anxiously attempt to elaborate the response they have just made, even if it is already complete and correct. In the original Structural Control section of the Speaking test, variable response-pauses were provided, the longest being 25 seconds in duration. When the tapes were scored, it was found that few students required as much as five seconds in which to make their response. As well as having a negative effect on the student's composure, the lengthy response-pauses made for slow and uneconomical scoring, since there was no way of eliminating them from the student's tape. In its original form, the scoring of this section of the Speaking test took a full five minutes per student.

Allied to the problem of timing is that of length. Since speaking tests are difficult and uneconomical to administer, the ideal test is one which is as short as the demands of efficiency and reliability will allow. In the original versions of the Speaking test, both the Oral Reading and the Fluency sections were found to be far too long. During the process of pilot-testing, it became clear that these sections of the test were approximately twice as long as was necessary: both performance and scoring suffered in consequence. In the Oral Reading section, for instance, it emerged that a sufficient number and variety of scoring points could have been provided within the framework of a much shorter and simpler text. The scoring of the original reading passages was an extremely lengthy process, involving a great deal of redundancy. Similarly, in the Fluency section of the test, where the student was required to describe the events depicted in two picture-sequences, it was found that the response to the second picture-sequence tended to be similar to, but shorter than, the response to the first one. This was partly due to the fact that the picture-sequences were somewhat alike in content. The first showed a woman buying fish from a fish-monger, cooking it and then eating it. The second showed two small boys at a counter apparently asking for and obtaining a number of bottles of lemonade and some ice cream. The boys were subsequently shown clutching their stomachs. The situations depicted in the two sequences were thus basically similar (buying and later consuming food or drink) and tended to call forth essentially similar responses. The students tended to concentrate on the first picture-sequence, producing only an abbreviated response to the second one. For example, in response to the first picture-sequence, one Population IV student said: "A young woman goes to a market in her city and here she wants to buy a fish. When she arrives at home she cooks it and, after some minutes, she eats it." In response to the second picture-sequence, the same student said: "Two young boys want to drink drinks. Their father gives them drinks but, after some minutes, they are ill." Similarly, another Population IV student's first response was: "I see that a lady is buying a fish and that the man is selling her a fish. The man has a hat on his head and a long nose. The lady goes home and prepares her dinner. It is ten to six. After ten minutes she eats her dinner." His second response was: "Two little boys buy something to drink and also ice creams. They take the ices and the drinks. But they drink too much and so they are sick." These examples are typical of the general trend of performance: it became clear that the second picture-sequence was adding little to the test but excess length.

Difficulty Level

It was found during pilot-testing that some parts of the original versions of the tests were pitched at too high a level of difficulty, particularly for the Population II students. In the Oral Reading section of the Speaking test, for example, it was found that the passages selected for reading aloud were apparently beyond the comprehension of most students. This was especially true of Population II students, who read aloud in such a halting, word-by-word manner that it was impossible to attempt to score intonation, except where intonation could be indicated by the stress placed on a single word. Similarly, in one part of the Fluency section of the Speaking test, where students were shown a single picture and asked to describe what had happened prior to the events depicted, what was actually happening in the picture and what was likely to happen next, it was found that the majority of the Population II students failed to understand what they were required to do, although most Population IV students coped quite well with the task. It was evident that the level of difficulty of the material was more appropriate to the stage of competence reached by the older students than by the younger.

Scoring

The scoring system originally adopted was found during pilot-testing to be too inflexible to cope with correct but unforeseen responses. In the original Structural Control section of the Speaking test, for example, all responses were scored on a right–wrong basis: to score a point, a response had to be correct in every respect; if the response contained any errors or omissions at all, it scored zero. This entailed a considerable loss of information. For instance, if, in answer to the question: "Are the men in the house?," a student were to answer: "No, they are not. They are on roof.", he would score zero. (Here again, this incomplete response was encouraged by the provision of only two blank spaces between the cue-words "They" and "roof" in the student's test booklet.) Further, some items had cues for a two-sentence response, but could be answered correctly in a single sentence. For example, the question: "Is the girl's hair short?" could reasonably have been answered by the sentence: "No, it's very long.", but this response would have scored zero in the original scoring system, since the required answer was: "No, it's not short. It's very long." There was an obvious need to devise a more flexible scoring system, which would permit the acceptance of a wider range of correct responses, making provision for unforeseen but acceptable alternative responses.

The original scoring system also tended to place too heavy an emphasis on the grammatical accuracy of the student's spoken and written responses to the neglect of the more stylistic and expressive features of fluency. It was agreed that a revised version of the scoring system should be developed, which would give more weight to aspects of fluency such as variety of tense and structure, range of vocabulary, and, insofar as written composition was concerned, to the quality of cohesiveness.

THE SPEAKING TEST

The Speaking test was administered to subsamples of each of the target populations, on an individual basis. The same test was used for Populations II and IV, except that, for Population IV students, the Fluency section of the test was extended to include further free-response material. The final version of the Speaking test was made up of three sections: Structural Control, Oral Reading, and Fluency. The Structural Control section consisted of ten tape-recorded questions, statements or instructions, to which the student was required to respond in English, relating his response to the appropriate picture in his test booklet. Each item was presented once only and the student was given six seconds in which to respond. His responses were tape-recorded for later scoring. In order to avoid lengthy silences, the student was instructed to answer: "I don't know," if he was unable to attempt a response. He was also informed that the test procedure required him to respond using a complete sentence with a subject and a verb, although it was recognized that in everyday speech replies such as "Yes" or "No" could constitute acceptable answers to some of the questions. All test instructions were given in the student's mother tongue.

The test items themselves were preceded by two untimed practice examples, to familiarize the student with the test procedure. For example, the first picture in the student's test booklet showed a bed. The tape-recorded question corresponding to the picture was "Can you see a bed?" If the student was unable to respond to this question, the test administrator was instructed to prompt him with the reply: "Yes, I can." The second picture in the test booklet showed a bowler-hatted, pipe-smoking gentleman carrying an umbrella and standing in front of a signpost indicating London and Liverpool. The corresponding instruction was: "Ask me if the man lives in England." If unable to respond, the prompt: "Does he live in England?" was given to the student. This practice session was not recorded and could thus be prolonged until the student understood what was required of him.

The student's responses to the test items were each scored on a three-point scale, as follows:

0=No response. "I don't know." Inappropriate or unintelligible response. Response employing an incorrect verb form.

1=Appropriate and intelligible response employing the correct verb form but containing a peripheral error, such as an article omitted or incorrectly given.

2=Appropriate and intelligible response employing the correct verb form and free from grammatical errors.

Scorers were instructed that the Structural Control section of the Speaking test was designed to test only the student's ability to produce an appropriate and grammatically correct response to a well-defined stimulus. Pronunciation and fluency were not in question: the student should not, therefore, be penalized for hesitancy, poor pronunciation or faulty intonation. The scorers were provided with a list of correct responses to the test items, but it was emphasized that the list was intended for guidance only and was not meant to be exhaustive. Scorers were instructed to transcribe on to the student's score sheet any response which they considered to be correct but which was not among those listed. These additional responses were then scrutinized by the scoring supervisor and, if accepted, were scored as described above.

In the Oral Reading section of the Speaking test, the student was required to read aloud a short passage of simple prose, which included conversation. He was given three minutes in which to familiarize himself with the text. He was informed that his score on this section of the test would depend on the accuracy of his pronunciation and the naturalness of his phrasing. After the student had studied the text for three minutes, he was instructed to read it aloud clearly and naturally. The student's reading of the passage was recorded for later scoring. There was no time-limit for this section of the test: the student was allowed to read at his own pace.

Thirty features of the reading passage were identified for scoring. These included the correct pronunciation of specified vowels and consonants as well as phrasing and intonational features. The student's rendering of each of the 30 features was scored on a right–wrong basis: each feature correctly rendered scored one point; each incorrect rendering scored zero.

The Fluency section of the Speaking test was in two parts. Only the first part was administered to both Population II and Population IV students; the second was restricted to Population IV students.

In the first part of the Fluency section, the student was required to describe in English the events depicted in a sequence of pictures. He was offered a choice of two picture-sequences and advised to choose the sequence about which he could say the most. He was given two minutes in which to study the pictures, make his choice and think about what he would say. He was told that he could say whatever he liked about the content of the picture-sequence he had chosen, provided that he spoke in English. He was encouraged to attempt to say at least three or four sentences about the picture-sequence. The student was also informed that his score on this section of the test would be based on the amount spoken, on the accuracy of grammar and pronunciation, and on the appropriateness and variety of vocabulary, tense and structure. When the student began to speak his response was recorded for later scoring. No time-limit was imposed.

The second part of the Fluency section, attempted by Population IV students only, was similar to, but more demanding than, the first. The student was presented with a single large picture of a party scene and was required to talk about it in English. He was instructed to describe what might have led to the party, what was happening in the scene depicted, and what might happen when the party ended. He was encouraged to say at least three or four sentences about the party and, as before, was informed that his score would be based on the amount spoken, on the accuracy of grammar and pronunciation, and on the appropriateness and variety of vocabulary, tense and structure. He was given three minutes in which to study the picture and plan what he was going to say about it. When the student began to speak, his response was recorded for later scoring. Again, no time-limit was imposed.

Both parts of the Fluency section were scored in the same way. The student's total response was, in each instance, scored for volume, accuracy and variety, as follows:

Volume. The scorer played the student's response-tape and counted the number of intelligible clauses spoken, up to a maximum of 30. This cut-off point was established before the scoring session began, from a sampling of the tapes.

Accuracy. The scorer replayed the student's response-tape and scored each intelligible clause for accuracy on a four-point scale within each of the following three categories: grammar, vocabulary, pronunciation. The rating scales used in each category are shown below:

Grammar
0=3 or more errors or omissions
1=2 errors or omissions
2=1 error or omission
3=No errors or omissions

Vocabulary
0=3 or more incorrect or unintelligible words
1=2 incorrect or unintelligible words
2=1 incorrect or unintelligible word
3=No incorrect or unintelligible words

Pronunciation (including word stress)
   0=3 or more errors
   1=2 errors
   2=1 error
   3=No errors

Variety. After the second playing of the student's response-tape, the scorer gave a global rating for the variety of the student's total response, using a four-point scale within each of the following two categories: variety of tense and structure, range of vocabulary. The rating scales used in each of these categories are shown below:

Variety of tense and structure
   0=No variety in either tense or structure
   1=Some variety in either tense or structure
   2=Some variety in both tense and structure
   3=Considerable variety in both tense and structure

Range of vocabulary. Basic word-lists were established for each picture-sequence and for the party scene. These lists contained the minimal vocabulary needed for description (six words for each of the picture-sequences, ten words for the party scene) and were used to establish the criterion of "range of vocabulary," as shown below:

   0=Vocabulary less than the basic word-list
   1=Vocabulary limited to the basic word-list
   2=Vocabulary exceeding the basic word-list, but to a minor extent
   3=Vocabulary exceeding the basic word-list to a major extent

When all three sections of the Speaking test had been scored as described above, the scorer made a global assessment of the student's performance on the whole of the test and assigned him a rating on a five-point scale, defined as follows:

   0=Extremely poor response
   1=Poor response
   2=Reasonable response

3 = Good response

4 = Extremely good response.

The assignment of a global rating completed the scoring of the Speaking test.

THE WRITING TEST

The same Writing test was used for Populations II and IV. It was a group test, the final version being composed of four sections, the first three of which called for "guided" responses of a fairly closely-structured kind, the fourth for "free" written composition. Each of the first three sections was preceded by appropriate practice examples, to familiarize the students with the test procedure. Before attempting the Writing test, students were told to read the test instructions and study the practice examples carefully. They were advised to work quickly but carefully and warned that words incorrectly spelled would be regarded as errors. They were also advised not to spend too long attempting to answer any given item: if unable to attempt an item, they were to proceed to the next item or to the next section of the test, as appropriate. The students were told that the time-limit for the first three sections of the test was 15 minutes and that, 15 minutes after the beginning of the test, they would be told to begin work on the fourth section. If they finished the first three sections of the test in less than 15 minutes, however, they were instructed to go straight on to the fourth section, without waiting to be told to do so. They were informed that the time-limit for the fourth section of the test was 25 minutes and that they would be reminded of the time five minutes before the end of the testing period. The time-limit for the whole of the Writing test was thus 40 minutes. Students who finished the test before the 40-minute period had elapsed were instructed to read their work through and to add to it if they wished. All test instructions were given in the student's mother tongue.

The first section of the final version of the Writing test contained 13 sentence-completion items, each requiring the student to supply a single word, correct in form and appropriate in meaning, to complete the given sentence. The items tested the students' ability to make correct use of a number of grammatical features, including prepositions, relative pronouns, adverbs and tense forms. The scoring of this section was on a right–wrong basis: each sentence correctly completed scored one point; any error scored zero. Only a limited range of response was possible in so structured a situation, as had been

143

established during pilot-testing, so it was a simple matter to provide an objective scoring-key which catered for the whole range of response on this section of the test.

The second section of the Writing test contained nine sentence-completion items, arranged in four short subsections. Unlike those in the first section of the test, the sentence-completion items in the second section often required the students to provide two or even three missing words to complete a given item correctly. The nine items in this section tested the correct use of pronouns, the ability to make required changes in the number of verbs, nouns and pronouns and in the tense of verbs, and the appropriate use of the active or passive voice. Suitable practice examples were provided before each of the four subsections. Again, each written response was scored on a right–wrong basis according to a scoring-key devised after pilot-testing had established the range of performance on this section of the test.

The third section of the Writing test contained eight sentence-completion items different in kind from those used in the first two sections of the test. These were multiple-choice items in which the students were provided with a sentence-stem and three words or phrases with which to complete the sentence. The words or phrases were given in random order and, for each item, a choice of four response-patterns was provided. The students had to select that response-pattern which employed the words or phrases in such an order that, added to the sentence-stem, a correct and meaningful sentence was created. Since a multiple-choice technique was employed, permitting only one correct response per item, completely objective scoring was again possible for this section of the test.

In the fourth section of the Writing test, the students were required to write a composition of not more than 200 words on the subject of travel. This section of the test called for a virtually free response: the only limiting condition, apart from the restriction on length, was that 12 words relevant to the subject of the composition ("ship," "car," "plane," "bus," "train," "interesting," "dangerous," "safely," "fast," "crash," "ticket," "holidays") must be used by the students when writing their composition, but could be used in any order or grammatical relationship. The students were informed that their score on the composition would reflect not only the accuracy of their writing but also the amount written, up to the stipulated limit of 200 words. They were instructed to write a rough draft of their composition first and then to copy out the final version neatly and legibly.

144

The scoring system used for the composition section of the Writing test was developed from that originally devised to score spoken fluency. Each composition was scored for volume, accuracy, variety and cohesiveness, as follows:

Volume. The scorer counted the number of intelligible clauses written, up to a maximum of 200 words, marking the end of each intelligible clause with an oblique line. Any unintelligible material was ignored. If a student had failed to finish copying out the final version of his composition, but had nevertheless completed the composition in draft form, the draft was retained and was used in scoring from the point where the final version had been left unfinished. If the final version of the composition was complete, the rough draft was destroyed.

Accuracy. Each intelligible clause was then scored for accuracy on a four-point scale within each of the following three categories: grammar, vocabulary, spelling. The rating scales used in each category are shown below:

Grammar
    0=3 or more errors or omissions
    1=2 errors or omissions
    2=1 error or omission
    3=No errors or omissions

Vocabulary
    0=3 or more incorrect or unintelligible words
    1=2 incorrect or unintelligible words
    2=1 incorrect or unintelligible word
    3=No incorrect or unintelligible words

Spelling
    0=3 or more spelling errors
    1=2 spelling errors
    2=1 spelling error
    3=No spelling errors

Variety. After the student's composition had been scored for volume and for accuracy, as detailed above, the scorer gave a global rating for the variety of the writing as a whole, using a four-point scale within each of the following two categories: variety of tense and structure, range of vocabulary. The rating scales used in each of these categories are shown below:

Variety of tense and structure

   0=No variety in either tense or structure
   2=Some variety in both tense and structure
   3=Considerable variety in both tense and structure

Range of vocabulary. The criterion for "range of vocabulary" was established by reference to the basic list of 12 words which the students had been instructed to include in their written composition. Rating was as follows:

   0=Vocabulary less than the basic word-list
   1=Vocabulary limited to the basic word-list
   2=Vocabulary exceeding the basic word-list, but to a minor extent
   3=Vocabulary exceeding the basic word-list to a major extent

Cohesiveness. After rating the composition for its variety, the scorer then rated the student's writing as a whole for its cohesiveness, using the following four-point scale:

   0=No attempt to link statements
   1=Minimal linking of statements (e.g., the repeated use of "and")
   2=Some variety in the linking of statements (e.g., "and," "but," "as well as," etc.)
   3=Use of subordinating conjunctions and embedded statements

When the student's script had been scored as described above, the scorer made a global assessment of the quality of the student's written composition as a whole and assigned him a rating on a five-point scale, defined as follows:

   0=Extremely poor response
   1=Poor response
   2=Reasonable response
   3=Good response
   4=Extremely good response

The assignment of a global rating completed the scoring of the Writing test.

THE SPEAKING AND WRITING TEST RESULTS

For purposes of analysis, the initial variables used in the scoring of the Speaking test and the composition section of the Writing test were combined and weighted to form new composite variables, giving measures of quantity, quality, and variety. (The determination of the weighting formulae and the calculation of inter-rater reliabilities for the Speaking and Writing test scores were carried out at Princeton by Dr John B. Carroll; he describes these procedures in detail in Part 2 of this chapter.) Means and standard deviations for the new composite variables, as well as for total test scores and overall global ratings, are presented in Tables 5.1 and 5.2. Table 5.1 presents the Speaking test data, Table 5.2 the Writing test data. It should be noted that, in Table 5.1, the scores shown for quantity, quality and variety represent Population II students' scores on the first part of the Fluency section of the Speaking test, but Population IV students' combined scores for performance on both parts of the Fluency section of the Speaking test.

Inspection of Table 5.1 shows that at the Population II level Swedish and French-speaking Belgian students obtain the highest mean global ratings and also the highest mean total scores on the Speaking test. Mean total scores for Finnish and Italian students are virtually identical and their mean global ratings are also of a similar level. Belgian and Swedish students also achieve higher mean scores than Finnish or Italian students for the quantity and quality of their test performance, but, when the variety of their spoken production is considered, Swedish and Finnish students lead the field, with Italian and Belgian students achieving an almost identical mean score well below that of the Scandinavian students.

At the Population IV level Swedish and Hungarian students achieve the highest mean total scores and also the highest mean global ratings; they also achieve the highest mean scores for the quantity and the variety of their test performance. When the quality of their performance is considered, however, the Swedish students maintain their lead, but are closely followed by the Finnish and the Hungarian students. The general test performance of the Belgian, Italian, and Finnish students at the Population IV level is, in the main, inferior to that of the Swedish and Hungarian students, but is consistently superior to that of the Chilean students, whose mean scores are the lowest in each of the categories assessed.

Table 5.2, presenting the Writing test data, shows that, at the Population II level, Swedish and Belgian students again achieve the highest mean scores, not only for all four sections of the Writing test but also for the global rating of the composition section. With regard to the quantity and variety of their written composition Belgian and Swedish students once more achieve the highest mean scores. When

147

the quality of the written composition is in question, however, the highest mean scores are achieved by the Swedish and the Finnish students, although mean scores for the Belgian students are only marginally lower. Apart from the one instance already cited, the test performance of the Finnish and the Italian students is generally inferior to that of the Swedish and the Belgian students.

At the Population IV level Swedish and Finnish students obtain the highest mean total scores for all sections of the Writing test. For the global rating of the written composition, however, the highest mean score is obtained by Swedish students, with Hungarian and Finnish students achieving an identically high mean score only fractionally lower than that achieved by the Swedes. The Swedish and Finnish students also achieve the highest mean scores for the quantity and the quality of their written composition. When the variety of their composition is in question, however, the Swedish students still retain the lead, but the Italian students achieve a higher mean score than the Finns. Nevertheless, on the whole, the test performance of the Scandinavian students surpasses that of all other students. As was observed with regard to the Speaking test results, the performance of the Chilean students on the Writing test is consistently inferior in all respects to that of the remainder of students tested.

Some amplification of the results outlined above may be obtained from an inspection of Tables 5.3 and 5.4, which show the percentage frequency distribution of the five points on the rating-scales used to assess the overall quality of the students' oral production and written composition. Speaking test data are presented in Table 5.3, Writing test data in Table 5.4. It will be recalled that, on the global rating-scales used, scores range from zero for an extremely poor response to four for an extremely good response.

Another interesting feature of the Speaking and Writing test results is the extent to which students' scores on the two tests correlate with one another. It has been suggested (Carroll, 1963) that the extent to which scores on tests measuring different foreign-language skills correlate with one another in a given learning situation may be a function of the degree to which each skill has been emphasized during the course of instruction. Accordingly, it might be expected that oral and written skills would be highly correlated at the end of a period of instruction in which equal emphasis had been given to each skill area, but less highly correlated after a period of instruction in which either skill-area had received lesser emphasis. It has also been found that scores on foreign-language tests tend to correlate more highly with one another as the student's competence in the foreign language develops over time. For example, Burstall (1973) found that the correlation coefficient for Speaking and Writing test scores was 0.70 at the end of a three-year period of instruction in French at the elementary level, but had risen to 0.81 after a further two years' instruction in French at the secondary level. Similarly, Carroll (1967) reported even higher correlation coefficients (ranging from 0.76 to 0.90) between French test scores at the undergraduate level.

Limitations on space do not permit the presentation in full of the correlational data derived from the English Speaking and Writing test scores, so discussion will be limited to the more salient features of the findings (See Tables 5.5–5.7). The total Speaking test score tends to correlate more highly with the total score for the first three sections of the Writing test (composed, it may be recalled, of "discrete-point" items) than it does with the total score for the fourth section of the test ("free" written composition). Correlation coefficients between the total Speaking test score and the total score for the first three sections of the Writing test are all positive and range from 0.30 to 0.79; correlation coefficients between the total Speaking test score and the score for the composition section of the Writing test are also all positive, but, in all but two instances (Population IV students in Hungary and in Italy), are lower than those between the total Speaking test score and the score for the first three sections of the Writing test, ranging from 0.24 to 0.54. Correlations between the global ratings for Speaking and Writing are uniformly positive but extremely variable, ranging from 0.30 to 0.80. The quantity and quality scores for Speaking and Writing also intercorrelate positively, but with considerable variation from country to country, the correlation coefficients ranging from 0.12 to 0.72 for quantity and from 0.09 to 0.66 for quality. Considerably lower correlation coefficients are obtained when the variety scores for Speaking and Writing are considered. Here, the coefficients range from mildly negative (–0.10) to relatively positive (0.56), but the majority are in the region of 0.20. There is no evidence of a general tendency for Speaking and Writing test scores to correlate more highly when older rather than younger students' scores are considered.

When total test scores are correlated with the composite variables contributing to those scores, it is clear that scores for quantity and variety correlate more highly with total scores than does the score for quality. For the Speaking test, the correlations between the quantity score and the total score are uniformly high, ranging from 0.68 to

0.93; for the Writing test, the corresponding values range from 0.89 to 0.94. Correlations between the total score and the variety score range from 0.49 to 0.90 for Speaking and from 0.80 to 0.93 for Writing. Those between the total score and the quality score, however, range only from 0.49 to 0.69 for Speaking and from 0.42 to 0.65 for Writing. As might be anticipated, correlations between the total score and the overall global rating are high, those for Speaking ranging from 0.62 to 0.89, those for Writing from 0.68 to 0.88. It is possible that the high correlations between the total test scores and the composite variable scores reflect primarily the fact that, although the different parts of the tests have attempted to tap different aspects of spoken and written fluency, they must all draw on a certain basic knowledge of English (its phonology, morphology, syntax and lexicon) and are thus less likely to measure discrete skills than to probe overall fluency in the language.

REFERENCES

Agard, F. B. and Dunkel, H. B. *An Investigation of Second-Language Teaching.* Boston: Ginn & Co, 1948.

Andrade, M.; Hayman, J. L.; and Johnson, J. T. *Measurement of Listening Comprehension via Television in Elementary School Spanish Instruction.* Stanford, California: Institute for Communication Research, Stanford University, 1961.

Andrade, M.; Hayman, J. L.; and Johnson, J. T. *Measurement of Speaking Skills in Elementary Level Spanish Instruction.* Stanford, California: Institute for Communication Research, Stanford University, 1963.

Burstall, C. "Second-Language Acquisition: Interactions of Attitudes and Achievement." Unpublished Ph.D. thesis, University of London, 1973.

Carroll, J. B. "Research on Teaching Foreign Languages." In Gage, N. L. (Ed.), *Handbook of Research in Teaching.* Chicago: Rand McNally & Co, 1963.

Carroll, J. B. *The Foreign Language Attainments of Language Majors in the Senior Year: A Survey Conducted in US Colleges and Universities.* Cambridge, Mass: Laboratory for Research in Instruction, Graduate School of Education, Harvard University, 1967.

Chaplen, E. F. "The Reliability of the Essay Subtest in a University Entrance Test in English for Non-Native Speakers of English." In Perren, G. E. and Trim, J. L. M. (Eds.), *Applications of Linguistics. Selected papers of the Second International Congress of Applied Linguistics, Cambridge, 1969.* Cambridge: Cambridge University Press, 1971.

Chomsky, N. "The formal nature of language." In Lenneberg, E. H. *Biological Foundations of Language.* New York: John Wiley and Sons, Inc., 1967.

Cotler, S. and Palmer, R. J. "Social Reinforcement, Individual Difference Factors, and the Reading Performance of Elementary School Children," *Journal of Personality and Social Psychology*, 18, 1971, pp. 97–104.

Dyson, A. P. *Oral Examining in French*. London: The Modern Language Association, 1972.

Finlayson, D. S. "The Reliability of the Marking of Essays," *British Journal of Educational Psychology*, 21, 1951, pp. 126–134.

Godshalk, F. I.; Swineford, F.; and Coffman, W. E. *The Measurement of Writing Ability*. New York: College Entrance Examination Board, 1966.

Graham, N. "Towards a Test of Language Production." *Educational Review*, 24, 1, 1971, pp. 34–46.

Johnson, C. E.; Flores, J. S.; Ellison, F. P.; and Riestra, M. A. *The Development and Evaluation of Methods and Materials to Facilitate Foreign Language Instruction in Elementary Schools*. Urbana, Illinois: University of Illinois Foreign Language Instruction Project, 1963.

Morrison, R. L. and Vernon, P. E. "A New Method of Marking English Compositions," *British Journal of Educational Psychology*, 11, 1941, pp. 109–119.

Palmer, A. S. "Testing Communication," *International Review of Applied Linguistics in Language Teaching*, 10, 1, 1972, pp. 34–45.

Patterson, G. R.; Helper, M. E.; and Wilcott, R. C. "Anxiety and Verbal Conditioning in Children," *Child Development*, 31, 1960, pp. 101–108.

Pimsleur, P. "A French Speaking Proficiency Test," *French Review*, 34, 5, 1961, pp. 470–479.

Plaister, T. H. "Testing Aural Comprehension: A Culture Fair Approach," *TESOL Quarterly*, 1, 3, 1967, pp. 17–19.

Rand, E. "A Short Test of Oral English Proficiency," *Language Learning*, 13, 1963, pp. 203–210.

Rivers, W. M. "Listening comprehension," *Modern Language Journal*, 50, 1966, pp. 196–204.

Sarason, S. B.; Davidson, K.; Lighthall, F.; and Waite, R. "Rorschach Behavior and Performance of High and Low Anxious Children," *Child Development*, 29, 1958, pp. 277–285.

Spearritt, D. *Listening Comprehension: A Factorial Analysis*. Melbourne: Australian Council for Educational Research, 1962.

Upshur, J. A. "Productive Communication Testing: Progress Report." In Perren, G. E. and Trim, J. L. M. (Eds.), *Applications of Linguistics. Selected papers of the Second International Congress of Applied Linguistics, Cambridge, 1969*. Cambridge: Cambridge University Press, 1971.

Vernon, P. E. and Millican, G. D. "A Further Study of the Reliability of English Essays," *British Journal of Statistical Psychology*, 7, 2, 1954, pp. 65–74.

Wilkinson, A. "Spoken English," *Educational Review Occasional Publications No. 2*. Edgbaston: University of Birmingham Press, 1965.

Wiseman, S. "The Marking of English Composition in Grammar School Selection," *British Journal of Educational Psychology*, 19, 1949, pp. 200–209.

Wright, A. "The Role of the Artist in the Production of Visual Materials for Language Teaching," *Educational Sciences*, 1, 3, 1967, pp. 139–149.

Part 2: The Determination of Scoring Formulas[2]

The writer was asked to perform the necessary computations and make appropriate decisions in regard to developing formulas for combining scores from the various parts of the English Writing and Speaking tests. In performing this task, he followed the same general procedures that were followed for the French Writing and Speaking tests (Carroll, 1975).

In analyzing French pretest data, he found evidence that suggested that two components of performance in free-response Writing and Speaking tests could be distinguished, namely, "quantity of correct response" and "relative quality of response." The first of these components is represented, at one end, by the individual who is able to provide a large volume of correct response, e.g., in writing a long essay which is correct in grammar and vocabulary, or giving a fluent oral response with good control of grammatical structure and word-choice, and at the other end by the individual who either gives no responses at all or gives responses that are very imperfect in grammar, vocabulary, or other aspects of linguistic accuracy. The second of these components has to do with the proportion of the response that is actually correct; two examinees could have the same proportion of their responses correct even though one has given very few responses and the other has given a large volume of responses. It was assumed that the English free-response data could be analyzed in terms of these two components, and perhaps others.

The initial scoring procedures for the English Writing and Speaking tests had been established, of course, by the International Committee of English as a Foreign Language. These procedures provided for the collection of "global ratings" that could be used as criteria for the determination of scoring and weighting formulas. A global rating on a scale of 0 (low) to 4 (high) was assigned to each student's total performance on the Writing test, and a similar global rating was assigned to each student's total performance in Speaking (including the Structural Control and Oral Reading tests, as well as the Fluency tests).

---

[2] This part was written by John B. Carroll of the University of North Carolina.

STATISTICAL PROCEDURES FOR
DETERMINING WEIGHTS OF
SCORES FOR COMPOSITES

The general procedure was to go through two or three stages of combining variables.

At the first stage, raw regression weights for the original variables and certain combinations thereof in the prediction of the global ratings were computed for different countries and populations. Relativized β-weights (i.e., raw regression weights multiplied by a factor such that the algebraically largest β-weight would become unity) for variables with generally significant β-weights were averaged over countries and populations, and a series of integers was selected as the first-stage raw-score weights so as to be approximately proportional to the averages of the relativized β-weights. However, in this stage, attention was paid to the possibility of forming two or three composites whose intercorrelations would be as low as possible, including, for example, the "Quantity correct" and "Quality" composites mentioned above. Separate sets of regression analyses were made to form these composites; in fact, it was usually the case that several alternative analyses were made so that the most satisfactory one could be found. Furthermore, separate sets of analyses were done for the two parts of a test where such existed (as Fluency A and Fluency B, for the Speaking test), partly in order to determine the consistency of the patterns of regression weights and partly (as a by-product) to determine the intercorrelations of the separate parts, including interform reliabilities.

Similar procedures were carried out at a second (and sometimes a third) stage of analysis, this time determining appropriate integer weights for the composites that had been formed in the first (or a prior) stage so as to optimalize, approximately, the correlation of the new composite (or composites) with the global rating criterion.

English Writing Test

The scoring system for the English writing test was determined on the basis of 8 049 cases screened from 8 711 cases by eliminating those that had zero scores on "number of intelligible clauses" or which had missing data of any sort. The reason for eliminating cases with zero scores on number of intelligible clauses was that the remainder of the part scores would automatically be zero, with the consequence that if these cases had been used they would produce artifacts in the correlational analysis. (These cases were not to be eliminated, however, in the main analyses; they would show up, in general, as cases with zero scores on the final output variables.) The 8 049 usable cases were from various populations and countries, as shown here:

	Finland	Hungary	Sweden
Population II	608	–	2 007
Population III	535	830	2 000
Population IV	–	576	1 493

Although the samples differed in character and size, no attempt was made to weight them by size, or otherwise to treat them differentially in the present analysis. Regression analyses were performed separately for each of the seven samples, and for all samples pooled.

The initial variables used in this analysis were as follows:

1. Global rating (scale 0 [low] to 4 [high])
2. "Volume," number of intelligible clauses
3. Accuracy 1: Grammar
4. Accuracy 2: Vocabulary
5. Accuracy 3: Spelling
9. Variety of tense and structure
10. Range of vocabulary
11. Cohesiveness

In the first stage of the analysis, the interest was in determining whether several somewhat independent composites could be formed from these variables. It was noted that the accuracy scores, variables 3, 4, and 5, could be regarded as measures of "Quantity of correct writing" since they represented sums of points (on a 0–3 scale) to each intelligible clause. If these scores were each divided by variable 2, the number of intelligible clauses, the resulting scores could be regarded as measures of relative *quality* of writing, since they would represent average points awarded per clause. Therefore three new variables were established:

6. Average accuracy: Grammar   − (Var. 3)/(Var. 2)
7. Average accuracy: Vocabulary   − (Var. 4)/(Var. 2)
8. Average accuracy: Spelling   − (Var. 5)/(Var. 2)

By means of the previously described regression analysis procedure where relativized regression weights were averaged, it was decided to form three composites:

Quantity score: Weights of 2, 1, 1 for variables 3, 4, 5 respectively
Quantity score: Weights of 2, 1, 1 for variables 6, 7, 8 respectively
Variety score: Weights of 2, 1, 2 for variables 9, 10, 11 respectively

In the pooled samples, the correlations of these variables among themselves and with the global ratings were as follows (N = 8 049):

	Quantity	Quality	Variety	Global rating
12. Quantity score	1.000	0.546	0.717	0.729
13. Quality score	0.546	1.000	0.502	0.537
14. Variety score	0.717	0.502	1.000	0.788

As will be seen, these three scores make independent and significant contributions to the prediction of the global rating, and it may be concluded that they measure different aspects of writing performance.

At the second stage of analysis, the problem was to form a total writing score composite from these three composite variables. Separate regression analyses were made for each population–country combination. In these analyses, the beta-weights for all three composites were uniformly positive; those for variable 12 (Quantity) and variable 14 (Variety) were in every case significant at the 1 % level, and those for variable 13 (Quality) were significant at that level in three of the seven cases. (This is partly a matter of different sample sizes.) Appropriate integer weights for the three variables, allowing for their different beta-weights and variances, were determined to be 1, 10, and 20, respectively. In the pooled sample, the β-weights for these three composites were 0.293, 0.115, and 0.520 respectively, with a multiple correlation of 0.828.

Table 5.5 shows selected correlations of global ratings, initial variables, and composite scores. The total writing score, as weighted by the formula established, correlates 0.819 with the global ratings in the pooled sample.

Although the univariate statistics give evidence of considerable skewness in some of the variables, inspection of certain relevant scatterplots of means of variables with mean global ratings over samples gave no indication that it would be worthwhile to carry out non-linear transformations on some of these variables. It was in any case thought best to leave the variables in their original forms, so that any desired transformations could be applied later.

A word should be said about the assumptions underlying the procedure of determining weights from regression analyses against global ratings as criteria. The assumption is that global ratings themselves are too much influenced by transitory subjective factors (such as variations in the perceived average quality of the material being judged) to be used as criterion variables, but that over the total sample of cases the global ratings do provide a measure—though an unreliable one—of quality. Thus, an optimal weighting of detailed scores based on their regression weights in predicting global weight-ings would provide a sufficiently reliable and quasi-objective set of criterion scores. It is assumed also that the detailed scores are less subject to the transitory subjective factors that would affect the global ratings.[3] (The reliabilities of the final scores are presented and dis-cussed in another section of this report.) (Note: Some concern may be expressed about the high weight of the variety scores in the for-mulas presented above. It is based on subjective judgments on short scales that might be affected by the same factors that would affect global ratings. The high weight reflects the relatively high correla-tions of the variety scores with the global ratings. A better evaluation of this problem may be possible when the overall results of the main analyses are available, for it will be possible to compare the final criterion variables with respect to their associations with background factors.)

English Speaking Test

The scoring system for English speaking was determined on the basis of 1 186 cases, screened from a total of 1 325 available cases by eliminating those with missing data on any of the parts of the speaking test or with zero scores on "Volume" (Number of intelligible clauses) on either Fluency A or Fluency B (when given, in Population IV). The reason for eliminating cases with zero scores on number of intelligible clauses was the same as before. The 1 186 usable cases were from various populations and countries, as shown here:

	Finland	Hungary	Sweden
Population II	200	–	200
Population III	162	122	191
Population IV	–	115	196

In the first stage of the analysis, the problem was to develop weighting formulas for compositing the elements of the Fluency tests. (As in the case of the Writing test, *relative* quality scores were formed by dividing the quantity correct scores by the volume (variable 4 below). Thus, the initial variables involved, with code numbers by which they are listed in the correlation matrix presented later, were the following:

1. Global rating (scaled 0 [low] to 4 [high], given over all aspects of the speaking test including structural control and oral reading)
4. (or 16) Number of intelligible clauses, Fluency A (B)
5. (or 17) Accuracy 1, Grammar, Fluency A (B)
6. (or 18) Accuracy 2, Vocabulary, Fluency A (B)
7. (or 19) Accuracy 3, Pronunciation, Fluency A (B)
8. (or 20) Relative accuracy, Grammar, Fluency A (B)
9. (or 21) Relative accuracy, Vocabulary, Fluency A (B)
10. (or 22) Relative accuracy, Pronunciation, Fluency A (B)
11. (or 23) Variety 1, Tense and Structure, Fluency A (B)
12. (or 24) Variety 2, Range of Vocabulary, Fluency A (B)

The analyses were complicated by the fact that Populations II and III took only Fluency A, while Population IV have scores on both Fluency A and Fluency B. Thus, in Population IV analyses, many more variables were available. As before, separate regression analyses against the global ratings were made for the various samples, using whatever variables were available. Variables 8–10 (or 20–22) were formed by dividing each of variables 5–7 (or 17–19) by variable 4 (or variable 16). By the techniques explained earlier, and considering the beta-weights and average relativized β-weights, the first stage analysis yielded three composites, as follows:

13. (or 25) Quantity score, variables 5, 6, 7 (or 17, 18, 19), weighted 1, 1, 1, respectively
14. (or 26) Quality score, variables 8, 9, 10 (or 20, 21, 22), weighted 3, 1, 2, respectively
15. (or 27) Variety score, variables 11, 12 (or 23, 24), weighted 2, 1 respectively

It was noted, incidentally, that variables 5, 6, and 7 were highly collinear, with the result that their beta-weights varied widely through sampling error, for this reason they were weighted equally.

In the second stage of the analysis, the variables considered were variables 13, 14, 15 (or 25, 26, 27), plus variables 2 (total score, Structural Control) and 3 (total score, Oral Reading). In these analyses, variable 2 usually had significant positive beta-weights, whereas variable 3 had either non-significant weights or significantly negative beta-weights. It was therefore decided to drop variable 3 from the final composites altogether. Variables 13, 14, 15 (or 25, 26, 27) nearly always had highly significant positive beta-weights. With account taken of average relativized β-weights, the integer weights for composing a final total Speaking score were as follows:

Variable 2 (Structural control): 8
Variable 3 (Oral reading): 0
Variable 13, 25 (Quantity): 1
Variable 14, 26 (Quality): 6
Variable 15, 27 (Variety): 15

The final weighting formulas were adjusted so that the Quantity, Quality, Variety, and total Speaking scores would be approximately comparable for all populations, i.e., regardless of whether only Fluency A scores, or both Fluency A and B scores, were present. (In effect, the A and B scores are averaged for Population IV.)

Tables 5.6 and 5.7 present selected correlations among the global ratings, the initial variables, and the final composites, for all samples from Populations II and III combined, and for all samples from Population IV. The validity of the total Speaking score is 0.859 for the first set of pooled samples, and 0.734 for the second set of pooled samples. Both values are subject to a restriction-of-range phenomenon.

INTER-RATER RELIABILITIES FOR WRITING AND SPEAKING SCORES

In order to obtain inter-rater reliabilities for the Writing and Speaking scores, the following plan was established for the International Scoring Committee:

1. All "regular" scoring of either the Writing test scripts or the Speaking test tapes was to be completed before any second scoring for reliability was done.

2. On the basis of the "global rating" given in "regular" scoring, either to the Writing test or the Speaking test (as the case might be), each rater was to select at random two cases with each of the possible scores, that is, ten cases in all.

3. Each rater would then be given ten cases selected at random from the pool, except that no rater would be given a case that he or she had already scored. These cases would then be completely re-scored, without reference to the first set of scores.

This procedure for selecting cases automatically produced a rectangular distribution of the first set of global ratings, and, apart from regression effects, also of the second set. This type of selection may also have influenced the means and variances of the remaining variables, with the consequence that these means and variances are probably less representative of the total achieved sample, even controlling for population. The likelihood is that the standard deviations of the reliability scoring data are greater than those for the achieved sample as a whole, and possibly the obtained rater reliabilities are slightly inflated as compared to those that might have been obtained for the achieved sample as a whole. The means and standard deviations of all variables involved in the reliability scoring, including the composites obtained by the scoring formulas, are presented in Tables 5.8 (Writing) and 5.9 (Speaking).

These statistics were obtained in Princeton on the basis of data supplied by the International Scoring Committee for English as a Foreign Language. They are based on all cases supplied, except that a few cases were eliminated for the presence of zero scores in the "number of intelligible clauses" in *both* original and second scorings. (All cases in which raters disagreed as to zero scores in number of intelligible clauses were left in the sample.)

The inter-rater reliabilities of the global ratings were 0.754 for Writing and 0.787 for Speaking. These correlations are quite respectable considering that they are for two raters; they may be taken as estimates of the reliability of a single rating.

The inter-rater reliabilities are quite high whenever they are based on quantity; they are lower when based on quality or variety. Nevertheless, all the final composite scores may be considered to have a sufficient degree of reliability for group comparisons and the other analyses performed in this project.

REFERENCE

The Teaching of French as a Foreign Language in Eight Countries: An Empirical Study. Stockholm: Almqvist & Wiksell, 1975

NOTE

[3] Support for these assumptions may be derived from the fact that, as shown later, there are considerable differences between means of global ratings for an original and a second scoring, whereas the means of the final scorer based on the original and the second scoring tend not to differ very much. Also, the rater reliabilities of the final scores are generally higher than those of the global ratings.

Table 5.1. *Means and Standard Deviations for the Speaking Test Scores*

Country	Popula-tion		Quantity Score	Quality Score	Variety Score	Global Rating	Total Score
Belgium (Fr.)	II	$\bar{X}$	47.5	84.2	16.0	1.2	208.6
		S.D.	29.1	12.4	15.5	0.8	73.6
Finland	II	$\bar{X}$	39.4	84.1	25.5	1.1	198.0
		S.D.	29.7	16.1	30.6	1.1	97.3
Italy	II	$\bar{X}$	32.4	79.5	16.3	0.9	197.6
		S.D.	16.1	15.2	19.0	0.6	76.8
Sweden	II	$\bar{X}$	43.5	87.1	37.0	1.3	235.5
		S.D.	22.1	15.0	31.6	0.9	87.4
Belgium (Fr.)	IV	$\bar{X}$	63.6	84.5	23.5	1.7	242.1
		S.D.	30.5	9.9	19.5	0.7	69.4
Chile	IV	$\bar{X}$	40.0	71.0	10.2	0.3	143.5
		S.D.	25.0	15.9	16.8	0.5	64.5
Finland	IV	$\bar{X}$	71.9	92.5	37.2	1.7	298.7
		S.D.	39.9	11.0	28.4	0.7	87.3
Hungary	IV	$\bar{X}$	93.5	90.0	49.3	2.3	302.6
		S.D.	63.7	9.1	29.7	1.1	122.7
Italy	IV	$\bar{X}$	58.6	86.0	43.2	1.7	270.1
		S.D.	27.4	12.9	20.5	0.7	72.1
Sweden	IV	$\bar{X}$	88.9	95.8	55.1	1.9	343.4
		S.D.	44.9	6.6	26.7	0.8	85.9

Table 5.2. *Means and Standard Deviations for the Writing Test Scores*

Country	Popu-la-tion		Quantity Score	Quality Score	Variety Score	Global Rating	Total Score (1, 2, 3)	Total Score (4)
Belgium (Fr.)	II	$\bar{X}$	162.2	97.1	128.9	1.5	12.5	388.2
		S.D.	81.2	15.0	66.1	1.8	6.8	138.4
Finland	II	$\bar{X}$	144.3	101.8	100.2	0.9	9.7	346.3
		S.D.	84.6	10.9	73.4	1.1	8.4	153.1
Italy	II	$\bar{X}$	88.5	85.4	119.3	1.1	11.3	293.8
		S.D.	55.7	17.0	70.6	0.8	7.0	127.9
Sweden	II	$\bar{X}$	162.9	98.9	122.5	1.4	14.2	384.3
		S.D.	82.0	11.6	64.2	0.9	7.4	140.1

Country	Population		Quantity Score	Quality Score	Variety Score	Global Rating	Total Score (1, 2, 3)	Total Score (4)
Belgium (Fr.)	IV	$\bar{X}$	177.6	99.3	154.0	1.8	20.5	430.9
		S.D.	74.7	10.1	62.9	0.8	6.0	124.7
Chile	IV	$\bar{X}$	76.8	86.5	98.9	0.8	7.2	262.2
		S.D.	50.0	13.6	54.5	0.8	4.8	104.9
Finland	IV	$\bar{X}$	205.3	108.4	172.0	2.0	26.6	485.7
		S.D.	65.1	6.6	52.8	0.7	3.2	102.8
Hungary	IV	$\bar{X}$	157.3	100.7	136.8	2.0	18.2	394.8
		S.D.	75.9	11.5	70.0	1.0	7.2	142.1
Italy	IV	$\bar{X}$	119.2	89.6	176.0	1.6	18.9	384.9
		S.D.	61.8	14.0	57.9	0.8	6.0	116.9
Sweden	IV	$\bar{X}$	241.3	106.7	197.3	2.3	25.3	545.3
		S.D.	73.7	8.3	57.3	0.8	4.6	120.0

Table 5.3. *Percentage Frequencies for Speaking Test Global Rating*

Country	Population	0	1	2	3	4
Belgium (Fr.)	II	21.6	39.6	34.7	3.5	0.5
Finland	II	38.2	22.8	28.1	8.1	2.8
Italy	II	23.3	63.3	12.5	0.9	0.0
Sweden	II	19.5	40.8	31.0	6.2	2.4
Belgium (Fr.)	IV	3.8	35.8	48.3	12.1	0.0
Chile	IV	69.5	26.5	4.0	0.0	0.0
Finland	IV	5.8	28.0	60.8	4.8	0.7
Hungary	IV	2.5	24.8	28.2	26.7	17.7
Italy	IV	0.0	42.3	40.2	17.5	0.0
Sweden	IV	3.8	23.6	56.9	13.1	2.6

Table 5.4. *Percentage Frequencies for Writing Test Global Rating*

Country	Population	0	1	2	3	4
Belgium (Fr.)	II	13.3	36.2	42.1	7.4	1.0
Finland	II	49.1	20.2	20.7	7.8	2.2
Italy	II	27.9	42.6	26.1	2.8	0.6
Sweden	II	19.2	38.9	31.4	9.2	1.3
Belgium (Fr.)	IV	6.5	21.8	54.5	15.3	2.0
Chile	IV	39.4	42.2	16.9	0.9	0.6
Finland	IV	1.3	20.9	57.6	17.7	2.6
Hungary	IV	7.4	22.3	39.6	23.0	7.7
Italy	IV	6.1	35.7	45.8	12.2	0.2
Sweden	IV	1.9	17.4	43.3	32.0	5.4

Table 5.5. *Selected Correlations of Global Ratings, Initial Variables, and Composites Formed for English Writing*

$N = 8\ 049$

Variable	$\bar{X}$	S.D.	Correlations				
			1	12	13	14	15
1. Global ratings	1.76	1.00	1.000	0.729	0.537	0.788	0.819
2. Number of intelligible clauses	17.28	7.85	0.687	0.979	0.409	0.684	0.902
3. Accuracy 1: Gammar	43.00	21.90	0.723	0.993	0.575	0.716	0.937
4. Accuracy 2: Vocabulary	46.30	22.05	0.719	0.988	0.500	0.704	0.923
5. Accuracy 3: Spelling	46.59	22.80	0.721	0.985	0.514	0.702	0.921
6. Relative accuracy: Grammar	2.42	0.40	0.456	0.497	0.895	0.457	0.559
7. Relative accuracy: Vocabulary	2.65	0.28	0.332	0.296	0.604	0.279	0.341
8. Relative accuracy: Spelling	2.65	0.37	0.386	0.354	0.630	0.320	0.395
9. Tense and structure	1.45	0.82	0.688	0.587	0.436	0.830	0.757
10. Range of vocabulary	0.71	1.05	0.467	0.428	0.276	0.625	0.554
11. Cohesiveness	1.67	0.93	0.673	0.644	0.443	0.873	0.804
12. Quantity score	178.89	87.72	0.729	1.000	0.546	0.717	0.939
13. Quality score	101.46	11.25	0.537	0.546	1.000	0.502	0.616
14. Variety score	139.10	72.71	0.788	0.717	0.502	1.000	0.909
15. Total writing	419.45	155.42	0.819	0.939	0.616	0.909	1.000

Table 5.6. *Selected Intercorrelations of Initial Variables, Composites, and Global Ratings, with Means and Standard Deviations of All Variables*

$N=875$ cases from Populations II and III

Variable	$\bar{X}$	S.D.	1	13	14	15	31
1. Global ratings	1.66	1.01	1.000	0.724	0.486	0.771	0.859
2. Total structural control	8.16	5.04	0.670	0.419	0.475	0.558	0.822
3. Total oral reading	25.32	6.46	0.402	0.243	0.295	0.340	0.448
4. Fluency A, No. clauses	6.51	4.03	0.671	0.979	0.232	0.628	0.726
5. Fluency A, Accuracy 1, Grammar	15.88	11.13	0.720	0.986	0.401	0.663	0.798
6. Fluency A, Accuracy 2, Vocabulary	17.20	11.37	0.697	0.986	0.315	0.633	0.750
7. Fluency A, Accuracy 3, Pronunciation	15.99	10.35	0.719	0.976	0.415	0.692	0.810
8. Fluency A, Relative acc., Grammar	2.36	0.52	0.442	0.372	0.876	0.388	0.567
9. Fluency A, Relative acc., Vocabulary	2.62	0.40	0.279	0.212	0.508	0.192	0.292
10. Fluency A, Relative acc., Pronunciation	2.43	0.53	0.324	0.223	0.744	0.301	0.436
11. Fluency A, Variety 1, Tense and structure	0.88	0.81	0.729	0.610	0.417	0.948	0.811
12. Fluency A, Variety 2, Range of vocabulary	0.69	0.81	0.603	0.578	0.301	0.777	0.686
13. Fluency A, Quantity	49.07	32.29	0.724	1.000	0.382	0.673	0.798
14. Fluency A, Quality	87.22	14.20	0.486	0.382	1.000	0.424	0.621
15. Fluency A, Variety	36.82	32.47	0.771	0.673	0.424	1.000	0.864
31. Total speaking	238.36	95.76	0.859	0.798	0.621	0.864	1.000

Table 5.7. *Selected Intercorrelations of Initial Variables, Composites, and Global Ratings, with Means and Standard Deviations of All Variables*

$N=311$ cases from Population IV

Variable	$\bar{X}$	S.D.	1	28	29	30	31
1. Global rating	2.13	0.90	1.000	0.693	0.472	0.645	0.734
2. Total structural control	11.65	5.67	0.439	0.327	0.471	0.406	0.743
3. Total oral reading	28.82	9.31	0.204	0.236	0.153	0.157	0.437
Fluency A							
4. Number of clauses	9.56	5.88	0.621	0.884	0.246	0.574	0.688
5. Accuracy: Grammar	25.09	16.79	0.642	0.881	0.348	0.592	0.719

Variable	$\bar{X}$	S.D.	1	28	29	30	31
6. Accuracy: Vocabulary	25.96	16.51	0.627	0.876	0.279	0.581	0.693
7. Accuracy: Pronunciation	24.44	16.00	0.643	0.902	0.383	0.624	0.755
8. Relative accuracy: Grammar	2.56	0.41	0.338	0.278	0.725	0.304	0.412
9. Relative accuracy: Vocabulary	2.69	0.27	0.184	0.130	0.370	0.196	0.219
10. Relative accuracy: Pronunciation	2.51	0.45	0.310	0.281	0.686	0.338	0.439
11. Variety, Tense and structure	1.18	0.77	0.513	0.520	0.358	0.800	0.624
12. Variety, Range of vocabulary	1.11	0.85	0.344	0.516	0.374	0.644	0.601
13. Quantity	75.49	48.80	0.644	0.895	0.340	0.605	0.729
14. Quality	92.46	10.79	0.415	0.351	0.899	0.408	0.537
15. Variety	52.04	30.64	0.529	0.605	0.424	0.869	0.719
Fluency B							
16. Number of clauses	12.48	7.01	0.605	0.929	0.324	0.688	0.790
17. Accuracy: Grammar	33.15	19.83	0.627	0.927	0.398	0.691	0.808
18. Accuracy: Vocabulary	34.56	19.78	0.625	0.931	0.361	0.697	0.801
19. Accuracy: Pronunciation	32.87	19.93	0.612	0.917	0.416	0.701	0.810
20. Relative accuracy: Grammar	2.62	0.27	0.328	0.276	0.630	0.238	0.374
21. Relative accuracy: Vocabulary	2.76	0.21	0.235	0.148	0.354	0.169	0.200
22. Relative accuracy: Pronunciation	2.58	0.35	0.291	0.281	0.684	0.356	0.424
23. Variety, Tense and structure	1.41	0.76	0.550	0.525	0.394	0.807	0.628
24. Variety, Range of vocabulary	0.58	0.94	0.439	0.597	0.180	0.649	0.590
25. Quantity	100.59	59.20	0.625	0.930	0.394	0.700	0.811
26. Quality	94.66	7.90	0.391	0.340	0.801	0.360	0.484
27. Variety	51.08	31.54	0.596	0.648	0.366	0.877	0.720
28. Total quantity	88.04	49.38	0.693	1.000	0.404	0.719	0.847
29. Total quality	93.56	8.01	0.472	0.404	1.000	0.452	0.600
30. Total variety	51.56	27.13	0.645	0.719	0.452	1.000	0.824
31. Total speaking	326.33	102.71	0.734	0.847	0.600	0.824	1.000

Table 5.8. *Rater Reliabilities of Part and Final Scores—English Writing Selected Cases (N =100) from Population II*

	Original Scoring		Second Scoring		
	$\bar{X}_1$	σ_1	$\bar{X}_2$	σ_2	γ_{12}
1. Global rating	2.11	1.36	1.53	0.88	.754
2. Number of clauses (Volume)	18.05	8.64	17.94	8.24	.980
3. Accuracy 1: Grammar	45.38	24.16	45.95	23.49	.949
4. Accuracy 2: Vocabulary	47.64	24.34	47.87	23.20	.963
5. Accuracy 3: Spelling	48.56	25.32	48.49	24.23	.963
6. Variable 3 / variable 2	2.45	0.43	2.49	0.34	.498
7. Variable 4/variable 2	2.62	0.30	2.65	0.27	.491
8. Variable 5/variable 2	2.64	0.40	2.64	0.38	.726
9. Variety of tense and structure	1.56	0.91	1.34	0.82	.647
10. Range of vocabulary	0.97	1.28	0.96	1.18	.598
11. Cohesiveness	1.75	0.99	1.75	0.82	.613
12. Quantity score	186.96	96.99	188.26	93.69	.966
13. Quality score	101.68	12.00	102.64	9.41	.663
14. Variety score	151.80	84.62	142.80	70.82	.773
15. Total writing	440.44	176.42	443.70	159.82	.929

Note: Composition of Sample

Belgium (French)	28
Finland	13
Sweden	59
Total	100

Table 5.9. *Rater Reliabilities of Part and Final Scores—English Speaking Selected Cases (N =82) from Population II*

	Original Scoring		Second Scoring		
	$\bar{X}_1$	σ_1	$\bar{X}_2$	σ_2	γ_{12}
1. Global rating	1.93	1.37	1.43	1.05	.787
2. Total score, structural control	8.72	5.90	8.71	5.82	.961
3. Total score, oral reading	22.62	6.65	23.34	6.85	.835
4. Fluency A, No. clauses	6.43	4.86	6.35	4.86	.980
5. Fluency A, Accuracy 1, Grammar	16.22	13.16	15.76	12.98	.972
6. Fluency A, Accuracy 2, Vocabulary	17.40	13.66	16.22	13.15	.946

	Original Scoring		Second Scoring		
	$\bar{X}_1$	σ_1	$\bar{X}_2$	σ_2	γ_{12}
7. Fluency A, Accuracy 3, Pronunciation	16.33	13.66	14.41	12.14	.960
8. Fluency A, variable 5/ variable 4	2.21	0.84	2.17	0.85	.714
9. Fluency A, variable 6 / variable 4	2.49	0.84	2.34	0.80	.662
10. Fluency A, variable 7 / variable 4	2.25	0.80	1.99	0.79	.640
11. Fluency A, variety 1, tense and structure	0.85	1.00	0.72	0.74	.655
12. Fluency A, variety 2, range of vocabulary	0.78	1.05	0.84	0.98	.832
13. Fluency A, Quantity	49.95	40.19	46.39	38.05	.966
14. Fluency A, Quality	81.72	26.97	77.06	28.11	.714
15. Fluency A, Variety	37.32	41.13	34.21	32.90	.780
16. Total speaking	238.74	134.09	227.31	124.90	.953

Note: Composition of Sample

Belgium (French)	10
Finland	55
Italy	1
Sweden	16
Total	82

Chapter 6

The Place of English in the Schools

SOCIAL AND ECONOMIC BACKGROUND

Introduction

To fulfill their purpose, systems of education, schools and their curricula as well as the methods of teaching, must reflect a country's culture, the pattern of its economic development and its broad political and social aims. This is especially true of the teaching of a foreign language which is usually justified in considerable part because it helps to ensure the opportunity for contact with other countries in economics, science and technology as well as in literature and the arts. Other factors which influence the place of a foreign language in the schools are the country's level of literacy and the extent to which it is linguistically homogeneous. The existence of sharp regional or social differences and the degree of a country's social integration are also relevant. If a country is socially integrated and economically advanced it is encouraged to be outward looking and to favor the acquisition of the means to ensure the continuance of that advance by maintaining its contacts with other advanced nations. Where a country is not so well integrated or advanced it requires the knowledge which other countries possess. It cannot obtain this knowledge unless its system of education provides for a "language of wider communication" such as English. In the end, whether a foreign language is taught and if so which language and to what segments of the population are mainly aspects of social integration and of economic development. The level of a country's industrialization and the extent to which international science and technology are required are intimately associated with the teaching of a foreign language.

Some social and economic factors of importance are the extensiveness of a country's international trade, tourism, and the currency of international mass communication media such as films, television and newspapers. Some countries have close historical and political ties with a particular foreign country, or because of war and the consequences of war they need to teach a particular foreign language for domestic reasons. Finally, the importance which a country attaches to its educational institutions, the financial support which it gives them as well as the economic and social status that it accords to its teachers will influence not only the quality of foreign language instruction but also the likelihood of a foreign language being taught at all and, when it is, to what proportion of the student population.

It is not suggested that there is a direct, causal relationship between these societal variables and achievement in English as a foreign language. Nevertheless, there is some evidence in the ten countries studied in this instance that achievement tends to co-vary with the way in which these societal variables operate. This relationshup is probably one of the most vital questions which requires further investigation. There is sufficient data now available to indicate how such an investigation should be planned.

Social Integration and Economic Development

The ten countries are almost without exception well-integrated national states, well advanced socially and economically. Generally speaking, their linguistic minorities, usually small where they exist, do not seriously affect the national system of education. This is relevant to this present study since it is evident that wherever minority cultures and languages are recognized in the education of the majority, and even more so when the minorities acquire the major national language as a second language, the organization of the curriculum in order to include a foreign language is affected. The actual teaching of a foreign language to minorities presents problems which do not affect the majority of the students in homogeneous countries to the same extent. In Finland the Swedish minority constitutes 7.4 % of the total population and the language and associated culture of that minority are recognized in their curriculum, whereas those of the much smaller Russian and Lappish minorities are not. In the Netherlands the linguistic minority in Friesland constitutes 3 % of the total population, and its importance, like that of the Swedish minority in Finland, is increased because it is compact and concentrated. The Fries language is recognized in the primary schools of Friesland, where there is a strong demand for the extension of the provision. In Thailand the Chinese (10 %), Malays (3.0 %), and Indians (1.0 %) are well represented in certain areas. Where the minorities are not recognized on a national level they may still be taken into account in regions or enclaves. Moreover, as is the case with Finnish Lapps or the minorities of Hungary, the minority culture may be given a place in the syllabuses of such subjects as history, music and dance. Greater recognition of these

169

small minority cultures is the overall tendency in education and to that extent the case for a foreign language is harder to make save in respect to a very select group.

Belgium and Israel are more linguistically heterogeneous than the other IEA countries. Belgium consists of two equally large language communities with associated divergencies in religious and cultural affiliations, and with two separate Ministries of Education. Furthermore, apart from the basic linguistic division, 10 % of the children in primary schools, most of them immigrants, are taught in a language other than their native tongue. In Israel Hebrew is spoken by nearly 60 % of the population and Arabic by just under 25 %. Both languages are recognized officially in the system of education though, generally speaking, Hebrew is the language of instruction, Arabic being included in the curriculum if it is requested. In addition, Israel has a large number of immigrants from very many different countries; consequently, the proportion of parents whose mother tongue in childhood was the national language was no higher than 16.4 % and 11.1 % in the two sample populations in Israel, whereas in most of the other ten countries the percentage reached 85 % and higher.

The influence of the existence of sizeable linguistic minorities cannot be ascertained from the results of the present study since it was not chosen as a separate variable. The evidence is inconclusive: heterogeneous countries like Israel and Belgium as well as linguistically homogeneous countries like Germany and Sweden have relatively high levels of achievement. But it is an area of interest which needs to be researched because of the considerations outlined already in this chapter.

National Economic Development
Most of the countries are well developed industrially, devoting major percentages of their Gross National Product (GNP) and of the employable population to nonprimary industries. Such industries require the support of commercial contact with foreign countries, and this is the case among the ten countries to varying degrees. The extent to which trade is oriented towards English-speaking countries is relevant to the present study. It is worth noting therefore that countries such as Israel and Sweden which emphasize English in the curriculum have far higher levels of trade with English-speaking countries than does Hungary where English is introduced relatively late into the curriculum and taught to a relatively small

percentage of students. If we take the level of industrial development, the extent of international trade (especially with English-speaking countries) and urbanization as constituting one set of indices, the countries which rank the highest—the Netherlands, Belgium, Sweden and Israel—also tend to have the highest mean levels of achievement. Chile, Thailand and Hungary, which rank lowest on the "development" indices, are not so favorably placed on the scale of achievement.

EDUCATIONAL DEVELOPMENT

The expansion of educational provision, like the level of social and economic advancement, affects the demand for a foreign language in society and, therefore, its place in the expanded provision. Compared with an indigenous second language or the mother tongue, a foreign language is very much a school-based subject. This is recognized in many of the ten countries by the policy of teaching it to increasingly large numbers of students and of introducing instruction in the language at progressively early ages. Therefore, where the educational provision is expanded overall, the foreign language tends to be assured of a broader social support in the future; the greater the reinforcement of the knowledge of a foreign language outside school the greater the motivation of the student in learning it, and the greater the possibility of higher achievements. It is not without significance therefore that the one thing common to all the ten countries is a considerable expansion of educational provision during recent years. However, it appears that comparatively high mean levels of achievement in English are associated less with the degree of recent expansion than with a tradition of extensive educational provision. Those countries which started late tend to have, relatively speaking, low mean levels of achievement.

It is also noteworthy that several countries have reported not only increasing interest in foreign language teaching but several practical teaching innovations as well, such as the development of language laboratories and the use of different kinds of technical aids. The conjunction of expansion of opportunity to learn, together with more sophisticated methods designed to enable students to teach themselves, means that a foreign language is ceasing to be an elitist acquisition and has begun to take its place with mathematics and science as the prerogative of majorities of students in many countries. How changes in the techniques and methods of teaching a foreign

171

language reflect the changes in the social and economic backgrounds of students learning the languages as well as large increases in the mere numbers of those learning a foreign language should be a subject of study in itself.

It may be interesting to note, without making too much of the matter, that a choice to study English or French, the two languages included in the IEA Six Subject Survey, appears to be related to differences in student motivation. Peaker compared the background characteristics of students in the French and English samples with the background characteristics of the students in the IEA Stage 2 sample. His results, which are based on a type of "standardized" mean difference between samples, are presented in tables 6.1 and 6.2. The pattern of findings reflects a striking contrast between the two language samples: the students studying French in the English-speaking countries and in the Netherlands tend to be higher in ability (as measured by the Word Knowledge test), come from more affluent homes and, in general, come from backgrounds of higher social status than the average Stage 2 student. This is not true of the students studying English in the Federal Republic of Germany, Finland, Israel, Italy and Sweden, who appear to be more representative of the total school populations. The choice to study English or French as foreign languages apparently is influenced by a set of social conditions and related to perceptions of the unique communication roles played by the two languages. Because of such influences the two languages are attractive to different segments of the school populations. The suggestion merits further research within countries where both languages are taught, and the results should be compared across countries.

DIFFERENCES IN THE PATTERN OF GENERAL EDUCATIONAL PROVISION

Table 6.3. gives selected structural features of the national systems of education for the countries participating in the English as a Foreign Language study.

The teaching of a foreign language should be seen within the structure of the total school system as well as against the social and economic background. The lowest age of compulsory schooling is usually 5 or 6, but it may be as high as 8 years (Thailand); but most countries make some provision for pre-schooling, though the percentage take-up is small except in Belgium, the Netherlands and Israel. The length of the period of compulsory education varies from four (Thailand) to nine years, e.g., Finland and Sweden. The percentage of students who remain beyond the terminal point of compulsory schooling varies quite considerably. The most consistently high retention rate, 65 % at 16, 53 % at 17 and 35 % at 18, is in Sweden which also tends to have relatively high mean achievement levels.

The countries differ to an even greater degree in the way in which they segment the total provision from pre-school to university, though, with the exception of Sweden, countries, tend to distinguish elementary from secondary schools. Even where elementary schools are distinguished from secondary, the point at which the change occurs differs by as much as four years among the ten countries. Some countries also have "intermediate or observation" phases of schooling. Most countries have some kind of examination at the modal age of transfer to secondary education. Such differences as have already been noted here accompany differences in type of post-primary education. Here the main interest from the standpoint of foreign language teaching is the speed with which countries are developing comprehensive education since this means that the admission of students to such studies is more broadly based, even if the foreign language is not taught to all students. The most advanced in this respect is again Sweden. Most countries tend, like the Federal Republic of Germany (also with relatively high mean levels of achievement), to retain selection in some form. The selective or non-selective character of the school system does not appear to have a decisive relationship with achievement in English. However, the countries which tend to retain the highest proportion of students in Population IV —Sweden and Belgium, tend also to have the highest levels of achievement in English. Those which retain the lowest proportion of students—Thailand, Chile and Italy—tend to have low mean levels of achievement. The Netherlands is an exception in so far as it tends to have low retention and high mean achievement levels.

Two other aspects of the organization of education may affect the teaching of a foreign language. The first is the amount of time which students spend at school. Secondary school students spend approximately 25 % to 33 % more time at school than do those in elementary schools, and this may contribute to the general tendency to delay the foreign language until secondary school. There is, very simply, more time for it. By the same token, since the difference in the total amount of time available for secondary education varies considerably between countries it is easier to understand why some are able to give a foreign language greater prominence than others do. The countries which tend to require the greatest number of hours of attendance in secondary academic schools—Sweden, the Federal Republic of Germany and Israel—also tend to have the highest mean levels of achievement. Those that tend to require the least number of hours—Chile, Hungary and Thailand—tend also to have the lowest mean achievement levels, comparatively speaking.

Finally, the teaching of a foreign language is influenced by the degree of specialization in an academic subject (like the English language) compared with the degree of emphasis in the curriculum of teachers in training which the "methodics" of teaching generally and the support subjects such as psychology receive. Although it applies less to teachers in primary schools, the teaching of a foreign language, like the teaching of science, demands a lengthy study of the subject itself, and in view of the normal length and the number of weekly hours of the English course in schools this study has to continue well beyond the period of secondary education. If a foreign language teacher is unable to obtain a specialist English course at college, his preparation in the subject may not extend beyond four and sometimes only three years. The proportion of time given to instruction in the English language as distinct from aspects of pedagogy varies from 20 % in Thailand to 90 % in Israel and Italy, and the difference tends to be associated with differences in mean achievement levels of students.

GENERAL CHARACTERISTICS OF THE SCHOOLS

Organization

Data concerning some general characteristics of the schools are displayed in Tables 6.4–6.7. The teaching of English and the level of achievement in types of schools may be influenced by the criteria adopted for selecting students for such schools and, in particular, the age or grade range for which a school caters. Countries differ in these respects: there is a between-country range of nearly four grades in Population II with respect to the lowest grade in participating schools, from 3.7 to 7.6; and in Population IV the range is between 3.3 to 9.3. Differences with regard to the highest grades catered for in Population II range between 8.8 to 12.3, and in Population IV between 10.1 and 13.0. Countries differ in the grade-span the schools cater for and so far as Population II is concerned in the age range of the students in those grades as well. There are therefore very different problems of organization, some countries having schools which are able to concentrate their teaching of English on limited specific age groups and others needing to adjust to problems presented by much wider age ranges.

Coeducation or separate instruction for boys and girls is another aspect of differentiated education and, in view of the general belief that girls at certain stages tend to be better than boys at foreign languages, the question of its importance merits some consideration. Swedish schools are all coeducational and so are nearly all of the schools in the Federal Republic of Germany included in the samples. Coeducation is least favored in Thailand in both Populations, and in Italy and Chile (Population IV). It might appear therefore that there is a tendency for coeducation to be associated with higher levels of achievement. But without more information about how the countries interpret coeducation, whether in the form of separate schools or of separate classes within mixed schools or some other organization, it would be premature to draw any definitive conclusions.

Countries differ a great deal according to whether they tend to recruit students to their schools from a specific area (usually the neighborhood) or use criteria, like examinations, which involve the exploitation of a possibly wider catchment area. In Population II few countries based their selection policy on residence in the school neighborhood. The criterion is used even less in Population IV. An entrance examination appears to have more relevance, but especially in Population IV this is generally less important than general academic performance. There appears to be an association between relatively high mean levels of achievement and the reliance on academic performance as a criterion for entry into a particular school or course. This appears to be so in Belgium, the Netherlands and Israel. Countries like Thailand which do not emphasize the criterion tend to have relatively lower means.

Criteria other than those included in Tables 6.4 and 6.5 assume some importance in one or two countries, though they are not significant in differentiating between countries. For instance "membership of a specific religious or national group" is of importance in Israel and to a lesser extent in the Netherlands and Thailand, but the data provided by the responses to questionnaires are not sufficient to enable any kind of conclusion to be drawn concerning relationships to achievement. It is an area which is of considerable importance in many countries, and research of a comparative nature, which would enable conclusions to be drawn about how much differences in selection policy affected not only general levels of achievement but also attainment in specific subjects like a foreign language, would be valuable.

Characteristics of the School—Curriculum and Community

Countries differ in the proportion of academic as distinct from vocational and general type schools in the two samples. There is a marked tendency for countries with high proportions of academic schools in the present sample to have, as could be expected, rather high mean levels of achievement.

One aspect of community background is specifically linguistic. Generally speaking, the overall characteristics of the school background do not appear from the present study to have much importance, but an exception needs to be made with respect to the linguistic features of the school environment. Differences between the language of instruction in schools and the native languages of some of the students and their families are relevant to the teaching of a foreign language, though possibly less relevant than to the teaching of other subjects. The differences between school and home language are most apparent in Israel where in Populations II and IV respectively 7.8 % and 5.7 % of the students speak a language other than that used in the school. Italy and Belgium (Fr.) have the same characteristic, but to a lesser extent.

The role of teachers in schools in decision making, the choice of materials and of course books, must be important on any count. In general the teachers tend to be involved in the selection of textbooks and the choice of method, but the association of these variables with levels of achievement tends to be inconsistent across countries. Teacher participation in the formulation of syllabuses tends to be low. However deeply involved in the choice of methods and texts the teachers may be, the effectiveness of this involvement is limited because they are not able to participate in the decisions concerning the syllabuses which determine the type of text or method which would be suitable. This tends to be the case in most of the countries.

Inspection is generally regarded as having a close association with the improvement of education and with the promotion of higher mean levels of achievement. It is noteworthy in all countries that the percentage of schools which are not inspected is low, the tendency being for inspection to occur more frequently than twice a year.

176

Reporting to the school authorities appears to be the main purpose of inspection in Population II, the next in order of importance being advising the school (principal or director) or the class teacher and assessing the competence of a teacher. Advice and assessment tend to be more important in Population II than in Population IV where reporting to authorities takes pride of place.

ENGLISH IN THE SCHOOLS

Status of the Language

Tables 6.8–6.10 give data relating to English in the schools. English is in many countries an optional subject and the option becomes available at different points in the grade pattern of the schools. Consequently there are differences between the overall percentage of students taking English and the distribution of the percentage of students taking English in the successive grades. The highest overall percentages of English students (virtually 100 %) are found in Israel, Sweden and Thailand, countries which nevertheless differ remarkably in levels of achievement. Of greater interest is the distribution of the total number of students in the different grades and the percentage of any grade taking English. Apart from Belgium and Italy the percentage of English students is very high from Grade 5 or 6 and tends to be consistently high almost to the end of the school course. Hungary, which has the task of teaching Russian as the first foreign language to all students is the exception. Since on this variable there is a fair uniformity across countries in the proportion of the total school population which takes English, it is difficult to estimate what association there may be between this variable and mean achievement levels.

We can also consider the number of English students as a percentage of the enrollment for each population in the sampled schools. Since these percentages are only with respect to those schools drawn into the sample it was to be expected, first, that they would be higher than those in Table 6.8. They are only marginally higher, especially in those countries where a very high percentage of the overall school population took English. The picture that emerges of English in these ten countries is therefore one of considerable national interest in the subject, and this high level of national interest is satisfactorily reflected in the school systems and in the schools actually sampled. Where English is an optional subject students may select it in consultation with the staff of the School or independently. The tendency is for students in Population IV to have greater freedom of choice than those in Population II. However the student's freedom to exercise a choice in this matter does not appear to have any consistent relationship across countries with mean levels of achievement. Both these countries where little choice is allowed, as in Israel, and countries where students choose freely, as in Belgium, may have high mean achievement levels.

Teachers

Several factors help to determine the number of teachers of English a school requires—the number of students, the amount of time devoted to English, the size of classes and the proportion of teachers who spend all or only part of their time on English. There is little correspondence, across-countries, between the level of English staffing in schools and achievement in the language. Countries like Belgium, the Federal Republic of Germany, and Sweden, with relatively high mean levels of achievement, tend to have high English staffing ratios. Countries like Thailand, also with high staffing ratios, tend to have a relatively low mean achievement; but the Netherlands with low staffing ratios for English has a relatively high mean achievement level. However, the picture of the status of English judged in terms of the size of the staff is rather imprecise because it is difficult to take all factors into account simultaneously.

Very few schools employ native speakers of English to teach the language—not surprisingly, Belgium, the Federal Republic of Germany, Israel and the Netherlands have the greatest number of such teachers, though Thailand which is usually regarded as outside the main stream of English language influence has a small complement. The present study cannot even hint at any association between the existence of native language teachers of English and levels of achievement because the numbers involved are too small, but the question is sufficiently important to merit further research. Such an investigation would have to relate the existence of native speakers of the language as teachers to the quality of the English teachers whose main language is not English. Improvement of the quality of the indigenous teachers of English may not be the most economical answer always. The value of more native speakers of English as teachers and as teacher trainers should be assessed carefully.

Grade of Introduction of English

English tends to be introduced not earlier than Grade 3 and not later than Grade 9 (see table 6.8). In theory this allows for a wide range of options, but in practice most countries choose Grade 5. However, the same grade does not correspond to the same age group across-countries, and it can be argued that age rather than grade (which is simply an administrative feature) has a more potent influence on achievement. For this reason it is necessary to bear in mind that, for instance, Grade 5 students are 11 years of age in Thailand and Hungary but only 10 years old in the Federal Republic of Germany, and that Grade 6 students in Italy are of the same age as Grade 5 students in Chile and Thailand. It should be noted that Thailand offers English in some kindergartens, and that the choice of beginning grade in Netherlands depends on the type of school. Such considerations make it advisable to avoid simple comparisons between age and achievement levels across-countries.

The mean of the grade of introduction of English for the sample for which data are available tends to differ from the stated policy, and the difference may be quite large in some instances. In Belgium the difference is between a policy stipulation of Grade 7 and an actual mean grade of 9.6 in Population IV. Differences in Population IV reflect the fact that large numbers of students commence their study of English later than the stipulated grade partly because it is their second foreign language and partly because the system of school options enables them to take up the study of a foreign language relatively late. Where Population II is concerned any discrepancy may be due to changes in policy which are working themselves through the school systems. This is partly the reason for a difference between a stipulated Grade 3 and a mean of 5.9 in Finland.

Time for English

The numbers of periods a week in which English is taught in Population II range at the beginning stage from two to six. The beginning stage in Population IV tends to be allocated a larger number of periods. The same wide range characterizes the intermediate and advanced stages in both Populations. However, the number of periods has to be related to the length of the period itself which may vary from 40 minutes in some countries to 55 or 58 in others.

Financial Support for English

The proportion of the school budget ear-marked for English in the ten countries is not ungenerous when account is taken of the number of subjects in the curriculum, and the fact that, generally speaking, though the language is chosen by large numbers of students, it is still an optional subject. Financial support is particularly generous in those countries like Sweden, the Netherlands and Finland, where the mean levels of achievement tend to be comparatively high. It is interesting that countries with relatively high budgetary allocations may not staff the teaching of English generously. On the other hand, Thailand, which has a comparatively moderate to low budgetary allocation, tends to staff the subject fairly generously. The index of financial support for the subject is probably a very complicated problem, and it is vitally important to identify the factors involved and the weight to be allocated to each of them if the cost effectiveness of the teaching of English is to be ascertained.

Aspects of Classroom Presentation of English

An interesting feature is that only in one country (Thailand) is speaking English taught for the first time later than the grade at which the language is introduced into the curriculum. Nevertheless, though reading English is taught before speaking, achievement in reading in Thailand does not compare favorably with achievement in those countries which begin with speaking English. Generally, most countries begin with an oral approach and it does not appear that this is associated with low levels of reading achievement or that a reading approach is associated with higher mean levels of achievement in reading.

The extensive use of English in teaching the language, though not a uniform practice, tends to be the general policy. Countries like Italy, which do not tend to conform to this practice tend to have relatively moderate means in reading, especially in Population II. The practice is more frequent in nearly all countries in Population IV. Countries which tend to rely on the use of English differ according to the point in the English course where the reliance on English to teach the language becomes pronounced. Thailand and Chile, with low mean levels of achievement, tend to do so earlier than most other countries, while Finland, with a high mean achievement, delays the use of the language as a general rule until Grade 7, and Belgium and the Netherlands until Grade 8. There is a tendency for high mean levels of achievement to be associated with moderately late dependence (Grades 6 or 7) rather than earlier dependence (Grades 4 or 5) on the use of English.

Table 6.1. *Comparison of the Samples for French as a Foreign Language and for Stage 2 for Population II*

Variable	Country					
	Eng-land	Scot-land	United States	New Zealand	Nether-lands	Mean
Grade	−.26	.28	.90	.64	1.57	.62
Father's occupation	.36	.22	.21	.45	0.55	.36
Student's sex	.10	.18	.24	.16	0.20	.18
Father's education	.20	.11	.32	.38	0.41	.28
Mother's education	.17	.07	.20	.33	0.32	.22
Expected education	.41	.62	.29	.60	0.66	.52
Homework	.35	.43	.27	.47	0.58	.41
Dictionary at home	.45	.30	.06	.14	0.03	.20
Books at home	.24	.29	.23	.29	0.14	.24
Siblings	.15	.19	.19	.15	0.53	.24
Mean	.22	.27	.29	.36	0.50	.32
World Knowledge	.19	.43	.47	.58	0.60	.42

Note: Each entry is (French Mean—Stage 2 Mean) /Stage 2 S.D.

Stage 2 refers to three other IEA Studies: Literature, Reading Comprehension and Science.

Table 6.2. *Comparison of the Samples for English as a Foreign Language and for Stage 2 for Population II*

Variable	Country					
	FRG	Finland	Israel	Italy	Sweden	Mean
Father's occupation	1.40	−.10	.30	.00	.08	.34
Student's sex	0.12	.00	−.08	−.22	−.04	−.04
Father's education	0.00	.00	.15	.10	.21	.09
Mother's education	0.10	.00	.16	.12	.27	.13
Expected education	0.15	.02	.22	−.02	−.04	.07
Homework	0.00	.16	−.17	−.22	−.22	−.09
Dictionary at home	0.05	.00	−.21	.09	.08	.00
Books at home	0.13	−.06	.14	.20	−.02	.08
Siblings	0.05	.04	.20	.00	.00	.06
Mean	0.22	.01	.08	.01	.04	.07
Word Knowledge	−.02	.14	.28	−.02	−.03	.07

Note: Each entry is (English Mean—Stage 2 Mean) /Stage 2 S.D.

Stage 2 refers to three other IEA Studies: Literature, Reading Comprehension and Science.

Selected Structural Features of National Systems of Education

	Bel-gium (Fr.)	Chile	FRG	Fin-land	Hun-gary	Is-rael	Italy	Nether-lands	Swe-den	Thai-land
Age of entry to compulsory education	6	7	6	7	6	5	6	7	7	8
Age at which compulsory education ends	14	14	15	16	14	14	14	15	16	12[d]
Duration of compulsory education	8	6[e]	9	9	8	9	8	8	9	4[d]
Modal age of transfer to secondary Education	12[a]	14	10–12[a]	11	14	14[b]	10–11	12	c	14
Age of terminal secondary groups	18–20	20	18	18	17	19	18	20	19	19
Number of hours instruction annually										
Primary	924	800–1 056	920	1 000	720	1 320	900	1 040	972	900
Academic Secondary	1 041	960–1 050	1 450	1 160	1 080	}1 544	1 100	1 140	1 260	}1 080
Vocational Secondary	1 228	1 296	94	–[f]	1 140		1 400	1 100	1 152	
Proportion of age groups in school										
Population II	90	71	94	99	83	–	55	98	99	90
Population IV	33	16	9[g]	21	28	–	16	13	45	10

e: Source of data: National Technical Officers' reports and the National Case Study estionnaires.

n some cases 12–16 years is period of observation.
Transfer at 12 to comprehensive schools.
Primary and secondary schools are not distinguished administratively.
Age at which compulsory schooling ends varies between 12 to 14 years.
The six years may be completed at any time between 7 and 15 years of age.
ot relevant in Finland.
Population IV was defined by the FRG as only those students in the *Oberprima*. If all the students in the relevant age group are considered, some 30% are still in school.

Table 6.4. *Selected Characteristics of Schools—General (1)—Population II*

	Belgium (Fr.)	FRG	Finland	Israel	Italy	Nether-lands	Sweden	Thai-land
School enrollment of boys								
Mean	463.9	289.0	225.7	225.7	342.1	405.4	353.9	856.1
S.D.	329.0	141.5	174.3	176.7	196.3	264.6	145.8	583.5
School enrollment of girls								
Mean	392.2	275.1	212.0	232.4	281.0	308.6	344.7	884.4
S.D.	283.1	104.6	167.7	160.4	179.9	190.3	143.9	640.0
School enrollment—total								
Mean	686.4	564.1	420.6	426.6	610.8	603.6	698.6	1 347.7
S.D.	325.4	234.8	270.2	260.8	245.4	396.1	288.3	531.3
Enrollment in Population II only								
Mean	133.0	87.5	104.6	120.4	118.2	64.8	309.4	178.3
S.D.	74.6	53.9	60.5	71.3	79.8	64.1	100.1	129.6
Full-time school staff								
Mean	64.6	22.7	22.4	34.7	43.4	33.0	48.7	59.9
S.D.	32.2	13.3	13.3	37.1	18.4	21.2	19.0	20.0
Number of students per teacher								
Mean	11.0	26.9	17.0	15.5	14.6	19.3	13.8	23.1
S.D.	8.2	6.5	4.5	4.3	6.9	4.1	2.7	7.7
Number of male teachers								
Mean	34.2	12.6	7.8	20.8	15.0	24.3	22.8	23.3
S.D.	25.7	10.2	4.9	23.5	9.2	17.6	6.3	19.5
Lowest grade in school								
Mean	4.5	4.0	5.8	7.6	6.5	6.9	3.7	5.1

Mean	12.3	9.2	10.8	8.8	11.5	10.0	10.1	9.6
S.D.	1.1	0.7	1.5	1.8	1.3	1.5	1.5	2.0
% of schools having coeducation	32.1	100.0	71.5	50.7	72.0	89.9	100.0	49.5
Streaming practices expressed in % having fast and slow learners:								
(i) taught separately	35.5	0.0	4.6	0.0	34.4	3.3	1.0	5.1
(ii) taught together								
always	34.1	100.0	79.1	98.9	30.7	92.2	38.4	52.8
sometimes	30.4	0.0	16.3	1.1	34.9	4.4	60.6	42.1
Number of hours schooling—weekly								
Mean	30.7	35.0	26.9	30.3	38.6	34.5	30.2	35.2
S.D.	1.7	0.0	1.5	3.4	1.2	1.3	3.1	2.4
Number of weeks schooling—annually								
Mean	37.4	40.0	40.0	33.4	34.2	34.6	39.7	37.5
S.D.	2.7	0.0	1.0	2.1	2.9	1.9	0.8	2.3
Use of criteria for admission expressed in % using:								
(i) local residency	13.6	93.4	26.6	30.4	63.0	10.7	70.9	0.0
(ii) academic performance	38.8	6.5	90.0	7.8	72.9	57.5	38.1	92.4
(iii) entrance examination	64.3	0.0	25.7	5.5	41.0	43.9	16.5	28.0
Number of schools in sample[a]	40	97	91	62	44	70	47	42

Note: % = Percentage.

[a] Not all answered every question on the questionnaire; percentages, means and S.D.'s are based only on those who answered the question seeking the information indicated here. Generally, 90 % or more of the sample responded to most questions.

Table 6.5. *Selected Characteristics of Schools—General (1)—Population IV*

	Belgium (Fr.)	Chile	FRG	Finland	Hungary	Israel	Italy	Netherlands	Sweden	Thailand
School enrollment of boys										
Mean	704.2	799.4	570.3	329.9	261.4	221.3	447.1	389.8	425.2	2 307.3
S.D.	480.2	495.7	261.3	195.8	169.8	197.0	248.6	257.5	280.6	1 248.3
School enrollment of girls										
Mean	324.6	850.5	439.9	400.4	468.4	250.9	386.0	301.9	351.4	893.9
S.D.	338.6	749.5	339.3	203.1	185.3	127.7	188.3	223.4	350.7	525.4
School enrollment—total										
Mean	771.3	1 124.3	851.6	695.5	716.7	457.5	791.6	688.7	776.6	2 433.3
S.D.	439.2	617.4	247.9	268.6	269.3	203.6	372.5	435.5	548.0	1 412.2
Enrollment in Population IV only										
Mean	54.3	107.5	61.5	65.9	161.5	77.9	119.5	57.3	212.9	75.7
S.D.	37.3	97.3	23.0	43.8	75.3	32.4	69.7	58.3	115.5	35.0
Full-time school staff										
Mean	66.2	39.2	45.2	30.2	41.7	40.5	64.3	41.2	49.3	90.0
S.D.	40.5	26.6	14.7	10.2	15.8	34.9	36.8	25.0	16.4	38.2
Number of students per teacher										
Mean	12.2	35.8	18.6	22.1	17.5	12.7	13.4	18.3	13.9	24.4
S.D.	2.9	28.9	2.8	4.9	4.5	3.4	3.6	2.9	2.4	5.7
Number of male teachers										
Mean	41.1	17.4	28.1	9.5	16.8	25.8	26.9	29.1	31.6	41.2
S.D.	28.2	15.5	13.3	3.9	8.8	26.8	12.6	18.8	13.4	25.3
Lowest grade in school										
Mean	3.3	6.9	5.0	5.6	9.0	8.7	9.0	7.2	9.3	4.6

Mean	13.0	12.0	12.0	13.0	12.2	12.0	12.1	13.0	12.1	10.1
S.D.	0.0	0.2	1.3	0.0	0.7	0.1	0.3	0.0	0.3	2.0
% of schools having coeducation	49.4	100.0	88.1	85.7	89.5	95.5	83.9	57.5	32.3	30.2
Streaming practices expressed in % having fast and slow learners:										
(i) taught separately	31.3	0.0	0.0	13.1	33.1	83.8	1.4	0.0	7.8	7.1
(ii) taught together										
always	13.3	100.0	96.9	86.9	31.9	15.2	98.6	99.4	68.9	76.3
sometimes	55.4	0.0	3.1	0.0	35.0	1.0	0.0	0.6	23.3	16.6
Number of hours schooling—weekly										
Mean	32.8	32.0	28.4	33.1	37.3	33.3	33.5	30.0	35.7	35.4
S.D.	2.9	0.0	2.2	2.6	1.9	1.4	3.5	3.7	1.1	3.1
Number of weeks schooling—annually										
Mean	36.1	40.0	39.8	33.8	34.3	33.0	36.1	40.0	32.9	37.8
S.D.	1.2	0.0	1.0	2.0	2.9	0.0	2.1	1.2	2.3	3.0
Use of criteria for admission expressed in % using:										
(i) local residency	11.7	34.3	17.7	8.4	48.9	83.3	1.1	35.8	71.0	0.0
(ii) academic performance	56.0	98.9	98.5	22.9	88.5	95.3	77.9	82.5	58.0	95.6
(iii) entrance examination	53.5	0.0	40.4	0.3	56.6	30.1	86.1	34.0	24.7	24.9
Number of schools in sample[a]	15	81	52	18	20	46	73	59	80	54

Note: % = Percentage.

[a] Not all answered every question on the questionnaire; percentages, means and S.D.'s are based only on those who answered the question seeking the information indicated here. Generally, 90 % or more of the sample responded to most questions.

Table 6.6. *Selected Characteristics of Schools—General (2)—Population II*

	Belgium (Fr.)	FRG	Finland	Israel	Italy	Nether-lands	Sweden	Thai-land
% of schools having a variety of courses	52.3	2.3	41.6	41.5	8.5	37.7	100.0	26.0
Of schools having only one type of course, % having:								
Academic	86.5	39.4	32.0	63.3	9.6	3.2	_[b]	100.0
Vocational/technical	13.5	0.0	17.0	30.9	30.9	44.1	_[b]	0.0
General	0.0	60.6	51.0	5.8	59.5	52.7	_[b]	0.0
Type of community served expressed in %:								
Urban	0.0	28.9	38.2	71.5	90.0	20.3	37.1	65.7
Suburban	5.4	25.0	3.2	5.6	5.0	18.1	16.3	33.6
Rural	6.3	2.0	26.0	22.9	5.0	30.4	12.2	0.0
Mixed	88.2	44.0	32.5	0.0	0.0	31.1	34.5	0.7
% having the following amenities in the community:								
(i) Public library	88.4	98.3	100.0	91.0	85.1	94.7	98.1	65.3
(ii) Foreign language societies etc.	46.2	96.2	21.7	57.8	64.1	37.6	94.2	36.3
% having teacher involvement in decisions regarding the selection of								
Texts	98.2	88.5	75.6	84.9	100.0	98.6	31.7	37.5
Method	22.3	96.5	77.9	81.3	78.5	94.1	97.3	80.9
Syllabus	0.0	0.0	16.5	27.1	20.5	63.1	0.0	57.7
% having inspection of school:								
Never	0.0	1.1	0.0	0.0	25.9	0.3	2.0	16.0
Twice a year	4.0	17.1	2.4	17.2	4.9	17.7	12.1	14.4
More than twice a year	64.6	47.5	9.5	75.8	6.0	94.5	91.0	45.8

Purpose of inspection expressed in % having it to:

(i) report for authorities	79.5	15.3	76.3	58.3	50.3	24.2	28.4	31.2
(ii) advise school on some problems	53.5	33.6	74.4	76.6	24.6	67.6	21.4	44.8
(iii) advise teachers	93.6	30.4	65.8	63.1	21.7	12.2	85.3	62.0
(iv) assess teachers	88.5	93.9	51.7	88.2	8.8	21.7	7.5	15.0
Number of schools in sample[a]	42	47	70	44	62	91	97	40

Note: % = Percentage.

[a] Not all answered every question on the questionnaire; percentages are based only on those who answered the question seeking the information indicated here. Generally, 90 % or more of the sample responded to most questions. Dashes (–) in the table indicate where no information was available because the question was not answered.

[b] Note that since 100 percent of Swedish Population II schools have a variety of courses, it is only appropriate that this question was not answered there.

Table 6.7. *Selected Characteristics of Schools—General (2)—Population IV*

	Belgium (Fr.)	Chile	FRG	Finland	Hungary	Israel	Italy	Nether-lands	Sweden	Thai-land
% of schools having a variety of courses	30.5	18.2	0.3	49.2	24.0	58.7	42.6	64.4	90.0	17.1
Of schools having only one type of course, % having:										
Academic	71.4	65.4	100.0	89.4	88.8	74.5	26.6	62.0	0.0	100.0
Vocational/technical	28.6	19.0	0.0	0.0	11.2	19.7	73.4	8.5	100.0	0.0
General	0.0	15.6	0.0	10.6	0.0	5.8	0.0	29.4	0.0	0.0
Type of community served expressed in %:										
Urban	3.0	85.4	35.4	63.5	15.7	76.1	93.5	24.0	48.2	41.6
Suburban	3.4	2.5	33.1	0.0	5.4	2.5	0.9	11.7	5.1	58.4
Rural	4.3	0.0	2.5	9.9	4.3	21.3	5.5	29.1	4.5	0.0
Mixed	89.3	12.1	29.0	26.6	74.6	0.0	0.0	35.2	42.1	0.0
% having the following amenities in the community:										
(i) Public library	84.7	85.3	91.4	100.0	100.0	94.3	98.8	100.0	99.0	68.7
(ii) Foreign language societies etc.	50.1	69.7	97.4	34.8	95.2	59.9	87.9	55.6	98.5	13.5
% having teacher involvement in decisions regarding the selection of:										
Texts	92.8	86.2	84.4	73.7	0.0	91.8	100.0	96.9	39.0	20.2
Method	22.9	84.0	100.0	41.1	38.9	93.6	98.1	95.9	98.2	94.9
Syllabus	1.3	16.7	0.0	2.3	0.0	20.6	4.9	47.0	0.0	67.3
% having inspection of school:										
Never	0.0	7.3	0.0	1.1	4.9	0.0	10.0	0.0	0.0	11.0

Twice a year	4.0	17.0	23.7	5.3	20.3	25.4	0.0	28.4	6.9	6.9
More than twice a year	63.7	12.9	19.9	1.4	22.7	74.6	31.0	28.6	91.1	59.9
Purpose of inspection expressed in % having it to:										
(i) report for authorities	76.6	66.0	41.3	90.0	54.6	81.6	58.3	24.6	68.8	48.4
(ii) advise school on some problems	54.5	37.2	45.7	63.7	16.4	89.5	33.4	71.1	11.0	23.9
(iii) advise teachers	89.0	14.6	34.0	70.9	89.9	91.5	0.0	4.8	95.5	36.7
(iv) assess teachers	83.9	6.7	71.7	43.7	83.8	83.4	4.9	33.1	6.5	41.2
Number of schools in sample[a]	54	80	59	73	46	20	18	52	81	15

Note: % = Percentage.

[a] Not all answered every question on the questionnaire; percentages are based only on those who answered the question seeking the information indicated here. Generally, 90 % or more of the sample responded to most questions.

Table 6.8. *Percentage of Total Student Population Enrolled in English Per Grade Level*

Country	3	4	5	6	7	8	9	10	11	12	13	Year reported
Belgium (Fr.)	–	–	–	–	20 %	25 %	85 %	85 %	85 %	85 %	–	1970
Chile	–	–	About 5–10 % begin at Grade 5, the majority at Grade 7 but the percentage for each of these grades is unknown.				95 %	95 %	95 %	95 %	–	1970
FRG	–	– ← 70 % of Primary →									67.9 %	1969
Finland			87.4 % ← 60 % of Primary →	78.7 %	80.1 %	77.0 % ← 52 % of Primary →	81.2 %	90.5 %	94.1 %	75.1 %	–	1970
Hungary	0.2 %	–	–	–	–	–	11.7 %	11.0 %	10.4 %	8.9 %	–	1970
Israel	–	–	100 %	100 %	100 %	100 %	100 %	100 %	100 %	100 %	–	1972
Italy	–	–	–	38 %	36 %	–	–	–	–	–	–	1970
Netherlands			← 75 % of Secondary (with English as a 1st F.L.) →		80 % (Gr. 7 or 8)		← 27 % of Secondary (with English as a 2nd F.L.) → The majority beginning English continue but the percentage for each of these grades is unknown.				–	1970
Sweden	–[a]	100 %	100 %	100 %	100 %	94.1 %	91 %	95 %	92 %	100 %	–	1970–1971
Thailand	–	–	100 %	100 %	100 %	100 %	100 %	100 %	100 %	100 %	–	1970

Note. Dashes (–) indicate that no percentage...

	Belgium (Fr.)	FRG	Finland	Israel	Italy	Netherlands	Sweden	Thailand
Estimated % of Population II studying English	72.5	89.0	75.8	74.4	55.4	97.3	94.1	97.6
% selecting students of English on the decision of:								
(i) Student only	97.0	42.2	75.3	0.0	81.9	31.8	100.0	13.4
(ii) Student and School personnel	3.0	17.6	7.1	18.5	3.7	60.4	0.0	79.6
(iii) School personnel only	0.0	40.2	17.6	81.5	14.4	7.9	0.0	7.0
Number of teachers of English								
Mean	6.6	6.5	2.3	3.5	2.3	3.2	8.8	18.3
S.D.	2.9	3.5	1.5	1.6	1.4	1.8	5.1	21.4
Full-time auxiliary staff:								
School librarian								
% having none	62.5	94.9	86.1	34.9	43.7	84.4	42.1	15.7
% having 1 or more	37.5	5.1	13.9	65.8	56.3	15.6	57.9	84.3
Foreign language laboratory technician								
% having none	98.7	100.0	98.6	96.3	93.7	87.1	97.9	69.2
% having 1 or more	1.3	0.0	1.4	3.7	6.3	12.9	2.1	30.8
Grade at which most students begin English								
Mean	7.1	5.1	5.9	5.1	6.5	6.6	4.0	5.9
S.D.	0.3	0.5	1.2	0.4	1.1	1.4	0.0	3.6
Grade of introduction of:								
Spoken English								
Mean	7.0	5.1	5.4	5.1	6.5	6.5	4.0	7.0
S.D.	0.5	0.5	1.5	0.4	1.1	1.9	0.0	3.0
Reading and writing in English								
Mean	7.0	5.1	5.6	5.1	6.5	6.5	4.0	6.3
S.D.	0.5	0.5	1.4	0.4	1.1	1.8	0.0	3.5

Table 6.9. (*Cont.*)

	Belgium (Fr.)	FRG	Finland	Israel	Italy	Netherlands	Sweden	Thailand
% conducting English classes in English:								
at Grades 1 thru 8 or more	88.7	82.4	74.7	74.4	25.3	68.9	67.7	55.7
not at all	11.3	17.6	25.3	25.6	74.7	31.1	32.3	44.3
No. of periods of English per week								
Beginning								
Mean	4.5	4.7	3.0	3.3	2.8	2.8	2.0	5.7
S.D.	1.3	1.1	1.2	0.7	0.9	0.7	0.0	1.2
Intermediate								
Mean	3.9	3.8	3.3	4.6	3.1	3.1	4.0	6.1
S.D.	0.5	0.7	0.9	0.5	0.7	1.0	0.0	1.2
Total number of minutes for English per week								
Beginning								
Mean	224.3	212.9	138.5	163.1	160.2	140.7	80.0	313.8
S.D.	64.6	51.1	52.7	27.6	48.4	33.1	0.0	75.8
Intermediate								
Mean	196.0	169.4	148.2	211.7	176.3	154.5	160.0	338.5
S.D.	25.6	33.6	36.5	27.7	34.4	49.1	0.0	67.5
Estimated % of the annual school budget for Foreign language instruction	–	10.4	12.9	7.6	10.2	16.9	17.1	13.1
Number of schools in sample[a]	42	47	70	44	62	91	97	40

Note: %=Percentage.

[a] Not all answered every question on the questionnaire; percentages, means and S.D.'s are based only on those who answered the question ... 90% or more of the sample responded to most questions. Dashes (–) in the table indicate

Table 6.10. *Selected Characteristics of Schools—English Specific—Population IV*

	Belgium (Fr.)	Chile	FRG	Finland	Hungary	Israel	Italy	Netherlands	Sweden	Thailand
Estimated % of Population IV studying English	87.1	97.6	74.6	88.4	35.6	92.8	67.7	98.2	91.3	93.6
% selecting students of English on the decision of:										
(i) Student only	89.4	70.1	100.0	90.8	27.4	0.0	46.2	61.3	100.0	0.0
(ii) Student and school personnel	5.8	0.0	0.0	6.0	61.8	0.0	0.0	38.7	0.0	100.0
(iii) School personnel only	4.8	29.9	0.0	3.2	10.8	100.0	53.8	0.0	0.0	0.0
Number of teachers of English										
Mean	5.5	3.6	9.1	3.9	2.6	4.4	3.8	3.4	7.6	22.0
S.D.	2.9	2.1	3.0	1.6	1.3	1.2	1.4	2.3	3.0	19.0
Full-time auxiliary staff:										
School librarian										
% having none	57.3	27.9	95.6	72.3	28.6	9.2	16.1	76.6	17.4	17.4
% having 1 or more	42.7	72.1	4.4	27.7	71.4	90.8	83.9	23.4	82.6	82.6
Foreign language laboratory technician										
% having none	83.0	90.9	98.6	94.5	93.5	100.0	91.2	78.2	85.5	59.6
% having 1 or more	17.0	9.1	1.4	5.5	6.5	0.0	8.8	21.8	14.5	40.4
Grade at which most students begin English										
Mean	7.6	7.4	5.3	5.6	9.0	5.4	9.0	6.9	4.0	4.9
S.D.	0.7	1.9	0.8	1.3	0.0	0.6	0.0	0.9	0.0	3.8

Table 6.10 (*Cont.*)

	Belgium (Fr.)	Chile	FRG	Finland	Hungary	Israel	Italy	Netherlands	Sweden	Thailand
Grade of introduction of:										
Spoken English										
Mean	7.5	7.0	5.3	5.5	9.0	5.2	9.0	6.9	4.0	5.3
S.D.	0.7	2.2	0.8	1.2	0.0	0.6	0.0	0.9	0.0	3.6
Reading and writing in English										
Mean	7.6	7.4	5.3	5.6	9.0	5.4	9.0	7.0	4.0	5.0
S.D.	0.8	1.8	0.8	1.2	0.0	1.0	0.0	1.0	0.0	3.5
% conducting English classes in English:										
at Grades 1 thru 8	100.00	54.4	92.2	83.8	81.2	96.1	0.0	71.6	80.9	64.4
not at all	0.0	45.6	7.8	16.2	18.8	3.9	100.0	28.4	19.1	35.6
No. of periods of English per week										
Beginning										
Mean	3.2	3.4	5.5	4.2	2.2	4.0	3.0	2.9	2.0	5.5
S.D.	0.8	1.1	0.8	0.7	0.6	0.0	0.0	0.5	0.0	0.9
Intermediate										
Mean	3.0	3.4	4.2	3.8	2.2	4.8	3.1	3.0	4.0	5.9
S.D.	0.7	1.0	0.6	0.6	0.4	0.4	0.3	0.7	0.0	0.4
Advanced										
Mean	2.7	3.3	4.0	3.7	–	5.0	3.3	3.1	3.0	6.8
S.D.	0.8	0.9	0.6	0.6	–	0.5	0.8	0.9	0.0	3.3
Total number of minutes for English per week										
Beginning										
Mean	161.3	147.5	248.4	186.4	109.0	200.0	176.1	147.1	80.0	322.3

Mean	149.4	152.2	187.9	171.5	98.8	217.2	179.3	152.1	160.0	345.0
S.D.	32.6	39.3	28.7	25.1	18.1	21.5	19.3	36.0	0.0	27.1
Advanced										
Mean	135.1	143.7	180.9	163.7	–	225.9	193.0	151.1	120.0	470.1
S.D.	38.9	37.4	25.5	23.0	–	25.8	50.1	47.8	0.0	137.6
Estimated % of the annual school budget for Foreign language instruction	–	10.1	16.1	22.6	17.5	9.8	7.9	16.3	14.0	8.5
Number of schools in sample[a]	54	80	59	73	46	20	18	52	81	15

Note: % = Percentage.

[a] Not all answered every question on the questionnaire; percentages, means and S.D.'s are based only on those who answered the questions seeking the information indicated here. Generally, 90 % or more of the sample responded to most questions. Dashes (–) in the table indicate where no information was available because the question was not answered.

Chapter 7

Characteristics of the Teachers

Teachers were asked to respond to two questionnaires. The first one was used to obtain general information. The second was designed to investigate the characteristics specific to teachers of English as a Foreign Language. It should also be remembered that many teachers of English teach other subjects also and that for this reason the responses may reflect the teachers' involvement in those subjects as much as in English.

GENERAL CHARACTERISTICS OF THE TEACHERS

There is considerable variation in the teacher-recruitment and training policies and practices of the ten countries. There are also considerable differences in the sizes of teacher samples in the ten countries. However, these differences do not affect the results of the investigation since we refer to percentages of the sample in reporting data. But it should also be noted that the sample is a satisfactory representative of each country. The between-country differences in the proportions of men and women in both samples are large, with the tendency being for the proportion of men in Population IV to exceed the proportion in Population II. Finland is an exception, and there the difference in the achievement rating of the two populations tends to be more favorable in Population IV than Population II. Tables 7.1 and 7.2 show some data regarding the general characteristics of teachers of English.

Teachers between the ages of 28 and 37 tend to constitute the largest single age group, estimated in decennial periods in all countries in both populations. Generally speaking, the tendency is for both populations to have higher proportions of teachers with relatively long rather than short experience, and for those teaching students in Population IV to be older than those in Population II. However, the differences in the age and sex composition of the teacher samples do not appear to be associated consistently with differences in mean levels of achievement in either population.

198

In both populations the percentage of teachers without any, or with less than 2 years post-secondary education tends to be low except in Belgium and the Netherlands. In both these countries it is probable that some courses in secondary schools, especially at the higher grades, are regarded as offering professional training for teachers. The general tendency is for a greater proportion of teachers in Population IV than in Population II to have had more than two years of post-secondary education. Further analysis of the data indicates that in Population IV high percentages of the teachers in the Federal Republic of Germany, Finland and Hungary have had more than four years of post-secondary education. In these countries there is a pronounced tendency to relatively high achievement levels. In most countries there are proportionately fewer teachers in both populations with long as opposed to short or mediumterm experience, though in Population IV the proportion with over 20 years of service tends to be greater than in Population II.

In view of the differences in age distribution, the extent of post-secondary education as well as extent of experience of teaching, it is worth noting that in all countries except Belgium and Sweden more than 75 % of the teachers in Population II devote all their teaching time to the subject in which they specialized in their professional training. In Population IV we note a similar tendency. Most teachers of English tend to be specialists.

The countries in Population II with the highest percentages of teachers spending more than 10 hours in lesson preparation are the Federal Republic of Germany and Sweden; these countries also tend to have relatively high mean levels of achievement. In view of the pre-university status of the Population IV students it is not surprising that their teachers might spend more time in preparation than do those in Population II. This is especially true of the Federal Republic of Germany, Finland, the Netherlands and Sweden, countries with relatively high mean achievement levels for that population. A further analysis of the data indicates that between 6 % and 14 % of the teachers in the same countries, as well as in Israel, tend to spend over 15 hours in preparation.

As regards correction of student assignments a fair proportion of teachers spend many hours (ten or more) on preparation, rather than very few (two hours), though the great majority, as was to be expected, spend between two and ten hours. Taking all ten countries together teachers in Population IV compared with Population II tend to spend more time in correcting students' work. It is interesting to note in this population that whereas Chile and Hungary (both testing Population IV only) reflect different tendencies in respect to time spent on preparation; they behave similarly in respect of correction. So far as other countries are concerned, in Population II Belgium, Israel, Italy and Finland behave somewhat similarly on preparation and correction, while the Federal Republic of Germany, and Sweden tend to give more attention to preparation than to correction. In the Netherlands and Thailand the opposite is the case. In Population IV greater stress appears to be placed on preparation than on correction in Belgium, the Federal Republic of Germany, Finland, Hungary and Sweden, while the position is reversed in Chile, Israel, Italy and the Netherlands. However these differences do not appear to have any consistent association with differences in mean achievement levels.

Another aspect of professional conscientiousness among teachers is their attitude toward professional affiliation, attendance at conferences, and the like. Of these indices, membership in a teachers' organization claims the highest percentage of teachers in all countries and in both populations, with higher figures in Population IV than in Population II. Attendance at conferences claims the next highest percentage in Population II, followed by the percentage of teachers subscribing to professional periodicals. In Population IV attendance at conferences seldom claims as high percentages as the other variables do in this set. The order in which these indices of conscientiousness or of professional awareness appear (in terms of percentages of teachers claiming involvement in them) may be related as much to the availability of facilities, like associations, conferences and periodicals, as to the choice made by the teachers. A professional union or association is likely to be an important if not an almost obligatory part of the professional life of every teacher, whereas the availability of periodical literature or opportunities to attend conferences are not only more infrequent but also make greater claims upon the teacher. Whatever the reasons for the differences in the degree of involvement, the degree of conscientiousness or of professional awareness, judged on this evidence, is moderately high in nearly all countries. The fact that the percentages tend to be higher in Population IV than in Population II may be the result in part of differences in the type of training of the two groups of teachers; also to be considered is the possibility that it is the more conscientious teachers who tend to become involved with pre-university students.

Between-country differences in the degree of professional awareness tend to be associated with differences in mean levels of achievement. A comparison of Finland, Israel and the Netherlands (Population IV) on the one hand, and Thailand and Italy (Population IV) on the other, suggests that. There are possible exceptions, as in the case of Sweden, which, though it has relatively high mean achievement levels, tends to have low percentages for involvement in professional activities, except affiliation with a professional organization.

Linguistic Qualifications and Competence

Tables 7.3 and 7.4 indicate selected language-specific characteristics of teachers of English. The percentage of teachers who claim the national language as their mother tongue is nowhere lower than 94 %, and would hardly merit a reference but for the position of Israel in both populations and of Belgium in Population IV. Of some interest from the standpoint of the English investigation is that 25 % of Israeli teachers on a further analysis of the data are found to claim English as their mother tongue. This is probably due to the strong English-speaking element in the composition of the Israeli immigrant population, the historical relationship with England and the continuing close association with the United States, and the status of English in the educational system which attracts native speakers of English from other English-speaking countries as teachers of the language. In Belgium there is an appreciably higher percentage of teachers in Population IV than in Population II who claim a non-national language as their mother tongue. A further analysis of the data suggests that this may be related to the greater number of Flemish or other Germanic language speakers who are included in the Population IV sample.

In Populations II and IV the great majority of the teachers commenced the study of English before the age of 16 (the end of the period of compulsory schooling in most countries), though there are some countries where teachers began to learn English after they had left school and sometimes even after the age of 21, as is the case in some instances in Finland and Italy. Israel has a high percentage of teachers who began the study of English well below the age of 16, while Hungary has a proportion of teachers who started quite late. Most teachers in Population II in nearly all countries tend to have had more rather than fewer than four semesters of further education in English beyond secondary school. In Population IV, apart from Sweden, this tendency is even more pronounced, a comparatively high percentage having received more than six semesters. There are

201

comparatively few teachers who have had only one or two semesters of post-secondary instruction in English—under 20 % in all countries except Hungary in Population IV. The length of the English course pursued by teachers, whether in secondary schools or later, does not appear to be associated consistently with relatively high or low mean levels of achievement in English. For instance, Israel and the Netherlands, with high means on achievement, and Thailand, which has low means on achievement, tend to have similar percentages of teachers with long periods of instruction. In Sweden (Population IV), with high mean achievement level, the percentage of teachers with relatively short periods of instruction tend to be as high as in Italy where the mean level of achievement is lower.

In all but two of the countries in Population II and in half of those in Population IV moderately high percentages of teachers (over 50 %) have resided in an English-speaking country up to three months. The percentages in Population II are higher than in Population IV. In Population IV Thailand, Hungary and Chile have high percentages of teachers who have spent less than three months in an English-speaking country. Furthermore, a more detailed analysis of the data indicates that in Population II over 10 % of the sample of teachers have spent over a year in an English-speaking country. However there is no consistent association between this variable and differences in achievement between countries.

In respect of understanding spoken English the percentage of teachers in Population II who admit to only an elementary competence tends to be under 16 % in all countries except Finland and Thailand where it exceeds 25 %. In Israel, the Netherlands and Sweden in both populations, the Federal Republic of Germany and in Finland in Population IV, large proportions claimed high levels of competence. The same is true of the teacher's estimate of their ability to speak English, although in Population II the estimates of ability are not as high as they are for "understanding spoken English." In Population IV the percentage of teachers claiming to have good ability to speak English—"able to speak fluently approximating to native speech"—are very high, especially in Israel and the Netherlands, and only slightly lower in the Federal Republic of Germany, and in Italy and Sweden. The percentage of teachers able to claim the ability to speak English at only an elementary level tends to be below 10 % in most countries, the most outstanding exception being Thailand where over 60 % of the teachers make such a claim. The percentages in

Population IV tend to be very low, especially in the Netherlands and Sweden where no teachers claim only an elementary competence. Thailand, in this population too, has the highest percentage of teachers claiming to have only an elementary speaking competence. The "ability to read English with reasonable ease with minimal use of lexical aids" is claimed by very high percentages of teachers in Population II in Israel, Italy, the Netherlands and Sweden. The figures in the Federal Republic of Germany and in Thailand are comparatively low. In Population IV the percentages are above 70 in all countries except Hungary and Thailand. The figures for teachers claiming only to be "able to understand the meaning of simple prose" tend to be below 3 % in nearly every country. The percentage of teachers able to write "summaries or oral discussions ... with appropriate choice of idiom ..." are relatively high in Italy, the Netherlands and Sweden and very high in Israel. The percentages for this high level of competence in writing are lowest in Finland and in Thailand in Population II. So far as concerns pronunciation, the percentage of teachers claiming to be able to pronounce English in a way which is indistinguishable from the way a native speaker pronounces it, is high in most countries.

Regarding overall aspects of English, Belgium and Israel, the Netherlands and Sweden tend to have the highest percentages of teachers claiming the highest of the three levels of competence stipulated in the questionnaire. These countries tend to have high mean achievement levels. Thailand, which has a lower mean level of achievement, is almost invariably included among those countries with the lowest percentages of maximum competence and the highest percentages of minimum competence in all five aspects of English in both populations. Pronunciation appears to be the aspect of English where most teachers claim the highest of the three levels of competence. The next in order tend to be Reading, Listening, Writing and Speaking. In all five aspects the percentages claiming high levels of competence are greater in Population IV than in Population II. The main general impression is that teachers of English in nearly all countries (Thailand is the clearest exception) have formed a highly favorable self-estimate of their competence in the language.

Participating countries differ greatly in the way they apportion the emphasis in the teacher training curriculum between "method of language teaching" and more academic aspects of the study of English. In both populations the countries in which relatively high percentages of teachers claim to have had a fair to large amount of "method" instruction are Belgium, Israel and Thailand, together with Chile in Population IV only. The reverse is true of The Federal Republic of Germany, Finland, Italy and Sweden and especially in the Netherlands (in both Populations), together with Hungary in Population IV only, where relatively high percentages claim to have had very little or no such training. Generally speaking "methodics" does not appear to have entered as much into the professional courses of Population IV teachers as of Population II. However, differences in types of training courses do not appear to be associated with differences in mean levels of achievement.

As regards the extent of the teachers' experience of foreign language teaching, in no country in Population II except Israel do more than 10 % of the teachers appear to have had above 20 years experience. In Population IV, on the other hand, only two countries have less than 10 % in that category.

In view of the differences in experience, length and type of training of teachers of English, it is interesting to note between-country differences in the use they make of specialist teachers of English as distinct from teachers of other subjects who may also participate in the teaching of English. Apart from Belgium and Sweden where the percentage of teachers of English who teach another foreign language tends to be high in Population II, the tendency is for teachers of English not to teach another foreign language. This is even more pronounced in Population IV. Specialization in English appears to be most pronounced in Israel, Netherlands, Italy and Thailand in both populations, together with Chile in Population IV. This aspect of teaching can be examined also in terms of the number of hours a teacher devotes to English. The countries where the majority of teachers spend 15 hours or more on a foreign language in both populations are Finland, Israel, Italy, the Netherlands and Thailand. These countries may be regarded as tending to specialize. This is even more evident in Population IV. The countries which tend to specialize by employing teachers to provide instruction in English in more rather than fewer grades are, except for Sweden, the same countries which tend to specialize in the other senses to which we have referred. It is fairly safe to assume that the greater the number of grades for which the teacher of English is responsible the less time he devotes to teaching other subjects. In Sweden, however, a language teacher as a rule teaches two or three foreign languages. The majority teaches English in several grades.

We are also entitled to assume that there is a high relationship between on the one hand membership in a specialist organization of teachers of a foreign language and specialist responsibility for that subject. However, the membership in a foreign language association is not high among the teachers of any country. But those countries which on other criteria tend to specialize (Finland, Israel, Italy and the Netherlands in both populations) also tend to have the highest percentages of teachers belonging to a foreign language association. The lowest percentages are in The Federal Republic of Germany, Belgium and Thailand in both populations, and in Italy in Population IV only. While it may be hazardous to exaggerate the tendency for specialization, there is some justification for identifying two sets of countries according to where they stand on specialization. Overall Finland, Israel, Italy and the Netherlands in both populations, together with Chile's Population IV, tend to have higher percentages of teachers conforming to the criteria already referred to. Sweden, the Federal Republic of Germany and to a lesser extent Belgium in both populations together with Hungary's Population IV, tend to have low percentages. It can be seen that there is little consistency between differences in mean levels of achievement and differences in tendency to specialize.

GENERAL CLASSROOM PRACTICES

Tables 7.5 and 7.6 contain some data related to *general* classroom practices used by English teachers. It must be remembered that these data refer to classroom practices and are not restricted only to the teaching of English since some teachers teach other subjects as well.

The relative importance of the five criteria which were employed in this study to determine the content of a course was assessed very differently by the teachers in the ten countries, though within any one country there was close agreement between the teachers of the two populations. Taking a general view of both populations in all countries the largest percentage of teachers tended to regard the post-school needs of students as paramount. This is particularly stressed in Belgium and Italy, and least emphasized in the Federal Republic of Germany and Thailand. The next largest percentage of teachers selected the "needs of the next grade or course," followed by the importance of "an external examination," "the use of a prescribed textbook" and finally "the requirements of an official syllabus." Conformity to the official syllabus is stressed as a course criterion by higher percentages of teachers in Thailand, Sweden and

Israel than elsewhere, and by lower percentages of teachers in Belgium and Italy. The use of a "prescribed text" is most emphasized by teachers in Sweden, Thailand and Israel and least in Belgium and Italy than elsewhere. It is in the Federal Republic of Germany and in Israel that we find the highest and in Sweden and Italy the lowest percentages stressing the importance of an external examination. Finally, the needs of the next grade or course tend to be favored by higher percentages in Italy and Thailand and by lower percentages in the Federal Republic of Germany and Sweden than elsewhere. While the tendency in any one country was for one criterion to stand out fairly clearly as the most important, in three countries this was not the case, fairly comparable percentages selecting different criteria. In Hungary moderate and in the Netherlands low percentages were recorded for all five criteria. In these cases it may be that teachers attached greater importance to a criterion not specified in the inquiry or that the teachers tend to act intuitively and pragmatically rather than according to any agreed principle. In Israel, Sweden, and Thailand high percentages were recorded for most if not all the criteria, and this may reflect the possibility that all five criteria enter into consideration in equal measure at different times—a sign of an eclectic and independent approach to teaching.

Two sets of variables were identified as having to do with actual use of materials and practical method rather than with the principles underlying types of courses. To that extent the responses may reflect their practice in handling other subjects as much as they do the teaching of English. Of teaching aids or methods "the use of text books" is the most consistently favored except in the Netherlands and in Hungary (testing Population IV only). The second most highly favored tends to be "the use of questioning" except in Belgium and the Netherlands in both populations and in Hungary, where the percentages tend to be very low. "Discussion" is the method which has the next most consistently high percentage, with the Netherlands and Sweden and especially Thailand in both populations, together with Chile in Population IV, tending to be exceptions. The most consistently low percentages are recorded for those activities involving small group or individual instruction. They seldom attract the adherence of more than 20 % of the teachers except in the Netherlands in both populations and Hungary in Population IV.

In addition to an understanding of the behavior of the individual aspects of method it is important to note the profile of the individual countries respecting the whole set. In Belgium the highest percentages are recorded for A/V methods, use of textbooks and discussion methods. The lowest are recorded for lecturing, project methods and programmed learning. Chile and Thailand resemble each other in tending to favor questioning, the use of textbooks and having low percentages for individual tutoring, projects and A/V methods. In Germany the highest percentages are recorded for textbooks and discussion, and this is also the case in Finland. In Hungary and the Netherlands the things which are most stressed tend to be those which are least favored in other countries, namely projects and programmed instruction, while those which are favored elsewhere are least emphasized in these two countries, namely text books and discussion. Sweden, Israel, and Italy tend to epitomize the general consensus or the median response across countries to most items.

As in the case of teaching aids, the highest percentages of teachers claimed to frequently use the more traditional rather than the more sophisticated types of evaluation. By far the highest percentages of teachers, except in Finland and Sweden, as well as in Thailand to some extent, claimed to use the "teacher-made essay" type of test. The next highest tended to claim the frequent use of "homework assessment," more particularly in Israel, Italy, Sweden, and Thailand. The third most frequently claimed was the "teacher's own objective tests," especially in Finland and Chile. While the percentages claiming "performance on term papers" as a frequent form of evaluation are not much below those claiming "teacher's objective tests," there does not appear to be any appreciable tendency to "use standardized tests" often. Nor is there any noteworthy difference in the behavior of these variables between populations in the same country.

The reluctance of teachers to adopt individualized instruction methods is reflected also in their attitude toward class organization. The percentage of teachers who claim to take account of the different learning rates and requirements of individual students by organizing small instructional groups within the total class is low in Population II and tends to be even lower in Population IV, where it might be expected to increase. Even when a further analysis is made of the data to discover the proportion of teachers having recourse to this system *occasionally* rather than *frequently* the percentages in both populations in the ten countries tended to cluster around 30%.

General Features of the Classroom Approach to English

Data regarding general classroom approaches to teaching English are presented in Tables 7.7 and 7.8.

There are very considerable differences between countries in the percentages of teachers who use "the mother tongue of the student" *often* in teaching English at any stage. At the beginning stage of Population II the percentages are fairly high, especially in Italy, Israel and the Netherlands, but relatively low in Finland. The differences in Population IV are not so wide. At the intermediate stage of Population IV the percentages are lower than at the beginning stage, and the between-country comparisons remain somewhat the same. The decline in the use of the mother tongue continues at the advanced stage, especially in Population IV. The countries which are least prone to use the mother tongue often are Finland, Belgium and the Federal Republic of Germany in both populations, together with Hungary testing Population IV only. Though the details are not tabulated for reasons of economy, it is worth noting that the countries which tend to use the mother tongue *often* tend in fact to do so *most of the time* even at the advanced stage. There does not appear to be any consistent association between differences in mean achievement levels among the countries and their approach to the use of the mother tongue in teaching a foreign language.

There appears to be a fair degree of unanimity between countries about which aspects of English should be introduced first, second or third in the course. The highest percentages of teachers select listening skills as those which should have priority, while writing skills demand least emphasis at the introductory stage. However, within this consensus there are some between-country differences.

The general significance of an audio/lingual approach is reflected in the teachers' assessment of the relationship of speaking and writing in teaching at the introductory stage. Relatively small percentages claimed to introduce writing before speaking, whether exclusively or supplemented by some speaking instruction, except in Thailand where approximately a third of the teachers took an uncompromising "writing" approach. The general tendency is to stress the use of speaking, though the majority of teachers tend to claim an approach which combines speaking and writing. Belgium and the Netherlands are the countries which most firmly support a speaking approach. In Population IV the choice of an oral approach, exclusively or modified, is not so pronounced as it is in Population II, though again with the exception of Thailand the proportion of teachers who claim to adopt an exclusively reading approach is negligible.

Aspects of English Teaching Method

Data on aspects of teaching method employed in English classes are presented in Tables 7.9 and 7.10.

In nearly all countries high percentages of teachers agreed on the emphasis to be placed on teaching pronunciation. There was not the same agreement on how this should be done, whether by "making pupils listen carefully and imitating" or "by practice supplemented by explanations." Only in Finland and Italy in Population II did imitation with explanation assume greater importance among the majority of teachers than imitation without explanation. Sweden followed by the Netherlands are the countries in which reliance on imitation without explanation was favored by the highest percentages of teachers. Thailand is the country where the highest percentage preferred to combine explanation with imitation practice. In Population IV the tendency is to emphasize imitation with explanation rather than without. Most teachers in both populations tend to adopt a pragmatic rather than an uncompromising approach.

In the interpretation of Tables 7.7 and 7.8 it was suggested that countries tend to give a higher priority at the introductory stage to speaking fluency rather than to writing. This tendency is confirmed in so far as higher percentages in most countries, particularly the Federal Republic of Germany, Israel, the Netherlands, and Sweden tend to prefer an emphasis on fluency of speech rather than correctness. However, an even greater percentage of teachers in most countries tend to approve of a combination of stress on fluency and correctness. And this appears to be more pronounced in Population IV than in Population II. In so far as teachers have chosen clearly between fluency and correctness there appears to be a consistent association between an emphasis on fluency and relatively high mean levels of achievement.

This tendency towards "liberalism" as opposed to "formalism" in teaching is evidenced in the responses of teachers to inquiries about the teaching of grammar. When teachers make a definite choice between methods involving first teaching the rules of grammar or promoting the learning of grammar by means of an approach "which first allows the pupils to learn to speak and understand English by imitating the teacher," the majority in most countries prefer the latter liberal approach. However, as we have noted elsewhere, the tendency is for teachers to compromise and to claim to adopt an approach which is a combination of inductive and deductive methods.

The traditionalism of teachers of English is evidenced in their attitude toward the choice of classroom teaching aids. The order in which teachers appear to place these items, in terms of percentages choosing to use them frequently, does not differ appreciably between countries. Generally speaking, the aids which are accorded frequent use by the highest percentages of teachers are the blackboard, pictures and real objects. In both populations Belgium, Finland, the Netherlands, and Sweden have higher percentages claiming to use tape recorders for whole classes in preference to real objects. The percentages claiming to use film strips and sound films, in most countries, are much lower than those claiming to use other aids. Two caveats must be entered at this point. First, not all aids lend themselves to being used with the same frequency in all cases. For instance, whatever the attitude of the teacher of English, it is unlikely that he will *need* to use sound films as frequently as the blackboard or real objects. In that sense teachers were not being asked to compare like with like. Secondly, whatever the attitude of teachers toward their use of aids, some of the more sophisticated aids may not be available. This undoubtedly accounts for the fact that the frequent use of language laboratories and individual tape recorders attracts the most consistently low percentages. The choice of aids is also a reflection of the type of training teachers have received, as well as the opportunity different countries provide for inservice training to give teachers an opportunity to familiarize themselves with the technology of education.

CONCLUSION

Although there are considerable between-country differences in respect to the type of English teacher employed in the schools, so far as training, extent of post-secondary preparation for teaching English, and relative emphasis on methodics or academic study of the language are concerned, there are several aspects which are common to most if not to all countries. Teachers have a refreshing confidence in their ability to speak English and to read and write it, though it is not clear whether their standards are those which they apply to themselves as teachers or as ordinary citizens of the country, and it is at least possible that in some countries teachers may be less confident or less willing to express their self-confidence than teachers in other countries. This may be so in Thailand. Second, from the evidence of this investigation teachers are more likely to be specialists than to be teachers of other subjects as well. This is in line with the relatively high level of professional awareness or conscientiousness claimed by teachers in their approach to English, especially where preparation of lessons is concerned. On the whole, teachers in nearly all countries emerge as realistic in their appraisal of the purposes of English teaching and of the principles which should guide them in formulating their courses. They are inclined to be pragmatic and to compromise rather than to adopt clear-cut and exclusive approaches. Where they do take a definite stance, however, they incline towards the more liberal and less formal approaches to English, to encourage fluency, for instance, and to prefer a practical rather than a rule-governed approach to the teaching of grammar. In one respect their traditionalism seems to conflict with their liberalism, namely in the tendency in very many of the countries to use the mother tongue even at a late stage in teaching a foreign language. These aspects of teaching practice in the ten countries are not without their exceptions, and it will be interesting to obtain detailed profiles of each country when the national reports appear. It may be hoped that those reports will be able to assess how far the responses of the teachers reflect their own attitudes to teaching and how much they reflect the availability of resources and the existence of long-standing national practices which may not always coincide with the views of teachers. Without a single unified measure of teaching practice or method, it is difficult and indeed pointless to estimate how far method variables relate to achievement. That they do goes almost without saying, and this is all the more reason for embarking on the production of such a unified and practical measure.

Table 7.1. *Selected General Characteristics of Teachers of English—Population II*

	Belgium (Fr.)	FRG	Finland	Israel	Italy	Netherlands	Sweden	Thailand
% of male teachers	38.5	49.0	24.6	33.2	19.1	71.1	38.8	22.9
% under 28 years of age	32	23.1	30.0	22.0	9.5	12.9	12.8	28.9
% over 28 years of age	67.7	76.9	70.0	78.0	90.5	87.1	87.2	71.1
% having post-secondary education of								
0 years	3.2	1.0	2.1	0.0	1.8	–b	2.0	9.1
> 0 but < 2 years	74.9	10.2	4.1	13.3	0.2	–b	4.7	7.7
> 2 years	21.9	88.8	93.8	86.7	98.0	–b	93.3	83.2
% teaching for								
< 5 years	24.1	40.8	48.3	14.3	31.9	16.6	28.9	30.0
5 to 10 years	37.4	23.9	26.0	36.3	42.1	16.4	28.7	22.5
10 to 20 years	31.4	23.5	22.0	21.6	17.4	46.9	31.3	33.4
> 20 years	7.1	11.8	3.7	27.8	8.6	20.1	11.1	14.0
In preparing lessons per week, the % spending								
< 3 hours	9.6	4.5	16.8	10.4	21.6	36.2	5.8	13.0
3 to 6 hours	19.4	33.0	40.2	34.7	38.3	38.1	28.1	39.8
6 to 10 hours	47.3	16.0	29.8	34.3	27.2	21.6	35.9	26.7
> 10 hours	23.7	46.5	13.2	20.6	12.9	4.1	30.2	20.5
For marking papers per week, the % spending								
< 2 hours	1.9	3.9	15.3	3.7	6.0	10.3	16.3	0.9
2 to 5 hours	45.4	61.0	41.0	30.2	48.3	42.4	46.5	15.3
5 to 10 hours	44.8	23.7	27.2	35.0	38.7	32.7	29.1	40.2
> 10 hours	7.9	11.4	16.5	31.1	7.0	14.6	8.1	43.6

% having membership in teachers' association

% reading professional journals regularly	20.3	30.1	60.1	43.7	50.1	45.7	56.3	25.6
% reading specialist professional journals regularly	40.5	31.1	54.0	50.2	51.3	49.5	35.2	48.1
% attending professional conference previous year	58.8	46.4	50.3	82.9	52.3	64.8	25.8	42.2
Number of teachers in sample[a]	105	248	187	70	126	146	492	310

Note: % = Percentage.

[a] Not all answered every question on the questionnaires; percentages are based only on those who answered the question seeking the information indicated here. Generally, 95% or more of the sample responded to most questions.

[b] No figures are given because of ambiguity in the wording of the question.

Table 7.2. *Selected General Characteristics of Teachers of English—Population IV*

	Belgium (Fr.)	Chile	FRG	Finland	Hungary	Israel	Italy	Netherlands	Sweden	Thailand
% of male teachers	63.1	32.8	57.9	18.3	39.3	24.2	29.9	88.4	43.9	30.2
% under 28 years of age	34.2	27.2	3.2	16.7	35.0	20.2	11.2	6.1	8.3	26.4
% over 28 years of age	65.8	72.8	96.8	83.3	65.0	79.8	88.8	93.9	91.7	73.6
% having post-secondary education										
0 years	0.6	1.5	0.4	0.0	0.0	0.0	2.9	—[b]	0.6	10.9
> 0 but < 2 years	54.3	4.1	5.0	0.8	0.5	16.9	3.7	—[b]	1.8	5.6
> 2 years	45.1	94.4	94.6	99.2	99.5	83.1	93.4	—[b]	97.6	83.5
% teaching for										
< 5 years	31.7	30.5	26.4	37.8	44.8	18.8	23.5	9.2	18.3	30.5
5 to 10 years	30.9	23.7	22.8	23.1	12.1	35.3	20.9	16.7	18.2	23.0
10 to 20 years	24.8	28.1	30.3	32.4	23.9	28.6	39.8	44.5	37.8	30.4
> 20 years	12.6	17.7	20.5	6.7	19.2	17.3	15.8	29.6	25.7	16.1
In preparing lessons, the % spending										
< 3 hours	4.0	30.5	1.7	7.8	7.8	6.6	28.6	11.1	3.7	17.1
3 to 6 hours	27.3	39.9	19.0	22.7	33.8	37.8	30.5	46.1	14.8	37.5
6 to 10 hours	43.7	23.8	10.9	43.9	38.9	30.1	30.7	27.0	38.2	24.7
> 10 hours	25.0	5.8	68.4	25.6	19.5	25.5	10.1	15.8	43.3	20.7
For marking papers, the % spending										
< 2 hours	5.8	17.5	0.8	7.0	9.5	10.4	12.8	1.9	5.7	0.4
2 to 5 hours	39.6	42.8	33.5	25.5	55.1	18.8	34.8	26.9	38.3	19.6
5 to 10 hours	42.4	32.7	18.5	47.4	28.5	38.4	44.9	57.0	35.4	35.7
> 10 hours	12.2	7.0	47.2	20.1	6.9	32.4	7.5	14.2	20.6	44.3

% having membership in teachers' association or union	76.3	72.4	69.3	91.7	96.3	96.2	64.7	85.5	93.9	51.9
% reading professional journals regularly	18.9	44.8	20.9	48.7	36.9	48.3	44.9	53.6	48.7	28.0
% reading specialist professional journals regularly	45.4	53.5	51.3	64.2	63.5	60.3	33.4	65.6	47.6	50.7
% attending professional conference previous year	53.8	47.9	41.5	61.1	57.4	91.1	42.0	49.3	21.0	42.2
Number of teachers in sample[a]	174	265	360	299	118	52	37	64	403	142

Note: % = Percentage.

[a] Not all answered every question on the questionnaires; percentages are based only on those who answered the question seeking the information indicated here. Generally, 95 % or more of the sample responded to most questions.

[b] No figures are given because of ambiguity in the wording of the question.

Table 7.3. Selected Language-Specific Characteristics of Teachers of English—Population II

	Belgium (Fr.)	FRG	Finland	Israel	Italy	Nether-lands	Sweden	Thai-land
% of teachers whose mother tongue is not the national language	3.0	2.2	0.8	75.0	0.6	5.4	2.1	4.1
% who began learning English								
under 16	92.4	99.7	82.8	96.3	56.7	99.5	99.1	99.3
16 and over	7.6	0.3	17.2	3.7	43.3	0.5	0.9	0.7
% having 0 to 3 months of residence in English-speaking countries	62.6	56.9	60.7	36.8	34.7	53.6	52.8	85.8
% having post-secondary education in English for								
0 semesters[a]	7.2	27.7	17.7	4.3	17.2	7.6	6.1	11.5
1–2 semesters	4.8	6.6	22.1	6.4	16.9	3.7	17.0	6.1
3–4 semesters	50.1	22.0	11.4	14.5	13.5	16.1	51.4	15.8
5–6 semesters	17.6	17.3	9.9	17.5	3.4	17.9	21.6	13.8
> 6 semesters	20.3	26.4	38.9	57.3	49.0	54.7	3.9	52.8
% having been trained in English teaching method								
None	2.2	39.5	40.3	4.1	50.1	13.3	35.6	11.1
Very little	21.0	42.0	23.4	12.2	23.3	81.9	48.4	16.6
A fair amount	45.8	17.4	19.1	62.0	22.8	3.5	14.0	61.3
A great deal	31.0	1.1	17.2	21.7	3.8	1.3	2.0	11.0
% having experience in teaching a foreign language								
< 20 years	92.9	95.2	98.3	74.7	91.2	92.7	91.1	97.3

in addition to English	70.8	16.7	27.0	1.9	11.5	14.5	64.2	4.2

% teaching English

< 5 hours	8.8	32.1	13.0	0.8	2.8	3.4	25.5	5.3
5 to 10 hours	15.8	32.3	17.7	7.8	2.5	6.9	51.5	11.8
10 to 15 hours	19.1	16.7	6.5	29.7	6.7	16.2	18.9	18.2
> 15 hours	56.3	18.9	62.8	61.7	88.0	73.5	4.1	64.7

% teaching English at

one grade level	21.5	34.2	16.2	5.7	9.5	7.7	11.5	56.4
two grade levels	30.0	31.2	23.9	34.3	28.9	9.8	27.2	29.8
three or more grade levels	48.5	34.6	59.9	60.6	61.6	82.5	61.3	13.8

% having membership in foreign language association	13.7	3.7	37.8	29.0	30.4	41.2	34.7	13.0

% claiming to have good to excellent competance in

(i) understanding spoken English	87.4	88.0	75.8	96.6	83.9	91.3	96.4	70.6
(ii) speaking English	92.3	84.5	75.4	96.4	94.8	92.5	96.4	37.7
(iii) reading English with minimal use of dictionary, etc.	58.4	35.3	51.5	91.0	78.4	76.0	73.3	29.4
(iv) writing English	93.2	89.4	71.6	98.8	94.4	87.1	98.0	66.0
(v) English pronunciation	96.0	99.9	81.9	98.3	94.0	100.0	98.4	58.9

Number of teachers in sample[b]	105	248	187	70	126	146	492	310

Note: % = Percentage.

[a] A full academic year is equivalent to two semesters.

[b] Not all answered every question on the questionnaires; percentages are based only on those who answered the question seeking the information indicated here. Generally, 95 % or more of the sample responded to most questions.

Table 7.4. *Selected Language-Specific Characteristics of Teachers of English—Population IV*

	Belgium (Fr.)	Chile	FRG	Finland	Hungary	Israel	Italy	Netherlands	Sweden	Thailand
% of teachers whose mother tongue is not the national language	19.1	5.3	3.4	1.5	2.0	76.7	0.5	3.4	4.0	2.7
% who began learning English										
under 16	88.5	94.6	97.7	81.0	75.7	100.0	58.0	100.0	97.6	99.6
at 16 and over	11.5	5.4	2.3	19.0	24.3	0.0	42.0	0.0	2.4	0.4
% having 0 to 3 months of residence in English-speaking countries	62.1	69.2	21.8	24.8	93.5	50.8	23.7	13.1	31.1	85.5
% having post-secondary education in English for										
0 semesters[a]	1.5	5.9	1.9	4.9	18.2	2.4	10.7	0.0	1.3	12.1
1–2 semesters	1.0	9.1	0.7	1.9	3.0	1.0	7.4	0.0	12.7	5.7
3–4 semesters	47.6	6.5	1.7	5.4	10.3	21.6	10.7	2.2	57.6	11.9
5–6 semesters	15.5	8.0	11.1	15.0	10.7	30.2	4.4	5.2	18.8	6.8
> 6 semesters	34.4	70.5	84.6	72.8	57.8	44.8	66.8	92.6	9.6	63.5
% having been trained in English teaching method										
None	8.2	0.9	34.5	37.9	13.2	11.8	51.8	12.8	39.7	16.4
Very little	25.2	9.1	52.7	21.6	63.2	6.0	13.0	81.7	49.0	13.1
A fair amount	39.6	37.8	11.1	8.9	18.4	58.8	22.9	5.5	10.1	59.4
A great deal	27.0	52.2	1.7	31.6	5.2	23.4	12.3	0.0	1.2	11.1
% having experience in teaching a foreign language										
< 20 years	89.4	83.7	81.8	91.9	84.3	87.5	80.8	70.6	76.8	95.2

	79.1	3.3	39.6	45.1	41.6	5.0	7.5	2.8	59.8	8.6
in addition to English	79.1	3.3	39.6	45.1	41.6	5.0	7.5	2.8	59.8	8.6
% teaching English										
< 5 hours	11.6	2.0	11.8	3.6	13.9	2.9	2.4	1.8	29.5	5.3
5 to 10 hours	34.0	13.0	29.8	12.0	27.0	9.8	0.0	2.6	44.7	8.9
10 to 15 hours	24.0	5.8	31.7	16.1	37.1	21.1	0.0	2.5	18.6	11.7
> 15 hours	30.4	79.2	26.7	68.3	22.0	66.2	97.6	93.1	7.2	74.1
% teaching English at										
one grade level	26.9	5.1	19.0	6.2	5.9	5.5	1.9	6.2	17.8	49.9
two grade levels	25.8	14.4	36.4	14.0	25.7	37.9	9.6	13.2	32.6	33.5
three or more grade levels	47.3	80.5	44.6	79.8	68.4	56.6	88.5	80.6	49.6	16.6
% having membership in Foreign Language Association	18.5	44.6	20.7	75.4	27.6	35.5	19.7	64.6	56.5	9.9
% claiming to have good to excellent competence in										
(i) understanding spoken English	90.7	88.3	99.7	94.8	90.6	98.8	86.2	95.4	98.9	73.0
(ii) speaking English	89.2	88.0	99.9	97.4	92.8	99.0	99.4	100.0	100.0	50.2
(iii) reading English with minimal use of dictionary, etc.	73.3	76.6	86.3	83.1	63.5	97.3	91.9	100.0	90.5	35.6
(iv) writing English	94.4	86.4	99.5	96.9	99.2	98.5	93.5	100.0	99.9	72.2
(v) English pronunciation	96.9	95.8	99.4	97.1	98.3	96.9	98.9	100.0	99.4	56.2
Number of teachers in sample[b]	174	265	360	299	118	52	37	64	403	142

Note: % = Percentage.

[a] A full **academic** year is equivalent to two semesters.

[b] **Not all** answered every question on the questionnaires; percentages are based only on those who answered the question seeking the information indicated here. Generally, 95 % or more of the sample responded to most questions.

Table 7.5. *Selected Features of General Classroom Practice—Population II*

	Belgium (Fr.)	FRG	Finland	Israel	Italy	Nether-lands	Sweden	Thai-land
% attaching great importance to each of the following in determining classroom practice:								
(i) Post-school needs of student	77.1	3.3	62.7	72.7	80.6	0.7	67.8	58.1
(ii) Requirements of official syllabus	6.8	10.5	16.2	69.6	11.7	9.8	43.6	46.9
(iii) Use of prescribed text	8.3	26.8	17.9	49.7	15.6	27.7	46.2	44.9
(iv) Requirements of external examination	27.2	74.7	30.6	63.7	26.2	8.2	22.0	47.7
(v) Preparation for work in next grade	63.2	11.8	51.4	83.4	73.2	4.4	52.7	75.4
% using the following types of teaching materials or approaches often:								
(ii) Text books	57.9	86.0	96.2	94.3	84.7	1.1	98.5	80.7
(ii) Printed drills material	33.8	28.7	84.5	45.9	11.4	40.2	60.2	15.8
(iii) Programmed instruction	2.6	5.3	1.9	9.3	6.3	86.9	4.6	18.4
(iv) Small group instruction	19.5	17.5	11.4	9.4	16.9	60.0	4.5	8.6
(v) Individualized work	23.4	13.2	11.7	10.7	25.8	81.4	26.8	49.7
(vi) A/V films, radio, etc.	69.8	24.3	18.8	35.9	14.1	19.6	60.5	3.8
(vii) Special projects and field trips	0.0	5.7	0.4	6.3	1.0	86.8	0.9	1.1
(viii) Lectures	1.3	18.8	1.1	7.4	2.3	0.0	0.7	18.9
(ix) Questioning	20.3	57.0	66.4	77.0	77.1	0.6	66.1	78.1
(x) Discussion	37.3	74.1	72.1	57.0	71.6	10.8	13.1	5.3
% using within-class grouping always or frequently	8.5	25.8	5.8	9.1	13.3	2.9	8.4	12.5

Regarding evaluation and assessment,
% frequently using:

(i) Standardized tests	3.8	3.3	6.3	6.3	9.4	8.6	7.1	6.4
(ii) Teacher-made essay tests	96.9	89.0	12.2	97.5	63.5	85.4	4.1	38.5
(iii) Teacher-made objective tests	38.2	10.8	65.2	14.4	67.1	15.4	38.0	55.9
(iv) Performance on homework	37.0	28.0	15.5	83.3	64.0	40.2	74.4	77.5
(v) Performance on term papers and projects	56.8	7.6	0.4	33.6	63.5	6.1	5.0	10.1
Number of teachers in sample[a]	105	248	187	70	126	146	492	310

Note: % = Percentage.

[a] Not all answered every question on the questionnaires; percentages are based only on those who answered the question seeking the information indicated here. Generally, 95 % or more of the sample responded to most questions.

Table 7.6. *Selected Features of General Classroom Practice—Population IV*

	Belgium (Fr.)	Chile	FRG	Finland	Hungary	Israel	Italy	Netherlands	Sweden	Thailand
% attaching great importance to each of the following in determining classroom practice:										
(i) Post-school needs of student	75.0	71.9	6.6	61.0	1.9	64.5	90.1	0.0	67.1	62.6
(ii) Requirements of official syllabus	7.0	28.1	19.3	14.1	10.0	74.6	13.4	0.0	37.1	50.8
(iii) Use of prescribed text	7.9	20.0	19.8	14.4	2.1	47.3	19.3	21.2	43.3	46.7
(iv) Requirements of external examination	23.1	24.3	77.8	56.3	5.4	62.8	35.2	1.1	24.7	44.3
(v) Preparation for work in next grade	63.5	54.7	4.2	41.8	3.2	85.0	86.5	6.2	40.3	74.0
% using the following types of teaching materials or approaches often:										
(i) Text books	64.3	46.5	91.3	98.8	0.0	97.3	74.3	1.1	99.1	80.9
(ii) Printed drills material	26.7	40.2	48.0	80.4	12.3	44.3	6.6	23.5	47.7	18.4
(iii) Programmed instruction	6.2	23.1	8.0	1.8	67.4	5.9	6.2	88.6	1.9	15.0
(iv) Small group instruction	10.9	13.5	7.1	3.7	18.4	7.4	6.2	55.6	8.4	6.9
(v) Individualized work	23.9	3.9	3.7	4.9	13.6	13.0	27.6	79.6	10.7	51.7
(vi) A/V, films, radio, etc.	43.2	17.4	12.0	22.1	28.3	52.3	8.5	20.7	56.7	2.3
(vii) Special projects and field trips	1.1	0.8	2.6	0.5	77.1	5.8	0.6	88.7	0.9	0.6
(viii) Lectures	0.7	15.8	16.0	3.2	44.6	7.8	0.0	0.0	1.3	17.5
(ix) Questioning	28.2	81.0	82.8	82.6	0.4	80.3	80.0	0.9	67.5	76.5
(x) Discussion	40.3	21.5	85.8	85.1	34.6	58.5	75.7	21.0	26.4	3.5
% using within-class grouping always or frequently	14.2	19.9	2.7	3.7	12.9	3.5	5.8	0.0	6.4	15.8

Regarding evaluation and assessment,
% frequently using:

(i) Standardized tests	3.2	9.3	6.0	10.8	0.0	2.4	18.4	11.7	2.9	7.4
(ii) Teacher-made essay tests	96.8	30.4	93.8	16.4	70.2	94.6	53.2	78.4	11.1	33.1
(iii) Teacher-made objective tests	21.7	82.6	8.5	67.0	8.3	10.3	31.3	17.4	23.6	48.7
(iv) Performance on homework	38.3	45.4	28.9	10.2	35.5	81.4	73.8	36.7	82.6	77.6
(v) Performance on term papers and projects	32.7	12.1	9.2	2.0	18.9	29.8	87.6	4.4	13.2	6.4
Number of teachers in sample[a]	174	265	360	299	118	52	37	64	403	142

Note: % = Percentage.

[a] Not all answered every question on the questionnaires; percentages are based only on those who answered the question seeking the information indicated here. Generally, 95 % or more of the sample responded to most questions.

223

Table 7.7. Classroom Approaches to English Teaching: General Features—Population II

	Belgium (Fr.)	FRG	Finland	Israel	Italy	Netherlands	Sweden	Thailand
% using students' mother tongue often in teaching:[a]								
Beginning English	44.3	39.3	33.6	70.7	77.8	72.5	53.6	65.4
Intermediate English	21.8	32.6	48.9	54.5	69.3	67.3	53.2	72.9
Advanced English	24.9	27.7	39.1	29.8	38.0	48.2	37.1	50.9
In teaching Beginning English, % whose first choice for emphasis is:								
(i) Listening comprehension	61.6	68.7	45.8	66.2	69.1	53.1	69.4	54.6
(ii) Speaking fluency	20.3	19.2	34.3	17.9	8.1	19.6	8.6	1.7
(iii) Correct pronunciation	13.3	10.7	13.4	3.6	17.7	18.8	17.0	28.2
(iv) Reading comprehension	4.5	0.8	4.1	8.2	3.8	8.5	4.6	10.4
(v) Ability to write	0.3	0.6	2.4	4.1	1.3	0.0	0.4	5.1
In teaching Beginning English, % whose second choice for emphasis is:								
(i) Listening comprehension	20.2	22.1	38.0	19.8	13.3	22.1	22.3	18.6
(ii) Speaking fluency	53.9	43.5	24.2	26.2	29.1	36.7	31.8	25.3
(iii) Correct pronunciation	21.2	28.0	27.4	25.9	40.9	22.1	22.5	29.9
(iv) Reading comprehension	4.7	5.0	9.4	28.1	15.5	17.7	23.1	20.1
(v) Ability to write	0.0	1.4	1.0	0.0	1.2	1.4	0.3	6.1
In teaching Beginning English, % whose third choice for emphasis is:								
(i) Listening comprehension	15.2	5.2	10.2	8.6	8.8	19.9	6.2	19.0
(ii) Speaking fluency	21.7	18.4	25.4	33.7	26.8	23.8	30.7	22.8
(iii) Correct pronunciation	38.1	35.5	26.2	15.8	24.5	29.6	23.9	19.0

(i) …comprehension	2.3	3.4	2.8	3.5	8.0	6.9	1.5	9.7
(ii) Speaking fluency	3.2	9.5	10.8	10.3	30.3	17.6	24.4	17.3
(iii) Correct pronunciation	14.0	17.4	20.4	25.8	11.6	21.8	23.5	14.4
(iv) Reading comprehension	53.0	49.4	47.7	24.4	37.4	43.1	34.4	34.5
(v) Ability to write	27.5	20.3	18.3	36.0	12.7	10.6	16.2	24.1
In teaching Beginning English, % whose fifth choice for emphasis is:								
(i) Listening comprehension	1.8	0.6	2.9	3.0	2.9	3.8	0.9	3.5
(ii) Speaking fluency	2.6	8.9	5.5	12.9	14.0	2.5	5.5	30.8
(iii) Correct pronunciation	11.6	9.0	13.7	28.7	3.4	8.2	12.6	7.8
(iv) Reading comprehension	14.6	9.1	9.0	1.9	7.8	4.6	0.5	3.3
(v) Ability to write	69.4	72.4	68.9	53.5	71.9	80.9	80.5	54.6
Regarding the order in which speaking and written forms are introduced, the % introducing:								
(1) Speech before written forms	81.4	37.2	44.1	32.9	37.3	52.1	26.8	33.3
(ii) Spoken forms first, but written and spoken forms are learned together	18.6	61.5	49.5	49.0	46.4	34.4	57.4	31.3
(iii) Written forms first, but written and spoken forms are learned together	0.0	1.3	6.4	16.7	9.9	13.5	15.6	5.1
(iv) Written forms before speech	0.0	0.0	0.0	1.4	6.4	0.0	0.2	30.3
Of those teaching subjects in addition to English, % using English as a teaching language in those subjects	15.5	13.3	34.4	91.7	93.9	6.5	2.5	86.5
Number of teachers in sample[b]	105	248	187	70	126	146	492	310

Note: % = Percentage.

[a] Note that for this topic, generally only 75 % or more of the sample responded to most questions.

[b] Not all answered every question on the questionnaires; percentages are based only on those who answered the question seeking the information indicated here. Generally, 95 % or more of the sample responded to most questions.

Table 7.8. *Classroom Approaches to English Teaching—General Features—Population IV*

	Belgium (Fr.)	Chile	FRG	Finland	Hungary	Israel	Italy	Nether-lands	Sweden	Thai-land
% using students' mother tongue often in teaching:[a]										
Beginning English	50.5	66.5	42.8	35.5	37.9	66.0	57.2	57.3	50.0	54.4
Intermediate English	35.1	63.4	31.1	38.1	22.2	54.4	68.6	62.7	57.1	63.7
Advanced English	23.1	62.9	14.9	51.6	14.0	24.2	36.9	45.6	46.0	63.0
In teaching Beginning English, % whose first choice for emphasis is:										
(i) Listening comprehension	56.7	81.2	59.7	51.3	25.9	66.3	73.9	53.5	55.0	56.4
(ii) Speaking fluency	25.0	6.3	24.9	29.9	40.3	13.8	2.0	11.2	8.7	0.7
(iii) Correct pronunciation	11.7	7.0	12.2	16.0	29.3	1.5	22.4	24.5	28.0	21.4
(iv) Reading comprehension	3.6	5.5	2.4	1.9	4.5	7.0	1.1	7.8	8.3	8.0
(v) Ability to write	3.0	0.0	0.8	0.9	0.0	11.4	0.6	3.0	0.0	13.5
In teaching Beginning English, % whose second choice for emphasis is:										
(i) Listening comprehension	20.0	12.3	26.0	30.9	42.1	18.0	22.5	17.6	28.0	13.7
(ii) Speaking fluency	45.2	39.9	30.4	28.2	29.1	25.2	24.2	36.6	31.4	30.2
(iii) Correct pronunciation	24.6	28.6	30.5	30.9	23.1	21.6	31.9	32.9	17.8	25.6
(iv) Reading comprehension	4.4	17.8	8.5	7.9	5.2	35.2	18.4	12.9	21.8	21.9
(v) Ability to write	5.8	1.4	4.6	2.1	0.5	0.0	3.0	0.0	1.0	8.6
In teaching Beginning English, % whose third choice for emphasis is:										
(i) Listening comprehension	19.6	3.5	9.1	11.0	24.3	7.0	8.9	16.8	12.5	18.3
(ii) Speaking fluency	22.4	33.2	19.2	27.1	21.9	37.6	51.5	34.8	26.1	16.6

(ii) Speaking fluency	7.3	15.7	13.5	6.5	10.3	13.1	11.6	11.4	27.1	14.4
(iii) Correct pronunciation	11.4	15.3	14.4	13.5	7.7	35.0	17.6	11.4	16.7	19.9
(iv) Reading comprehension	58.2	45.6	44.2	52.8	53.4	20.4	59.7	60.5	40.2	31.0
(v) Ability to write	21.1	22.3	24.1	21.9	23.6	20.6	8.0	12.1	13.2	23.3
In teaching Beginning English, % whose fifth choice for emphasis is:										
(i) Listening comprehension	5.6	0.5	1.4	2.1	1.2	7.4	0.0	8.5	0.2	5.5
(ii) Speaking fluency	1.1	5.9	12.7	8.8	0.8	15.7	5.7	6.9	7.0	32.8
(iii) Correct pronunciation	16.9	15.6	9.9	10.9	12.2	24.8	5.7	0.0	9.5	11.4
(iv) Reading comprehension	12.5	6.9	19.5	13.3	14.5	0.0	7.8	5.8	2.5	5.6
(v) Ability to write	63.9	71.1	56.5	64.9	71.3	52.1	80.8	78.8	80.8	44.7
Regarding the order in which speaking and written forms are introduced, the % introducing:										
(i) Speech before written forms	56.7	51.7	23.6	33.5	41.0	40.0	31.8	31.0	21.2	32.9
(ii) Spoken forms first, but written and spoken forms are learned together	38.1	40.8	74.6	55.6	52.2	42.2	35.6	50.0	48.8	26.7
(iii) Written forms first, but written and spoken forms are learned together	5.2	6.9	1.8	10.9	6.1	16.5	23.7	19.0	29.2	6.2
(iv) Written forms before speech	0.0	0.6	0.0	0.0	0.7	1.3	8.9	0.0	0.8	34.2
Of those teaching other subjects in addition to English, % using English as a teaching language in those subjects	17.8	57.9	12.2	31.6	2.2	100.0	100.0	0.0	2.8	88.7
Number of teachers in sample[b]	174	265	360	299	118	52	37	64	403	142

Note: % = Percentage.

[a] Note that for this topic, generally only 75 % or more of the sample responded to most questions.

[b] Not all answered every question on the questionnaires; percentages are based only on those who answered the question seeking the information indicated here. Generally, 95 % or more of the sample responded to most questions.

Table 7.9. *Classroom Approach to English Teaching—Features of Presentation and Methods—Population II*

	Belgium (Fr.)	FRG	Finland	Israel	Italy	Netherlands	Sweden	Thailand
In teaching pronunciation, % emphasizing:								
(i) Listening and imitation	59.8	52.5	38.4	58.2	46.2	65.3	87.9	20.2
(ii) Imitation and explanation	40.2	46.9	61.6	40.6	53.8	34.7	11.5	79.5
In teaching speaking skills, % emphasizing:								
(i) Fluency	19.7	21.7	21.3	28.9	23.5	30.2	22.2	5.0
(ii) Correct pronunciation	19.9	9.7	22.2	25.8	32.3	7.4	5.8	39.2
(iii) Fluency and correct pronunciation equally	60.4	68.6	56.5	45.3	44.2	62.4	72.0	55.8
In teaching grammar, % that:								
(i) first teach rules followed by translation exercises	0.3	0.0	2.8	5.4	2.2	3.0	5.6	8.5
(ii) teach correct spoken patterns only	16.1	18.6	19.2	7.1	11.1	27.3	2.1	21.7
(iii) teach correct spoken patterns followed by grammar rules	83.6	81.4	78.0	87.5	86.7	69.7	92.3	69.8
% of teachers frequently using:								
(i) Blackboard	65.8	90.0	99.1	99.0	86.3	88.7	96.6	96.4
(ii) Pictures	66.4	55.7	82.7	35.8	63.4	35.5	29.7	27.6
(iii) Real objects	31.7	57.3	37.2	27.2	46.2	6.2	8.0	24.0
(iv) Film strips	58.6	1.8	0.0	1.7	3.4	0.3	19.4	0.9
(v) Sound film	2.2	0.3	0.5	7.5	3.9	1.3	1.0	2.4
(vi) Phonograph records	19.7	41.4	27.7	1.1	42.0	8.4	7.2	13.9
(vii) Tape recorder (whole class)	78.5	17.8	55.0	7.2	20.8	69.5	97.2	13.3
(viii) Language laboratory (individual recorders)	10.5	4.1	1.2	0.0	9.1	8.2	9.5	2.4
Number of teachers in sample[a]	105	248	187	70	126	146	492	310

	(Fr.)	Chile	FRG	Finland	Hungary	Israel	Italy	lands	Sweden	land
In teaching pronunciation, % emphasizing:										
(i) Listening and imitation	55.7	60.0	32.3	40.8	22.7	50.2	37.7	50.3	79.8	23.2
(ii) Imitation and explanation	44.3	38.4	67.0	58.8	75.9	47.8	62.3	49.7	19.4	76.8
In teaching speaking skills, % emphasizing:										
(i) Fluency	11.0	21.7	12.6	23.0	12.1	25.2	20.5	18.8	17.3	6.3
(ii) Correct pronunciation	31.3	15.7	6.3	11.8	4.1	16.0	22.7	2.8	8.7	33.9
(iii) Fluency and correct pronunciation equally	57.7	62.6	81.1	65.2	83.8	58.8	56.8	78.4	74.0	59.8
In teaching grammar, % that:										
(i) first teach rules followed by translation exercises	5.2	1.9	1.4	7.0	11.2	2.9	5.9	12.3	5.7	8.9
(ii) teach correct spoken patterns only	11.6	20.9	3.6	4.8	6.8	13.6	10.5	14.0	1.5	25.3
(iii) teach correct spoken patterns followed by grammar rules	83.2	77.2	95.0	88.2	82.0	83.5	83.6	73.7	92.8	65.8
% of teachers frequently using:										
(i) Blackboard	71.6	94.7	94.9	98.9	91.8	100.0	80.7	78.1	96.4	97.8
(ii) Pictures	44.4	57.9	43.7	74.9	63.9	36.3	43.7	32.5	17.1	20.9
(iii) Real objects	20.1	63.1	34.0	30.1	38.4	33.4	31.5	2.9	5.3	19.0
(iv) Film strips	31.3	1.0	1.6	0.9	12.3	3.0	2.2	1.2	12.3	1.5
(v) Sound film	0.0	0.0	1.2	0.2	0.3	15.1	1.1	0.6	1.2	1.1
(vi) Phonograph records	9.1	6.6	17.1	17.4	16.7	1.5	8.2	17.7	4.7	11.3
(vii) Tape recorder (whole class)	56.6	10.9	13.9	57.0	66.8	3.2	8.8	70.3	95.1	9.5
(viii) Language laboratory (individual recorders)	21.1	1.6	7.4	9.3	11.6	0.0	12.2	11.1	8.9	3.3
Number of teachers in sample[a]	174	265	360	299	118	52	37	64	403	142

Note: %=Percentage.

[a] Not all answered every question on the questionnaires; percentages are based only on those who answered the question seeking the information indicated here. Generally, 95 % or more of the sample responded to most questions.

Chapter 8

Characteristics of the Students

The student variables which are analyzed and described here are in four sets: those having to do with general, personal characteristics and home background; those concerned with general educational experience; those having to do with the language experience of students outside school; and finally those variables having to do with the exposure of the students to English in the school program. In addition to these four sets, the students' self perception of ability in speaking, understanding, reading and writing English are examined, together with the students' stated intention of achieving good standards in the same aspects of English, the students' perceived difficulty of doing so, as well as the degree of industry students claim to exercise in English. The three scales, Interest in English, the Utility of English and English Activities Outside School are also discussed in this chapter.

GENERAL BACKGROUND OF STUDENTS

Tables 8.1 and 8.2 give data regarding the general background variables for students.

The age of students in Population II ranges from 14:5 to 14:8 years, and in Population IV from 17:8 to 19:2 years. Most students in Population II are in Grade 8; in Population IV they tend to be in Grade 12. Population IV parents tend to have more formal education than do the parents of students in Population II, although there are wide variations between countries. The mothers tend, in most countries, to have had less formal education than the fathers.

In the Mathematics study (Husén, 1967) the same Parental occupation scale was employed by all countries. Some found it more appropriate than others did, and it was decided that the countries in the present study should adopt their own classification, using a maximum of ten categories. In some cases all teachers were included in one professional category; in others distinctions were made between pre-school, elementary and secondary teachers, who were assigned to different categories. The same inconsistency is evident in the handling of different types of social-service employment. Further, all countries did not employ the same number of categories, and those that did, frequently did not agree on the occupations to fit the various categories. For these reasons, the suggested procedure proved not to be entirely satisfactory, and the number of categories was reduced so as to eliminate the most glaring anomalies.

The contents of the descriptions of the occupations which the National Centers supplied were re-sorted and the four categories below were established. In no country does the present classification ensure an entirely normal curve of distribution, but in most of them the categories which account for the smallest percentage of parents are at the two extremes, and the two middle categories are not too far out of line compared with either of the two extremes or with each other.

Category I: Unskilled, casual and manual labour.
Category II: Semi-skilled, skilled manual laborers, small traders, clerical and sales operatives, lower level public service employees.
Category III: Teachers, middle level public service employees (including middle and lower level police and armed forces employees), technicians, managerial staff and sub-professions.
Category IV: Higher administrative and executive professions; the learned professions.

The parents of Population IV students tend to be in higher occupational categories than the parents of students in Population II, a fact which is in line with the difference noted in the parental education of the two populations and due to social selection for upper secondary education.

GENERAL EDUCATIONAL EXPERIENCE OF STUDENTS

Tables 8.3 and 8.4 provide information concerning the general educational experiences of students of English. This information is in terms of their total educational experience rather than limited to experiences in English study. The level of parental support for the educational activities of students varies greatly between countries, between populations in the same country, as well as between the several activities which are referred to. Usually a general declaration of interest in school activities claims support among a higher percentage of parents than does actual participation in specific activities. Thus, in Belgium (Population II) 37.9% of the students claim that their parents "often show an interest in school activities" compared with 5.9% who are said to "help with homework." In Germany the disparity between interest and involvement seems to be more pronounced over the whole range of activities. Nevertheless, though parents may be reluctant, comparatively speaking, to participate in the activities, the general level of support is higher in Population II than in Population IV in most countries.

The order of the educational activities, in terms of the degree of parental support received tends to be the same for all countries in both populations, with the exception of Finland where "correcting speech" is the activity in which parents intervene most infrequently. But whatever the variations of parental support between the various activities, the level is usually higher in Population II than in Population IV, and this is true of "general interest" as well as of "actual practical participation."

Apart from encouraging the students and actually helping them at their work, parents provide support for educational activities by ensuring adequate facilities and materials, such as a separate room, books and dictionaries. The extent of the provision of a separate room in which the student may work, the use of a dictionary in the home and the availability of books in the home, tends to be greater in Population IV than in Population II, although there is considerable between-country variation.

The tendency is for reading for pleasure to be more popular in Population IV than in Population II and also for the percentage of those who read for the longer period (more than three hours) to be higher in Population IV than in Population II. At the same time, the tendency in Population IV for students to listen to radio and look at TV for fewer rather than more than ten hours is greater than it is in Population II, though in both Populations the percentages that prefer radio and television are higher than the percentages that prefer reading.

The percentage of those who spend less than two hours at their homework for all subjects varies considerably between countries, but less so in population IV than in Population II. There is marked tendency in Sweden (and in Finland to a lesser extent) to spend fewer hours on homework than is the case in most other countries, and to have less regular working habits as well. This suggests that for all subjects homework is given less weight in these two countries than in others or that less pressure is exerted in the homes of the students' experience in learning English (Tables 8.5 and 8.6). There does not appear to be any consistent association between differences in the behavior of these variables and differences in mean levels of achievement between countries.

SELECTED FEATURES OF THE LANGUAGE EXPERIENCE OF STUDENTS

Tables 8.5 and 8.6 provide information related specifically to students' experiences in learning English as opposed to their general learning experiences. It should be noted that these learning experiences are not limited to the school setting.

The tendency is for the great majority of the homes in nearly all ten countries to be linguistically homogeneous, though this does not mean that only the national language is spoken in the homes which are to all extents and purposes homogeneous. Whether this potential complexity is manifested in the actual day-to-day practice of parents and pupils is not known from the returns of this inquiry; it is a question which could have some bearing on foreign language achievements and attitudes and, therefore, deserves further research. Where there is a pattern of linguistic complexity in the home it does not follow that English enters into it. Nevertheless, it should be noted that in some countries as many as 25 % to 50 % of the parents have studied English. Israel, Thailand, Sweden and the Netherlands have the highest percentages in Population II, Finland and Italy the lowest.

Belgium, Thailand, and especially Israel are the countries where the linguistic background of students is likely to be the most complex. In the former, though only the French-speaking region was investigated, 20 % of Population II and 24 % of Population IV students claimed a tongue other than the national language as the first language of the parents. In Thailand, where the samples are not limited to a single linguistic community, the figures vary from 20 % to 29 %. However, in Israel the percentages exceed 80 %. Where the national language is not the only means of communication it is sometimes and to only some extent replaced by English. Where both the national language and another are spoken in the home the position of English is more interesting. Though there are comparatively few such homes where English is the regular means of communication, the status of English as an auxiliary home-language is high. For instance in Germany, the French language is no better placed than English as the principal means of communication in the home; but as an auxiliary language English is more frequently used than French. It may be possible that if French is used at all in the home it is because it is the first home language. Exceptions are in Finland where French is more frequently used in the home than English and in Hungary where French is used to an even greater degree.

Though the national language may be the first language of the home, it does not follow that it is the mother tongue of either or both of the parents. The percentage of parents whose mother tongue is different from the national language is highest in Israel and Thailand. In Israel the cause is reasonably clear, namely, the considerable proportion of the population who are first generation immigrants, very many of them from English-speaking countries. More students appear to belong to linguistically heterogeneous homes in Population IV than in Population II. In Thailand the reason for the complex language pattern of some of the homes is the existence of traditional language minorities.

Of the homes which possess any English books at all more than half are shown by a detailed analysis to possess fewer than ten volumes. The same limitations on the student's background experience of English appears from an analysis of visits to English-speaking countries. The difference between Populations II and IV, though slight, may be indicative. Population IV students are usually about four years older than those in Population II and have probably acquired greater independence. They are in the terminal year of secondary education and usually are not only better able to profit linguistically from a visit abroad, but probably are committed as well to a course of further or higher education and to the choice of a career where English as a language of wider communication may be required. In Populations II and IV a higher percentage of students in Israel than elsewhere claim to have opportunities to speak English. The next highest percentages are in Sweden and Belgium. The percentages of students claiming to speak English sometimes are invariably higher in Population IV than in Population II. In almost every country the figures for students reading English books, seeing English language films and television, and listening to English radio often are higher than they are for those actually participating in speaking English outside school. But the variabilities between countries are considerable. All considerations point to the relatively low level of societal support for English in the ten countries. Whatever may be said on theoretical grounds about the relative importance of the school or the social background in boosting achievement, it is fairly clear that a background of social support for the English language (apart from attitude) exists to only a very small extent in these ten countries. The role of the school is almost unique. It is not surprising that social support should be so tenuous, bearing in mind how "academically" oriented the teaching of English has been in most countries, to how small a proportion of each generation of students it has been taught until recently, and for how limited a period of their careers in school. The low level of societal support is further reflected in the low percentage of students in all countries who have a fair to good knowledge of English before they commence their English course. In view of the behavior of the sampled populations in Israel on the variables that we have already discussed it is not surprising that they should have the highest percentages of students with prior knowledge of English. But it is also worth noting that Thailand in Population II has a higher percentage of students in this category than every other country except Israel. Forty percent of Thai students begin English at Grade 1 or 2; this fact, together with the high level of parental occupation and education, should be taken into account in considering the level of prior knowledge of English in Thailand. Apart from Belgium all countries report higher percentages of prior knowledge in Population II than in Population IV. The former students are four years younger than the latter and will have had more opportunity to profit from the intensification of the impact of the English language upon society which has occurred during recent years. To this extent the level of societal support for English may be increasing.

The amount of parental help with student's English studies tends to be small, and smaller in Population IV than in Population II. This is probably not due to the inability of Population IV parents as compared with parents of Population II to provide that help; it is probably because the older students are less willing to ask for such help or to need it. But despite differences between the characteristics of parents of the two populations in the extent of actual help to students, parental attitude to the study of English by their children generally is highly favorable for both populations. The percentage of students claiming to have parents whose attitude towards English is unfavorable never rises above 7.5 %. The proportion favorable is never less than 8 % except in Finland and Thailand.

ENGLISH LANGUAGE EXPERIENCE OF STUDENTS IN SCHOOL

Tables 8.7 and 8.8 give information regarding student learning of English in the school setting.

English is introduced to most students in nearly all countries between grades 5 and 8, though in Sweden, Finland, and Thailand appreciable numbers commence their studies at much earlier ages. Other countries, e.g., Hungary and Italy, tend to introduce it later. Although Finland is among the countries where entry into the English course occurs early, it also has substantial numbers who begin English at ages 15 to 16, mainly because they study English as a second foreign language. However, age of entry may be more relevant than grade; as was noted in Chapter 6, there is no uniformity among countries in the relationship of age to grade.

In Population II the great majority of students have studied English for three to four years, and in some countries, Thailand for instance, for longer periods. It is noteworthy that by the age of 14+, 42% of the Thai students in the sample have studied English for more than seven years. In Population IV in nearly all countries the majority of students have studied English for at least five years, and usually longer, except in Hungary where nearly 90% of those sampled have studied English for between three and four years. It does not necessarily follow that Population IV students have studied English for more years than Population II students, but in view of the criterion (18 months to 2 years study) which was used in preparing the samples of students, the percentage of those who have studied English for less than two years is nowhere more than 2.7%, and generally below 1%.

In Sweden only 16% of the Population II sample and in Population IV 15% spend more than two hours at their English homework. In most countries the tendency is for at least 40% of the Population II sample to do homework for more than two hours and for over 20% of Population IV to spend between three and five hours on it. This may reflect the belief in Sweden that the encouragement of homework simply tends to exaggerate the advantages which students from more favorable homes already possess. Generally speaking, there appears to be an interesting correspondence in many countries between the amount of time students spend on English homework and the number of hours of instruction they receive in school in the subject. In both populations the countries which spend the least number of hours on classroom instruction in English are also those where the students tend to devote the least time to English homework. In the countries which spend more time on teaching English the students tend to spend more time on homework. The correspondence may be because that both variables reflect in much the same way the degree of national interest in English or teaching English. Or it may arise from the possibility that students adjust their homework schedule to the curriculum priorities without necessarily reflecting the level of national interest.

Both variables appear to be related to the size of English classes. In both populations the tendency is towards comparatively small classes. The countries which spend the least amount of time on homework and instruction tend to have the highest percentages of students in small classes. For instance, in Belgium (Population IV), even though the tendency is to devote fewer than three hours to instruction and fewer than two hours to English homework, over one third of the students in the same sample are taught in classes consisting of fewer than 15 persons. On the other hand, Israel, which has the highest percentage of students in the sample receiving more than three hours instruction, as well as devoting over two hours to English homework, tends to have relatively large classes; more than 45 % have over 25 students. Either fortuitously or as a matter of policy, countries tend to balance the amount of time devoted to English and the size of the English class. This may ensure that, between countries, the impact of English on the students is equalized but more needs to be considered.

The activities in which the highest percentages of students claim to participate "often" rather than "rarely" or "never" in most countries are Speaking to teachers in English, Writing exercises in English, and Translating from or into English. The activities in which the highest percentages of students claim to participate "rarely or never" in most countries tend to be Writing essays in English, Repeating broadcasts or taped oral exercises in English, and Reading for pleasure. Translation tends to be the most frequently employed exercise of those listed. These generalizations do not hold without exception in all countries. For instance, contrary to the general tendency high percentages of students in Chile and Thailand claim to "speak in the mother tongue." Again, contrary to the general tendency, high percentages of students in Chile claim that they rarely or never "speak to the teacher in English." Listening to records claims a high percentage of students in Israel but not in other countries.

While the behavior of students in the two populations tends to be similar in regard to these activities, there are some important changes of emphasis between Populations II and IV. For instance, Belgium, the Netherlands and Finland have higher percentages of students in Population II than in IV claiming frequent use of English in speaking to the teacher. In all other countries the reverse is reported. The use of English and of the mother tongue in the English lesson both claim higher percentages in some countries in Population IV than in II. One would expect the use of the mother tongue to decline as the use of English increased. While the percentage of frequent use of written exercises in English is lower in Population IV than in II in the Netherlands and Sweden, a higher percentage is recorded in Population IV than in Population II in Finland. As for translation, there is a strong tendency towards higher percentages for frequent use in Population II than Population IV in the Federal Republic of Germany, and towards higher percentages in Population IV than in II in Finland and the Netherlands. Higher percentages of students claim to write essays frequently in Population II than in Population IV in Belgium and the Netherlands, but the reverse is claimed in the Federal Republic of Germany, and in Israel, Italy and Thailand. Similarly, in Italy, for both types of reading, higher percentages in Population II than in IV claim to participate in the activities. But the situation is reversed in the Netherlands and Sweden. The one activity where the change of emphasis between Population II and Population IV is consistent across all countries is repeating exercises (recorded or taped oral exercises), where higher percentages claim to practice the activity frequently in Population II than in Population IV. The general picture is of considerable variability between countries and between populations in the same country, as well as of little consistency in the association between the behavior of the variables and achievement.

STUDENT INTENTIONS: ACHIEVEMENT IN
UNDERSTANDING, READING, SPEAKING AND WRITING

Table 8.9 shows data regarding student intentions to succeed at learning English.

Although the great majority of students of both populations in nearly all countries intended or proposed to achieve relatively high standards in English, there were some exceptions. For instance, the tendency in Finland's Population II is to aim at only moderate achievement; but the aim for Population IV is higher. In line with the achievement levels of these two populations in Finland, the mean scores of Population IV are superior. Similarly, that a very large percentage of students in the two populations in Italy do not propose a high or moderate achievement may simply reflect the fact that their actual mean level of performance does not compare very favorably with that of students in some other countries. On the other hand, their actual performance may be influenced by a fairly modest intention to succeed. Though not quite so negative, the attitude towards achievement among Thai students is not unlike that of students in Italy, and the same comments may be appropriate.

Looked at generally, and disregarding for the moment the between-country differences, the highest percentages of students seek a good understanding of spoken English; the next highest percentages propose good achievement in reading, followed by the percentages aiming for good standards of speaking and writing. It was not unexpected that the two decoding or receptive skills should attract higher percentages of students interested in doing well than do the two encoding or productive skills. The between-country differences are few, the most important being in Chile (Population IV), where the possibility of writing English well attracts as high a percentage as is drawn to the possibility of reading well, and higher than is attracted to the possibility of achieving a good understanding of spoken English. In most countries (for instance, the Federal Republic of Germany, and Finland and Sweden) higher percentages in Population IV than in Population II have an aspiration to achieve well or very well in the overall aspects of English.

STUDENTS' SELF-PERCEPTION OF ABILITY IN ENGLISH

Table 8.10 indicates students' self-perceptions of their ability in various aspects of English.

In spite of the comparatively high aspirations for achievement in English of the majority of students, no appreciable percentage of the sample of students in any country think very highly of their ability in English. It is noteworthy that in some countries, notably Belgium and Thailand, a greater percentage of students in Population IV appear to rate themselves more moderately than the students in Population II rated themselves. Elsewhere the tendency is for higher percentages of Population IV students than of Population II to assess their ability as being above "fair." If we regard all four skills together, the general tendency is for Italy and Thailand in Population II and IV, and Chile and Hungary in Population IV only, to have the highest percentages rating themselves as "fair" compared with "well," or "very well," which in the light of their mean level of performance may be an indication of how realistically the students of those countries assess their abilities. The greatest percentages of students rating themselves highly over all four skills are found in Israel, Belgium and Sweden, although in Sweden there is a fair percentage in Population II who rate themselves moderately in writing, compared with those in other countries. The countries which rate themselves rather highly tend to compare favorably with other countries in actual mean levels of achievement.

Although there are exceptions, reading is the skill on which the highest percentage of students consistently give themselves a high rating, the next skill being understanding spoken English, with writing having precedence in Hungary. Speaking and writing English well tend to claim approximately the same percentages of students who profess to have a good level of competence. As with students' statements of intention, it is noteworthy that the percentage of students who tend to give themselves a high rating in the productive (encoding) skills tends to be smaller than the percentage rating themselves highly on the receptive (decoding) skills.

STUDENTS' ESTIMATE OF THE DIFFICULTY OF ENGLISH

Generally speaking, more students in both populations in the present samples found English "hard" or "very hard" rather than "easy" or "very easy," with the exception of Chile (Population IV), Israel (Population IV but not Population II), and especially Thailand in both populations. This is shown in Table 8.11. In view of the comparative performance of Chile and Thailand this tendency was not expected. Apart from the students of Belgium, Israel, Italy, and Thailand the tendency is for higher percentages to find English "hard" in Population IV than in Population II and apart from the students in Israel and Thailand there are higher percentages in Population II than in Population IV finding it "easy" or "very easy." The more mature the student is, or the greater his experience in the language, the more realistic he appears to be in assessing the difficulty of English. However, by far the highest percentages of students in all countries and in both populations found English neither difficult nor easy when compared with other subjects. The greatest percentages of students who found English difficult, compared with other subjects, are in Belgium, the Federal Republic of Germany, the Netherlands, and Sweden (both populations). Finland and Thailand (both populations), Italy (Population II), and Hungary and Chile (Population IV only) are the countries where the highest percentages found English easy compared with other subjects.

STUDENTS' SELF-PERCEPTION OF THEIR INDUSTRIOUSNESS IN ENGLISH

In nearly all countries higher percentages of students claim to work harder rather than less hard at English as compared with other subjects. See Table 8.12. Across countries, the percentages claiming to work less hard at English than at other subjects are almost invariably higher in Population II than in IV. The countries with the highest percentages of students claiming to be more industrious in English than in other subjects are Finland, Israel and Sweden in Population II, together with Belgium, Hungary and Sweden in Population IV. This result should be considered together with the mean level of achievement in these countries. Across the ten countries approximately 40 % to 60 % in Population IV and between 50 % and 75 % in Population II claim that English requires just about the same amount of effort as other subjects.

The measures of intention in respect to levels of accomplishment, difficulty of English and industriousness required for the subject are entirely subjective and relative. The criterion of measurement in any of these indicators in one country may differ from that which is characteristic of another; what is regarded as easy in one country, may be regarded as difficult in another. Students measure themselves according to what they feel is the consensus in their country. Further, irrespective of differences in subjective criteria of measurement, students are likely to differ among themselves in terms of modesty or diffidence about their ability or industriousness. Neither within nor across countries is there an objective criterion against which students measure themselves. The countries which tend to have high percentages of students who regard English as easier than other subjects, for instance Israel and Thailand, tend also to be those with the highest percentages of students claiming to work less hard at English than at other subjects. They are also the countries with the highest percentages of students having a relatively low estimate of their ability in English. Yet the mean level of achievement in these two countries is not comparable.

AFFECTIVE SCALES

Three affective scales were administered to the English students. These are Interest in English, Activities in English outside School and the Utility of English scales. The items in each scale were factor analyzed and the results were used to formulate a scoring model. In this chapter and Tables 8.13–8.16 we refer only to the percentages of students who expressed an affirmative or negative response. Those "uncertain" or not leaning either way, are omitted. The items for each scale are in the appendix for this chapter.

Interest in English

There is a general tendency towards a high degree of between-country uniformity in the responses to the Interest in English scale, whether the percentage responding affirmatively to a given item is high or low. There is least uniformity in response to Item 4 ("English gets more interesting all the time"), where the percentage of students agreeing ranges between 33 % (Finland) and 81 % (Belgium), in Population II. The items which tend to claim the highest percentages of student-affirmation are 5, 8 and 10 in both populations. ("I would like to be able to speak more languages than my native tongue"; "I think everyone would benefit from learning English" and "It is important to learn English while still at school.") Almost as high a percentage of students tended to *deny* that "I cannot profit from learning English because it is too difficult for me" (7), which is equivalent to a positive response to English. The items with which the lowest percentages expressed agreement in most countries were the first one, "The marks I get in English are usually better than in most other subjects," and the second, "I like English more than most other subjects." Taking all ten items into account, the countries which tend to have the highest percentages of students with a positive attitude to or offering their strong agreement with the statements are Belgium, Hungary, and Thailand (except for Items 9 and 10 in Thailand). The differences between the two populations are few and not especially striking. However, it is interesting to note that there is a tendency for the Population IV students to have higher percentages reporting affirmatively than Population II for Items 5–10. These items tend to stress the utilitarian aspects of English. The percentages are higher in Population II than in IV for Items 1–4 which tend to reflect the aesthetic or emotional response to English. There does not appear to be any consistent association between the mean scores on this scale and the mean level of performance for the various countries on the Reading test.

English Activities outside School

As can be seen in Table 8.14, there do not appear to be strong tendencies for students to participate in the English Speaking, Reading or Listening activities itemized in this scale. There are very low percentages on Items 1, 3, 4, 5 and 6 in all countries and in both populations. The items which claim the highest percentages participating, though the figures are seldom higher than 20 % in any case, are "Listening to English radio and T.V. etc." (2) and "Corresponding in English with a pen pal" (4). The lowest percentages of all are recorded for "Visiting an English-speaking country" (6) and "Reading English newspapers and magazines" (1). However, countries differ to some extent in their preference of items. For instance, Israel tends to have the highest percentages for Items 2 and 3 ("Listening to radio in English" and "Talking with English speaking people"). In Hungary, on the other hand, Item 4 tends to attract the highest percentages. In Sweden Item 2 ("Listening to English") is the item which attracts the most positive response for Populations II and IV.

If we compare the overall pictures in each of the ten countries separately, bearing in mind that the percentages are low for nearly all items, the highest positive response tends to characterize Israel and Hungary, with Finland (except for Item 2) and the Federal Republic of Germany recording slightly lower percentages. Lower levels of positive response appear in Belgium, Chile, Sweden and Italy (except for Item 2), with Thailand tending to record very low percentages in both populations. This is an ambiguous scale, since it measures the *opportunities* for participation as much as, if not more than, it does the *actual* student participation. The extent of the latter can only be satisfactorily assessed in terms of the former. Consequently, any between-country comparison of participation as a measure of student "involvement" is difficult to establish. The one item on which there are reasonably high or moderately high percentages of positive response is "Listening to English language radio and T.V." Where the opportunity to participate occurs, students appear to take advantage of it; where there is little or no opportunity they obviously cannot participate. Consequently, the main value of the analysis of this scale is to confirm what has already been stated about the low level of background or societal support for English in most, if not all the countries.

Utility of English

Tables 8.15 and 8.16 give data regarding the students' perception of the utility of English.

Contrary to their behavior on the other two scales, the students in the different countries tended to react in very divergent ways to the items on the Utility of English scale, especially in Population II. In Population IV the countries tend to be more uniform in their general response. It is noteworthy that in Population IV nearly all students in all countries agree or strongly agree with the propositions expressed in Items 7–12. With the exception of Item 10 these items reflect a cultural rather than utilitarian concept of the use of English. Items 1–5 tend to reflect the more practical possibilities of English. The analysis of this scale tends to confirm the tendency noted in the response of Population IV to the items in the Interest in English scale. Students tend in each case to stress the "vehicular" use of English, its utilitarian value as a language of wider communication for industry, science and administration.

Generally speaking, the results of the three measures appear to be consistent with each other to a fairly high degree. The interest in English and the students' ideas about its utility tend to be more specific and practical among the older students. It is also probable that the limited opportunities for participation, which the English Activities outside School scale appears to demonstrate, influences the ideas students have about the use to which English may be put.

Appendix

List of Statements in the Three Scales

A. *Interest in English*

1. The marks I get in English are usually ... better than in most other subjects.
2. I like English ... more than most other subjects.
3. I would like to study English after the end of this school year.
4. English gets more interesting all the time.
5. I would like to be able to speak more languages than (mother tongue).
6. I hope that in my career I will be able to make some use of the English I learned at school.
7. I cannot profit from learning English because it is too difficult for me.
8. I think that everyone would benefit from learning English.
9. There are many subjects more important to learn at school than English.
10. It is important to learn English while still at school.

B. *English Activities outside School*

1. Read English newspapers or magazines.
2. Listen to English language radio programs or watch English language films or English language T.V. programs.
3. Talk with English-speaking children or adults.
4. Correspond in English with a pen pal.
5. Attend meetings of English language societies or other English language cultural organizations.
6. Have visited an English speaking country.

C. *Utility of English*

1. Studying English may someday help me to get a good job.
2. I need to study English because a foreign language is required in the school curriculum or to be admitted to a higher school.

3. I need to study English because it is used in school in the higher grades.
4. I need to study English in order to read books, newspapers, or magazines that I want to read.
5. Studying English will help me if I need to study another foreign language later on.
6. Studying English will allow me to make friends more easily with English-speaking people.
7. Studying English will enable me to meet, talk or correspond with a greater variety of people.
8. One is well educated only if one knows at least one foreign language.
9. I am studying English because I enjoy it.
10. I am studying English because I was given no choice in the matter.
11. Studying English will help me to understand my own language better.
12. Studying English will help me know and appreciate the way of life of people who speak English.

	Belgium (Fr.)	FRG	Finland	Israel	Italy	Netherlands	Sweden	Thailand
Age in months								
Mean	173.6	173.0	174.5	176.0	174.6	174.3	173.9	173.7
S.D.	3.5	3.7	3.6	4.1	3.3	3.1	3.7	5.5
Grade of student								
Mean	8.7	8.3	7.7	8.9	8.5	8.7	7.6	8.7
S.D.	0.5	0.8	0.6	0.4	0.5	0.5	0.6	0.7
% of male students	47.2	50.3	51.1	53.2	57.8	47.5	50.9	52.4
Number of children in family, assuming none have more than five								
Mean	2.9	3.0	3.8	3.7	2.9	3.9	2.9	–[b]
S.D.	1.6	1.6	1.7	1.7	1.5	1.7	1.4	–[b]
Father's education in years								
Mean	10.7	9.0	7.3	8.3	7.2	9.0	–[b]	7.3
S.D.	4.7	2.8	3.8	5.2	5.0	3.9	–[b]	5.4
Mother's education in years								
Mean	10.0	8.5	7.5	7.5	5.9	8.0	–[b]	5.1
S.D.	4.3	2.3	3.4	5.2	4.3	3.4	–[b]	4.6
Father's occupation,[c] %								
Category I	6.0	0.2	10.3	7.2	23.6	0.1	12.7	9.2
Category II	78.7	59.0	66.4	46.3	28.9	43.5	48.3	46.8
Category III	15.3	37.6	22.6	42.6	40.0	53.2	38.1	42.8
Category IV	0.0	3.2	0.7	3.9	7.5	3.2	0.8	1.1
Number of students in sample[a]	725	1 110	2 164	1 096	809	2 098	2 454	1 957

Note: % = Percentage.

[a] Not all answered every question on the questionnaires; %, means and S.D.'s are based only on those who answered the question seeking the information indicated here. Generally, 95 % or more of the sample responded to most questions.

[b] Note that no data is available because these questions were ambiguous in the questionnaires of the respective countries.

[c] Refer to the definitions of Categories I–IV given earlier in the chapter.

Table 8.2. *General Background of Students—Population IV*

	Belgium (Fr.)	Chile	FRG	Finland	Hungary	Israel	Italy	Netherlands	Sweden	Thailand
Age in months										
Mean	220.3	225.1	224.5	229.6	220.0	211.9	228.7	215.1	231.2	215.8
S.D.	13.9	16.7	9.8	12.6	4.5	14.2	12.9	13.9	14.3	14.6
Grade of student										
Mean	12.0	12.0	13.0	12.1	12.0	12.0	13.0	11.3	11.7	11.9
S.D.	0.0	0.1	0.0	0.3	0.0	0.1	0.0	0.5	0.5	0.4
% of male students	65.0	52.4	49.9	41.5	34.2	45.3	55.9	57.9	48.5	59.6
Number of children in family, assuming none have more than five										
Mean	2.9	4.4	2.6	3.4	2.2	3.3	2.7	3.7	2.8	—[b]
S.D.	1.7	1.7	1.4	1.6	1.1	1.7	1.3	1.7	1.4	—[b]
Father's education in years										
Mean	10.9	9.5	11.7	8.6	12.7	9.5	7.1	10.5	—[b]	8.2
S.D.	4.4	5.1	4.1	4.3	4.5	5.0	4.6	4.3	—[b]	5.4
Mother's education in years										
Mean	9.4	8.4	10.0	8.4	10.6	8.5	5.9	8.9	—[b]	5.6
S.D.	3.5	4.5	3.3	3.6	3.8	4.7	4.1	3.5	—[b]	4.7
Father's occupation,[c] %										
Category I	5.2	0.5	0.0	4.4	4.9	8.5	13.2	0.0	11.4	3.4

Category II	81.4	78.9	16.9	54.7	39.2	67.0	37.7	18.0	36.2	45.8
Category III	13.5	19.5	62.0	38.9	55.9	20.6	43.8	70.4	47.8	49.7
Category IV	0.0	1.0	21.2	2.0	0.0	3.8	5.4	11.6	4.5	1.0
Number of students in sample[a]	1 485	2 314	1 379	2 369	1 063	614	329	1 568	1 767	936

Note: % = Percentage.

[a] Not all answered every question on the questionnaires; %, means and S.D.'s are based only on those who answered the questions seeking the information indicated here. Generally, 95 % or more of the sample responded to most questions.

[b] Note that no data is available because these questions were ambiguous in the questionnaires of the respective countries.

[c] Refer to the definitions of Categories I–IV given earlier in the chapter.

Table 8.3. *General Educational Experience of Students—Population II*

	Belgium (Fr.)	FRG	Finland	Israel	Italy	Netherlands	Sweden	Thailand
Hours of schooling per week								
Mean	35.2	30.2	34.5	38.6	30.3	26.9	35.0	30.7
S.D.	2.4	3.1	1.3	1.2	3.4	1.5	0.0	1.7
Number of books in home								
Mean	52.0	45.8	42.5	54.7	44.5	53.9	54.4	41.9
S.D.	20.2	21.1	22.3	17.8	22.3	18.6	17.6	24.3
% using dictionary in home								
Often	44.6	30.9	16.8	34.2	36.9	33.5	11.9	29.3
Occasionally	49.1	59.0	51.8	50.7	57.5	58.0	70.6	53.4
% reading for pleasure								
>1<2 hours/week	25.3	20.9	18.6	16.8	26.6	24.4	22.6	26.5
>3 hours/week	34.5	42.0	38.1	49.0	29.4	31.9	27.5	18.6
% listening to radio or watching TV								
<10 hours/week	64.0	45.7	45.6	51.2	52.0	40.1	51.4	78.9
>10 hours/week	36.1	54.3	54.4	48.9	48.0	59.9	48.6	21.1
% with own room for homework	70.7	64.4	61.2	64.7	73.8	71.0	77.4	36.7
% with less than 2 hours/week homework for all subjects	4.1	9.2	25.2	9.2	9.1	7.1	46.0	6.7
% having a fixed time for homework	84.2	43.3	31.4	47.7	44.6	61.3	13.4	60.0
Parental support expressed in %:								
(i) Showing interest in school activities								
Often	37.9	53.4	19.1	50.7	71.6	46.7	23.0	21.1

Often	5.9	5.5	9.8	8.5	5.3	14.1	11.5	6.5
Occasionally	23.1	23.2	31.0	26.8	19.5	41.6	55.1	28.7
Never	69.9	69.5	58.2	64.3	74.5	44.0	29.1	64.2
(iii) Checking spelling								
Often	29.6	38.3	10.7	23.0	32.2	19.6	17.5	10.6
Sometimes	58.6	43.8	35.7	44.7	30.8	41.9	40.6	58.7
Rarely or never	11.8	18.0	53.7	32.3	37.0	38.5	41.8	30.7
(iv) Correcting speech								
Often	43.8	27.5	4.3	34.1	54.4	20.3	9.4	18.8
Sometimes	46.8	47.2	56.9	46.8	29.9	45.0	60.2	53.1
Never	9.3	25.3	38.7	19.1	15.8	34.7	30.3	28.1
(v) Encouraging cultural activities								
Often	10.6	6.6	3.0	9.6	18.7	2.5	2.5	8.2
Occasionally	34.3	39.4	21.5	23.8	28.8	21.1	10.9	45.0
Rarely or never	55.2	54.0	75.5	66.6	52.5	76.4	86.6	46.9
(vi) Encouraging reading								
Often	41.4	29.8	19.3	51.8	61.5	29.7	11.3	52.0
Sometimes	34.7	39.8	65.0	40.8	31.2	52.8	57.1	42.4
Never	23.9	30.4	15.7	7.3	7.3	17.5	31.6	5.6
Number of students in sample[a]	725	1 110	2 164	1 096	809	2 098	2 454	1 957

Note: % = Percentage.

[a] Not all answered every question on the questionnaires; percentages, means and S.D.'s are based only on those who answered the question seeking the information indicated here. Generally, 95 % or more of the sample responded to most questions.

251

Table 8.4. *General Educational Experience of Students—Population IV*

	Belgium (Fr.)	Chile	FRG	Finland	Hungary	Israel	Italy	Nether-lands	Sweden	Thai-land
Hours of schooling per week										
Mean	35.4	35.7	30.0	33.5	33.3	37.3	33.1	28.4	32.0	32.8
S.D.	3.1	1.1	3.7	3.5	1.4	1.9	2.6	2.2	0.0	2.9
Number of books in home										
Mean	56.3	43.8	60.7	57.9	63.3	59.2	50.9	58.3	60.0	46.9
S.D.	16.6	22.8	12.2	14.4	8.0	13.6	20.2	15.2	12.7	22.4
% using dictionary in home:										
Often	51.4	44.9	38.5	21.6	11.0	27.0	22.0	31.9	26.3	35.0
Occasionally	43.2	51.4	57.1	60.9	66.9	59.0	67.3	62.2	65.7	55.2
% reading for pleasure										
>1<2 hours/week	23.8	27.6	15.2	17.9	10.8	18.5	24.9	22.6	23.2	22.8
>3 hours/week	37.3	31.4	56.8	45.0	66.4	41.4	34.4	34.7	42.3	29.2
% listening to radio or watching TV										
<10 hours/week	75.1	77.6	67.5	73.2	67.0	60.9	57.5	64.0	68.3	73.2
>10 hours/week	24.9	22.4	32.4	26.8	33.0	39.1	42.4	36.0	31.7	26.9
% with own room for homework	73.3	54.7	80.5	77.6	51.4	57.0	70.4	78.9	87.5	44.0
% with less than 2 hours/week homework for all subject	3.9	15.4	6.0	3.2	7.8	9.5	7.1	2.4	10.4	0.9
% having a fixed time for homework	74.0	33.4	30.7	47.0	64.5	44.4	39.8	65.0	38.2	60.8
Parental support expressed in %:										
(i) Showing interest in school activities										
Often	21.7	45.5	45.5	15.6	65.2	50.9	54.0	40.3	23.2	16.4
Sometimes	55.7	45.4	45.4	71.9	97.9	36.8	35.2	45.4	62.9	65.2

Often	1.3	4.7	0.5	1.4	2.9	1.5	1.7	2.5	1.8	2.8
Occasionally	6.7	26.8	2.6	7.1	10.2	15.5	3.8	17.7	22.2	16.6
Never	90.3	67.8	95.7	91.1	85.5	82.4	93.7	78.4	74.8	79.6
(iii) Checking spelling										
Often	17.7	36.8	11.9	3.7	2.9	13.6	5.2	16.3	9.3	3.7
Sometimes	48.0	32.6	16.0	15.1	14.5	37.5	13.0	32.7	25.7	35.9
Rarely or never	34.3	30.6	72.1	81.2	82.6	48.9	81.8	51.0	65.0	60.5
(iv) Correcting speech										
Often	36.1	46.7	15.6	0.5	15.4	25.0	24.7	18.6	4.0	12.2
Sometimes	38.2	39.0	26.3	35.3	53.8	46.9	29.5	42.5	44.0	43.5
Never	25.7	14.3	58.1	64.1	30.8	28.1	45.8	38.9	52.0	44.3
(v) Encouraging cultural activities										
Often	13.7	8.2	18.2	3.3	33.3	6.8	9.8	6.3	2.7	5.1
Occasionally	38.0	32.6	36.7	27.7	42.6	27.3	26.7	30.4	15.8	35.6
Rarely or never	48.2	59.1	45.1	69.0	24.1	65.9	63.5	63.3	81.5	59.3
(vi) Encouraging reading										
Often	28.3	31.5	36.2	21.9	53.8	37.3	41.8	37.6	20.3	50.3
Sometimes	38.0	45.8	17.1	58.7	35.2	45.4	33.8	45.2	49.2	40.1
Never	33.7	22.7	46.8	19.4	11.0	17.4	24.4	17.2	30.5	9.5
Number of students in sample[a]	1 485	2 314	1 379	2 369	1 063	614	329	1 568	1 767	936

Note: % = Percentage.

[a] Not all answered every question on the questionnaires; percentages, means and S.D.'s are based only on those who answered the question seeking the information indicated here. Generally, 95 % or more of the sample responded to most questions.

Table 8.5. *Selected Features of the Language Experience of Students—Population II*

	Belgium (Fr.)	FRG	Finland	Israel	Italy	Nether-lands	Sweden	Thai-land
% having fathers whose first language was not the national language	20.0	3.8	3.1	83.7	2.0	8.7	7.7	26.5
% having mothers whose first language was not the national language	22.6	5.1	2.7	81.5	2.4	9.2	9.1	20.2
% having fathers whose first language was English	0.2	0.2	0.2	3.5	0.2	0.3	0.9	0.5
% having mothers whose first language was English	0.8	0.2	0.2	2.4	0.0	0.4	0.4	0.0
% having fathers who have studied English	35.4	22.1	15.5	45.8	15.6	38.1	41.0	42.9
% having mothers who have studied English	24.9	22.3	16.0	38.2	6.5	31.3	46.8	22.3
% having no English books in home	25.0	38.3	41.4	11.6	20.8	37.8	25.5	25.2
% having parental interest in English	92.3	86.7	74.3	88.6	92.5	88.5	95.0	83.4
% having parental help with English	32.3	12.8	15.7	33.5	12.4	26.1	40.6	16.5
% having opportunity to speak English out of school	59.8	65.0	46.5	86.0	48.3	54.2	55.4	55.9
% having never spent time in English-speaking country	84.4	92.6	93.7	86.8	91.8	89.5	84.8	91.7
% having fair to excellent knowledge of English prior to entry	2.2	2.5	3.4	11.4	3.7	8.9	3.2	9.3
Number of students in sample[a]	725	1 110	2 164	1 096	809	2 098	2 454	1 957

Note: % = Percentage.

[a] Not all answered every question on the questionnaires; percentages, are based only on those who answered the question seeking the information indicated here. Generally, 95 % or more of the sample responded to most questions.

Table 8.6. *Selected Features of the Language Experience of Students—Population IV*

	Belgium (Fr.)	Chile	FRG	Finland	Hungary	Israel	Italy	Nether-lands	Sweden	Thai-land
% having fathers whose first language was not the national language	23.6	5.6	2.5	4.1	1.2	89.0	3.1	10.7	5.3	28.9
% having mothers whose first language was not the national language	23.6	5.0	3.1	3.0	0.8	85.6	2.6	11.4	6.5	21.4
% having fathers whose first language was English	0.4	0.9	0.2	0.1	0.0	1.4	0.0	0.3	0.1	0.2
% having mothers whose first language was English	0.2	1.1	0.0	0.1	0.0	1.1	0.5	0.2	0.4	0.2
% having fathers who have studied English	37.1	37.7	49.3	23.2	21.2	39.0	13.5	60.4	48.3	49.6
% having mothers who have studied English	25.5	31.6	48.4	26.5	17.0	38.2	8.3	49.7	51.0	24.6
% having no English books in home	27.1	11.6	14.1	16.0	24.6	10.2	23.7	17.0	15.1	15.0
% having parental interest in English	89.5	86.8	92.9	81.5	88.7	90.0	92.1	91.2	93.5	68.1
% having parental help with English	15.3	19.6	2.6	4.1	6.0	20.1	4.2	8.5	10.6	10.6
% having opportunity to speak English out of school	49.5	55.3	72.8	66.9	62.4	90.1	57.6	67.4	66.3	57.3
% having never spent time in English-speaking country	68.8	95.1	54.6	87.1	92.5	84.8	88.4	67.3	63.5	96.1
% having fair to excellent knowledge of English prior to entry	2.5	1.8	1.2	2.9	9.7	7.9	1.9	5.7	1.6	2.5
Number of students in sample[a]	1 485	2 314	1 379	2 369	1 063	614	329	1 568	1 767	936

Note: % = Percentage.

[a] Not all answered every question on the questionnaire; percentages are based only on those who answered the question seeking the information indicated here. Generally, 95 % or more of the sample responded to most questions.

Table 8.7. Selected Features of the English Language Experience of Students—Population II

	Belgium (Fr.)	FRG	Finland	Israel	Italy	Netherlands	Sweden	Thailand
% beginning English in								
Grade 1 or 2	0.6	1.1	2.8	3.3	3.9	2.6	0.0	43.3
Grade 3 or 4	1.0	10.4	42.5	2.9	5.1	0.5	92.4	8.1
Grade 5 or 6	9.6	78.2	34.4	82.6	70.8	6.0	5.2	47.0
Grade 7 or 8	88.3	10.3	19.7	10.3	9.3	90.6	0.5	0.8
Grade 9 +	0.5	0.0	0.5	0.9	10.9	0.3	0.4	0.7
% studying English								
2 years or less	23.6	7.8	29.6	5.2	14.0	21.0	2.2	2.0
3–4 years	74.0	55.3	41.6	71.0	74.7	77.3	50.3	24.3
% having instruction in English								
less than 3 hrs/wk	9.6	31.7	54.1	10.3	74.2	74.9	90.0	44.9
between 3–5 hrs/wk	88.6	65.3	45.2	78.3	25.1	25.0	9.6	33.6
% doing English homework								
less than 2 hr/wk	40.3	47.4	57.1	29.2	36.3	69.6	83.1	18.9
between 2–5 hrs/wk	55.3	49.9	39.3	51.5	57.4	29.3	16.1	50.1
% whose English class has								
<15 students	25.2	6.6	10.0	7.6	6.5	5.9	8.6	1.0
15–20 students	33.7	13.3	24.3	14.9	25.7	22.3	29.3	1.9
21–25 students	32.3	24.9	9.9	11.8	35.2	42.2	34.3	3.1
% of students whose English classroom activities include								
(i) Speaking English to teacher								
Often	35.7	57.0	47.4	48.9	36.0	43.2	31.0	14.2

Rarely or never	42.2	61.9	35.5	49.7	47.1	44.0	43.6	15.3
	9.6	24.9	20.9	28.8	8.4	7.4	5.1	2.9
(iii) Listening to records, radio, etc. in English								
Often	35.5	29.0	12.8	67.3	18.1	44.6	54.1	15.1
Sometimes	33.4	43.9	49.3	23.6	31.9	22.8	36.7	60.2
Rarely or never	31.1	27.2	37.9	9.1	50.0	32.6	9.2	24.7
(iv) Repeating exercises in English								
Often	32.9	3.1	10.3	15.7	7.7	26.5	20.3	5.0
Sometimes	28.1	22.8	40.7	31.4	22.0	30.5	44.8	32.4
Rarely or never	39.0	74.2	48.9	53.0	70.3	43.0	34.9	62.6
(v) Writing exercises in English								
Often	70.8	51.4	68.5	53.2	79.6	69.8	48.1	75.8
Sometimes	26.1	42.7	24.8	28.4	18.2	26.2	44.7	20.2
Rarely or never	3.1	5.9	6.6	18.4	2.3	4.0	7.2	4.0
(vi) Translation into or from English								
Often	42.3	37.9	55.0	34.8	88.1	37.7	42.9	48.3
Sometimes	38.9	56.2	35.3	48.0	10.0	39.2	49.3	47.0
Rarely or never	18.8	5.9	9.7	17.2	1.9	23.1	7.8	4.7
(vii) Writing essays in English								
Often	37.9	9.2	2.5	21.0	34.9	5.5	5.8	12.8
Sometimes	43.8	43.1	25.0	50.3	40.0	24.9	40.2	40.0
Rarely or never	18.4	47.7	72.5	28.8	25.1	69.6	54.1	47.3
(viii) Intensive reading								
Often	16.5	57.8	64.8	21.0	28.5	38.5	33.3	29.6
Sometimes	40.1	37.1	24.8	44.9	33.0	48.3	44.7	55.7
Rarely or never	43.4	5.1	10.5	34.1	37.9	13.2	22.0	14.7

Table 8.7. (*Cont.*)

	Belgium (Fr.)	FRG	Finland	Israel	Italy	Nether-lands	Sweden	Thai-land
(ix) Reading for pleasure								
Often	20.0	13.9	10.3	25.8	26.9	10.6	10.0	14.7
Sometimes	49.0	36.2	43.9	50.1	46.7	48.3	51.0	54.7
Rarely or never	31.0	49.9	45.8	24.1	26.5	41.1	39.0	30.6
Number of students in sample[a]	725	1 110	2 164	1 096	809	2 098	2 454	1 957

Note: % = Percentage.

[a] Not all answered every question on the questionnaires; percentages are based only on those who answered the question seeking the informa-tion indicated here. Generally, 95 % or more of the sample responded to most questions.

	Belgium (Fr.)	Chile	FRG	Finland	Hungary	Israel	Italy	Netherlands	Sweden	Thailand
% beginning English in										
Grade 1 or 2	0.5	17.5	6.3	3.7	0.8	1.2	0.0	4.9	0.0	35.0
Grade 3 or 4	0.3	8.6	5.3	4.5	0.5	0.2	3.2	0.5	62.4	9.2
Grade 5 or 6	2.2	14.4	75.5	58.0	0.8	87.1	21.9	5.3	33.8	53.3
Grade 7 or 8	62.1	51.8	11.4	5.9	7.1	8.2	4.3	88.9	1.4	1.5
Grade 9 +	34.8	7.7	1.5	27.9	90.7	3.2	70.6	0.4	0.4	0.4
% studying English										
2 years or less	2.3	1.1	0.5	1.9	0.1	2.7	0.8	0.2	0.4	0.2
3–4 years	35.9	9.3	1.6	26.7	89.5	4.3	3.8	1.3	1.4	0.4
5–6 years	54.6	47.0	11.0	10.0	8.9	21.0	68.0	74.3	5.7	7.6
7 years or more	7.2	42.6	86.9	61.5	1.6	72.0	27.4	24.2	92.5	91.7
% having instruction in English										
less than 3 hrs/wk	82.1	73.2	18.8	20.9	71.9	9.5	74.3	48.8	95.9	42.9
between 3–5 hrs/wk	17.5	25.1	80.1	78.6	24.4	67.8	25.2	51.1	4.1	23.7
% doing English homework										
less than 2 hr/wk	69.9	65.8	38.4	25.8	52.4	25.7	53.4	57.5	84.3	22.5
between 2–5 hrs/wk	28.6	32.0	55.9	65.1	39.3	53.0	44.8	39.2	15.0	52.0
% whose English class has										
<15 students	35.0	3.3	27.2	10.8	18.5	14.0	6.5	6.6	8.0	1.1
15–20 students	36.4	8.5	42.0	23.0	37.9	18.0	15.2	34.1	30.0	10.0
21–25 students	17.2	8.0	22.2	30.5	13.1	19.6	27.4	31.8	37.7	8.6
% of students whose English classroom activities include										
(i) Speaking English to teacher										
Often	31.7	12.0	61.2	41.4	81.6	52.7	33.0	40.9	42.4	9.8
Sometimes	49.4	50.8	28.8	45.5	16.5	36.8	57.6	39.0	46.8	57.3
Rarely or never	18.9	37.2	9.9	13.2	1.8	10.5	9.4	20.0	10.8	32.9

Table 8.8. (Cont.)

	Belgium (Fr.)	Chile	FRG	Finland	Hungary	Israel	Italy	Netherlands	Sweden	Thailand
(ii) Speaking in mother tongue										
Often	44.9	70.2	17.2	32.8	12.6	13.0	45.2	51.3	30.7	79.1
Sometimes	41.9	27.2	49.7	53.1	61.2	42.3	44.5	38.7	58.1	18.2
Rarely or never	13.2	2.6	33.0	14.1	26.2	44.8	10.3	10.0	11.2	2.8
(iii) Listening to records, radio, etc. in English										
Often	30.4	27.7	26.2	5.0	37.2	58.4	20.5	39.1	39.6	7.4
Sometimes	33.7	42.6	30.6	42.8	41.4	32.7	32.5	29.0	49.8	60.2
Rarely or never	35.9	29.7	43.2	52.2	21.4	8.8	47.0	31.9	10.6	32.4
(iv) Repeating exercises in English										
Often	12.2	14.9	1.7	5.4	23.1	6.3	4.9	4.2	4.8	2.0
Sometimes	33.4	33.6	11.0	31.0	39.7	23.8	11.9	14.0	30.9	27.7
Rarely or never	54.4	51.5	87.4	63.5	37.2	69.9	83.3	81.9	64.2	70.2
(v) Writing exercises in English										
Often	37.8	43.2	32.8	82.4	47.3	39.9	63.6	27.8	15.3	66.9
Sometimes	53.0	44.3	52.5	13.5	43.9	43.3	34.1	27.3	54.6	27.7
Rarely or never	9.2	12.6	14.7	4.0	8.9	16.8	2.3	44.9	30.2	5.3
(vi) Translation into or from English										
Often	31.3	44.4	29.9	95.6	77.8	25.6	82.8	75.0	31.8	35.4
Sometimes	50.0	46.7	46.6	3.9	21.1	54.2	15.5	11.1	56.3	52.2
Rarely or never	18.6	8.8	23.5	0.5	1.0	20.2	1.7	14.0	11.9	12.4

(vii) Writing essays in English

Often	23.5	7.3	26.2	2.5	32.8	34.9	42.3	2.5	9.7	18.9
Sometimes	52.4	26.9	45.6	18.0	56.5	53.9	45.3	15.2	59.8	67.3
Rarely or never	24.0	65.7	28.2	79.5	10.7	11.2	12.3	82.3	30.4	13.8
(viii) Intensive reading										
Often	28.9	32.6	57.4	59.5	22.8	18.2	15.5	52.0	42.3	27.7
Sometimes	37.5	47.8	35.3	31.2	46.1	53.9	30.7	35.3	42.6	56.2
Rarely or never	33.6	19.5	7.3	9.3	31.1	28.0	53.8	12.7	15.2	16.1
(ix) Reading for pleasure										
Often	12.5	23.2	71.1	5.5	23.5	24.6	14.0	22.9	12.6	10.3
Sometimes	43.6	46.4	25.2	51.2	57.5	53.1	36.2	58.3	56.3	57.8
Rarely or never	43.9	30.3	3.6	43.2	18.9	22.4	49.8	18.8	31.0	31.9
Number of students in sample[a]	1 485	2 314	1 379	2 369	1 063	614	329	1 568	1 767	936

Note: %=Percentage.

[a] Not all answered every question on the questionnaires; percentages are based only on those who answered the question seeking the information indicated here. Generally, 95 % or more of the sample responded to most questions.

Table 8.9. *Percentages of Students Aiming to Achieve Well or Only Moderately Well in Understanding, Reading, Speaking and Writing English—Populations II and IV*

	Belgium (Fr.)		Chile		FRG		Finland	
	II	IV	II	IV	II	IV	II	IV
Speaking English								
Fair	28.0	45.7	–	56.5	28.6	16.9	61.6	49.1
Well or Very Well	70.2	51.8	–	39.8	71.2	82.0	35.8	50.5
Understanding spoken English								
Fair	28.3	35.4	–	52.0	27.8	8.2	56.1	35.9
Well or Very Well	70.2	62.9	–	44.9	71.3	90.7	41.1	63.8
Reading English								
Fair	25.9	32.8	–	49.7	28.1	16.1	53.6	36.4
Well or Very Well	72.4	65.1	–	46.9	71.5	82.6	43.2	63.3
Writing English								
Fair	30.0	41.3	–	50.1	30.4	23.2	54.9	44.4
Well or Very Well	67.6	55.1	–	46.3	69.3	75.9	41.7	55.3

Note: Since the percentages of students who indicate an entirely negative intention are negligible they have been excluded.

Table 8.10. *Students' Perception of Ability in Various Aspects of English—Populations II and IV*

	Belgium (Fr.)		Chile		FRG		Finland	
	II	IV	II	IV	II	IV	II	IV
Speaking English								
Fair	74.6	83.2	–	88.2	79.4	77.3	92.0	88.8
Well or Very Well	23.3	9.7	–	5.9	20.4	22.2	4.1	10.1
Understanding spoken English								
Fair	75.0	78.3	–	85.2	82.1	58.1	89.7	84.4
Well or Very Well	22.9	16.4	–	6.8	17.6	41.4	5.1	14.9
Reading English								
Fair	62.6	74.2	–	86.2	68.6	56.7	90.4	87.4
Well or Very Well	36.3	3.1	–	10.9	31.1	43.0	6.8	12.2
Writing English								
Fair	69.9	80.1	–	86.0	75.0	73.4	88.9	89.4
Well or Very Well	28.5	14.2	–	7.8	23.9	26.2	5.2	9.6

Note: Since the percentages of students who indicate an entirely negative intention are negligible they have been excluded.

Hungary		Israel		Italy		Netherlands		Sweden		Thailand	
I	IV	II	IV	II	IV	II	IV	II	IV	II	IV
	32.1	27.3	26.3	89.0	90.3	46.3	40.8	52.0	40.2	88.4	87.2
	67.0	70.1	72.1	5.8	4.1	51.7	57.3	46.9	59.7	8.7	9.7
	30.2	36.6	41.7	84.3	82.1	38.6	29.1	46.9	27.5	86.0	84.5
	68.9	59.0	56.1	6.4	4.5	60.4	70.0	52.5	72.5	11.2	13.9
	24.5	23.3	21.7	83.1	85.3	38.6	28.1	49.2	36.3	71.8	74.4
	74.7	74.2	76.7	14.7	12.7	60.0	70.9	50.0	63.6	27.4	25.1
	30.3	20.9	22.8	85.2	86.1	40.9	44.8	58.5	50.5	68.1	72.7
	68.2	76.3	75.7	11.1	12.0	57.3	53.3	40.0	49.0	30.7	26.3

Hungary		Israel		Italy		Netherlands		Sweden		Thailand	
I	IV	II	IV	II	IV	II	IV	II	IV	II	IV
	91.3	65.9	63.1	89.8	89.6	85.3	69.5	81.8	63.3	94.0	94.6
	6.2	32.3	35.0	3.5	5.9	13.4	30.0	16.4	36.0	4.2	3.5
	88.4	62.6	50.9	89.0	88.6	76.9	53.3	71.0	49.0	94.3	92.6
	5.0	34.2	47.2	2.5	3.5	22.4	46.6	28.0	50.9	3.7	6.5
	78.6	59.3	61.6	89.0	87.3	80.1	57.0	72.0	60.9	80.3	83.6
	20.9	39.8	38.0	9.2	10.5	19.5	42.9	27.4	39.0	18.7	15.2
	80.5	66.8	70.2	88.3	90.2	79.2	75.2	84.5	74.4	82.9	87.5
	14.5	30.5	27.2	5.7	7.6	17.8	23.9	12.3	24.4	15.4	11.4

Table 8.11. *Percentage of Students Who Found the Study of English Hard or Easy—Populations II and IV*

Population	Belgium (Fr.)		Chile		FRG		Finland		Hungary	
	Hard	Easy	Hard	Easy	Hard	Easy	Hard	Easy	Hard	Easy
II	37.1	17.4	–	–	29.1	9.1	25.8	35.2	–	–
IV	35.7	16.3	23.6	26.0	32.3	7.2	28.4	28.2	38.1	21.6

Note: Hard='Very hard' together with 'Somewhat hard'. Easy='Very easy' together wit 'Somewhat easy'.
Not all responses are indicated; those indicating learning English as neither hard nor eas are omitted.

Table 8.12. *Students' Estimate of their Industry in English Studies*

Population	Belgium (Fr.)		Chile		FRG		Finland		Hungary	
	+	−	+	−	+	−	+	−	+	−
II	18.1	14.5	–	–	13.0	9.2	18.3	14.7	–	–
IV	40.5	7.3	32.2	16.3	34.8	8.7	24.4	13.2	41.1	12.5

Note: +=I work harder in English than in other subjects, expressed as a percentag
−=I do not work in English as hard as I do in other subjects, expressed as a percentag
Not all responses are indicated; those indicating equal effort in all subjects are omitte

Table 8.13. *Percentage of Students in Populations II and IV Expressing Positive Intere in English*

	Items									
	1		2		3		4		5	
	II	IV	II	IV	II	IV	II	IV	II	IV
Belgium (Fr)	19.1	15.6	41.2	28.6	59.7	53.3	81.2	67.8	94.1	95.
Chile	–	18.1	–	21.3	–	44.0	–	59.7	–	94.
FRG	9.9	12.5	19.2	18.9	67.2	46.2	52.3	23.5	60.8	92.
Finland	15.4	14.5	22.0	35.9	51.7	55.4	33.2	43.3	89.6	99.
Hungary	–	15.9	–	39.7	–	64.2	–	75.8	–	92.
Israel	20.5	14.0	27.9	24.1	58.1	33.6	56.5	45.1	78.8	78
Italy	11.3	10.9	28.5	24.8	40.3	55.8	70.7	64.6	88.7	96
Netherlands	15.3	16.3	24.1	31.0	47.4	40.0	42.3	33.2	89.5	97
Sweden	13.3	15.1	20.5	23.1	66.9	39.4	42.1	41.6	92.1	98
Thailand	14.4	11.2	25.3	22.8	56.2	75.3	74.8	67.3	96.2	98

Israel		Italy		Netherlands		Sweden		Thailand	
Hard	Easy	Hard	Easy	Hard	Easy	Hard	Easy	Hard	Easy
24.3	17.4	26.5	25.0	42.3	15.2	40.1	20.0	14.8	27.7
22.1	24.7	25.1	23.0	45.7	10.2	43.6	15.2	9.5	41.3

Israel		Italy		Netherlands		Sweden		Thailand	
+	−	+	−	+	−	+	−	+	−
23.0	28.3	10.8	24.3	16.6	9.4	20.1	8.4	12.6	24.3
28.6	23.8	25.7	15.8	36.5	6.4	43.9	5.0	21.2	19.7

6		7		8		9		10	
II	IV	II	IV	II	IV	II	IV	II	IV
81.0	70.7	63.9	69.8	83.1	86.4	42.5	48.8	88.8	84.1
–	50.2	–	50.7	–	66.0	–	9.2	–	87.2
62.5	78.0	70.1	88.1	87.2	92.8	20.0	33.4	94.9	98.4
60.7	85.9	65.5	92.1	75.9	90.3	17.5	30.5	83.5	94.4
–	83.8	–	64.8	–	84.2	–	23.9	–	57.6
77.6	82.4	64.3	68.9	63.3	73.6	25.9	32.5	90.0	89.8
66.7	56.0	43.7	56.5	76.1	84.0	23.4	25.1	83.7	80.1
90.5	94.5	71.7	87.7	81.5	86.6	22.8	26.3	81.7	90.7
86.1	95.5	69.9	89.7	82.8	91.9	13.9	14.6	81.3	88.8
83.8	77.7	83.0	80.7	81.9	80.6	15.5	19.8	74.6	76.3

Table 8.14. *Percentage of Students in Populations II and IV Claiming Frequent Participation in English Activities*

Item	Belgium (Fr.)		Chile		FRG		Finland		Hungary	
	II	IV	II	IV	II	IV	II	IV	II	IV
1	5.1	4.8	–	5.7	0.9	6.0	2.1	6.6	–	9.7
2	21.4	19.8	–	15.3	11.3	17.8	52.6	59.3	–	31.4
3	8.9	4.7	–	6.8	5.0	12.7	2.5	4.6	–	7.8
4	9.2	9.6	–	5.4	9.7	16.5	12.3	12.3	–	20.1
5	1.1	0.3	–	3.3	0.4	1.1	0.7	1.2	–	8.5
6	4.2	5.6	–	3.7	1.6	12.2	1.7	6.4	–	3.4

Table 8.15. *Student Perception of the Utility of English; Percentage of Students Responding Negatively and Positively—Population II*

Items ...	1		2		3		4		5		6	
Country	B	A	B	A	B	A	B	A	B	A	B	A
Belgium (Fr.)	1.4	87.9	21.9	48.8	64.7	14.6	23.6	55.4	14.7	50.0	3.4	84.7
FRG	5.0	69.1	28.7	56.5	30.7	47.4	38.5	38.1	15.9	51.2	5.0	83.1
Finland	9.3	55.2	11.7	59.2	26.1	46.4	35.4	36.2	10.0	62.8	6.1	76.2
Israel	1.7	83.7	18.5	67.2	25.1	55.9	19.6	55.8	10.6	61.1	3.5	86.7
Italy	4.1	72.7	29.1	57.1	28.4	50.0	17.9	65.8	17.6	45.6	4.8	88.3
Netherlands	3.1	75.4	17.2	60.6	48.3	27.2	47.9	28.8	30.9	31.7	6.7	82.5
Sweden	3.6	73.0	11.0	70.9	15.8	59.5	38.8	33.5	16.7	45.8	3.7	84.3
Thailand	0.8	88.1	17.2	73.8	4.8	89.3	8.3	77.0	12.6	56.4	1.6	90.6

Note: (A) indicates agreement or strong agreement with statement constituting the item. (B) indicates disagreement or strong disagreement with statement constituting the item. The middle term of the scale 'Uncertainty' is omitted and the percentage responding to this can be inferred.

srael		Italy		Netherlands		Sweden		Thailand	
I	IV	IV	II	II	IV	IV	II	II	IV
0.4	9.7	2.9	2.7	1.9	8.1	2.5	8.8	4.6	5.7
1.1	53.7	5.6	8.6	70.1	68.7	54.1	54.0	11.8	6.6
7.9	15.5	3.7	6.7	4.2	9.8	3.6	7.3	6.3	4.1
1.2	18.1	6.5	10.3	6.5	14.7	10.0	16.3	2.2	2.8
2.6	2.4	0.9	1.0	0.2	0.4	1.0	0.8	4.9	6.5
6.9	9.3	3.8	3.4	2.7	7.8	4.3	17.2	1.1	0.4

		8		9		10		11		12	
	A	B	A	B	A	B	A	B	A	B	A
7.5	76.0	49.5	31.2	41.4	37.0	90.7	4.3	48.9	15.8	10.9	61.5
8.7	72.7	43.7	35.2	15.3	67.0	57.4	24.8	25.3	28.4	10.3	62.0
0.5	68.2	57.6	11.3	32.7	35.2	36.6	39.9	51.7	11.7	12.8	47.5
4.7	77.9	39.5	28.2	25.6	42.8	52.0	24.1	68.8	12.2	24.7	43.5
5.2	83.3	19.9	55.3	12.0	72.0	74.4	15.1	31.5	34.4	5.6	85.0
1.7	52.6	7.6	75.6	25.1	49.8	34.7	46.8	50.2	11.0	19.4	46.9
4.4	84.7	16.3	46.9	25.7	48.2	53.8	27.7	60.6	7.7	16.4	44.1
4.1	77.2	27.9	52.0	8.9	66.0	51.4	30.0	24.9	43.0	6.8	75.0

Table 8.16. *Student Perception of the Utility of English; Percentage of Students Respondin* *Negatively and Positively—Population IV*

Items ...	1		2		3		4		5		6	
Country	B	A	B	A	B	A	B	A	B	A	B	A
Belgium (Fr)	3.2	89.1	33.2	47.4	70.4	15.9	23.4	55.9	25.4	42.0	3.9	86.2
Chile	9.4	64.1	17.4	67.3	18.1	71.3	18.0	65.8	18.7	53.4	8.3	78.7
FRG	1.3	89.5	40.0	53.9	52.7	35.7	24.5	61.4	25.5	48.2	2.9	90.9
Finland	8.7	61.9	16.0	75.5	37.9	51.4	24.2	59.8	9.1	68.0	2.0	91.
Hungary	11.9	46.9	66.7	24.3	97.7	0.6	14.9	63.2	9.5	66.9	3.6	85.
Israel	1.4	81.9	13.8	74.8	16.9	67.4	16.5	61.6	10.6	62.7	1.1	89.9
Italy	4.6	77.4	39.0	50.0	49.6	37.9	19.0	66.6	23.6	37.7	2.5	91.8
Netherlands	4.0	78.5	23.4	63.9	60.1	29.8	28.1	53.0	26.7	31.9	6.1	83.8
Sweden	5.3	75.4	32.9	52.5	29.5	52.5	27.7	50.0	17.3	46.1	2.2	90.7
Thailand	0.9	91.8	22.6	71.0	4.1	92.8	5.6	76.4	15.7	47.2	1.7	89.4

Note: (A) indicates agreement or strong agreement with statement which constitutes the ite (B) indicates disagreement or strong disagreement with statement. The middle term of t scale 'Uncertainty' is omitted from the table and the percentage responding to this can inferred.

		8		9		10		11		12	
B	A	B	A	B	A	B	A	B	A	B	A
0	30.1	0.0	93.0	0.0	51.0	0.0	93.6	0.0	98.8	0.0	98.3
0	48.5	0.0	89.1	0.0	90.1	0.0	95.6	0.0	97.0	0.0	96.7
0	11.6	0.0	96.9	0.0	66.2	0.0	99.5	0.0	98.4	0.0	98.9
0	7.8	0.0	97.3	0.0	69.4	0.0	98.2	0.0	99.7	0.0	99.5
0	35.3	0.0	97.1	0.0	75.9	0.0	82.1	0.0	99.7	0.0	99.2
0	30.6	0.0	94.5	0.0	66.5	0.0	96.1	0.0	99.5	0.0	99.7
0	43.5	0.0	96.4	0.0	74.6	0.0	91.3	0.0	99.4	0.0	98.9
0	12.3	0.0	97.0	0.0	73.6	0.0	97.6	0.0	98.3	0.0	98.4
0	9.9	0.0	98.4	0.0	85.4	0.0	97.4	0.0	94.7	0.0	99.2
0	19.1	0.0	94.8	0.0	80.0	0.0	91.4	0.0	99.6	0.0	99.0

Chapter 9

Factors Associated with Individual Student Differences in Achievement in English: The Regression Analyses[1]

What accounts for differences in achievement in English as a foreign language? It was to this basic question that the investigators addressed themselves. Since English as a foreign language is chiefly a school-based subject area, it was expected that the influence of the school and its teachers would be of considerable importance. However, the effects of influences outside the school are not to be overlooked.

To determine the extent to which achievement in English could be predicted, it was determined to use regression analysis. *An Empirical Study of Education in Twenty-One Countries: A Technical Report* (Volume VIII in the series of reports concerned with the IEA Six Subject Survey) by Gilbert Peaker describes in detail the technical and methodological aspects of the data analysis. In addition, *The IEA Six Subject Survey: An Empirical Study of Education in Twenty-One Countries* (Volume IX in the series) by David Walker presents a general summary of the data analysis. What follows here is intended to be a brief and relatively nontechnical description of the procedures used in analyzing the English as a Foreign Language data in order to give those who are not statistical specialists a general idea of some of the problems and the conduct of the analysis as related specifically to this area of the survey.

PLANNING THE ANALYSIS

The Unit of Analysis

It was decided that the student was to be the unit of analysis. This could be undertaken in two ways. First, the analysis could determine what factors were associated with differences between the individual

---

[1] This chapter was written by Carolyn Emrick Massad of the Educational Testing Service.

student's achievement score in English and the mean achievement score of the students in the school he attended. This would be an investigation of students within schools. However, because such an analysis is not concerned with differences between-schools and since it is not likely that each school in every country provides the same educational environment for all its students, this form of analysis was not used.

The second approach, that of between-students across the total sample within each country, was preferred. In such an analysis each student is assigned the school mean scores for the variables describing the school and the teachers within the school he attends, but he retains his own individual scores for those variables characterizing him as an individual. For each country relationships are then examined between the school, teacher, and student measures but with the student as the unit of analysis. It should be noted, however, that the variations in the school environment may be underestimated since the mean school and teacher scores were used.

Strategy of the Analysis

For the study of English as a Foreign Language, as well as the other areas in the IEA Six Subject Survey, the regression analysis was carried out in stages by adding *blocks of variables* in an order that would reflect the chronology of impact upon the student. The principle underlying the use of blocks is that events occurring early in one's life history may determine later events, but the later events cannot influence the earlier events.

The *home variables* are outside the control of the school but do determine the kind of input available with which the school can work. Because the child comes to school from a home environment which has influenced his previous learning, it is necessary to take this into consideration before examining the effects of other predictor variables on achievement in English. For this reason, Block 1 in the regression analysis includes the home circumstances together with the sex of the student (determined even before birth). However, since there are no direct measures of home circumstances available, surrogates were used to form a compound variable which came to be labeled as the School Handicap Score. The six variables[2] used to comprise this score were: Father's occupation, Father's education, Mother's education, Number of books in the home, Size of family, Use of the dictionary in the home. The integer weights used for forming

271

the composite School Handicap Score were the same as those determined by Gilbert Peaker for the other subject areas in the IEA Six Subject Survey.

To arrive at the weights, the six variables in the composite were entered in regression analyses with Reading Comprehension, Science and Literature as the criteria. The averages of these weights were calculated and rounded to give integer values which were then used for combining the six variables to form the composite. The process of averaging across criteria and rounding was designed to give maximum stability and generality to the weights. It is to be noted that this was developed using Population II data and was applied without modification to Population IV, the reason being that Population II appeared to be the more heterogeneous group, and therefore the more representative of the country. However, since English as a foreign language—unlike the three subject matter areas used to determine the weights—often is not part of the required curriculum which inevitably restricts the English population of a country and the sample in a way not common to the other three areas, future research might well include a re-evaluation of the appropriateness of the weights used to form the composite School Handicap Score for the analysis of the English data.

It should be noted that it was found necessary to use the process of criterion scaling (Beaton, 1969) for Father's occupation because of substantial proportions of unclassifiable and missing responses as well as the fact that in some countries a validated occupational scale was not available and classifications used were arbitrary. Since criterion scaling for Father's occupation had also already been done for the Reading Comprehension, Science and Literature studies, the same scales, when available, were used for the English data analyses. Here the criterion employed for scaling Father's occupation was the Reading Comprehension measure, using unweighted corrected student scores at Population II. However, in some instances it was necessary to calculate Father's occupation scales for the English data analyses. When this was done, the Word Knowledge measure was used if it was available and if it led to sensible results. Otherwise, the English Reading achievement score was used.

Block 2 in the analysis was comprised of *Type of school and Type of program* since these variables provide an index of the student's learning experiences received prior to the time of the survey. In some instances parents have been able to select the student's school and/or program while in other instances the school has selected the student and/or determined his type of course or program. In yet other cases where there is a comprehensive school structure, all students from a given area may attend the same school and may or may not follow the same type of program. As a result, it was necessary to take into consideration the nature of the school and program or course in which the student was enrolled. The Type of school variable came from the sampling design of the IEA Six Subject Survey in which the schools were stratified according to type. The Type of program variable resulted from the process of criterion scaling. Because some countries found it impossible to set up an appropriate classification scheme for type of program and others developed a system of classification with a preponderance of students in one category, the criterion scaling was used. The criterion scaling allowed for a suitable scale to be developed and as well enabled the missing and unclassifiable data to be treated in an appropriate way.

Four *time variables* comprised Block 3: Years studied English, Grade (in which the student was currently enrolled), Grade beginning English and Age. These variables are interdependent and also related to the school in that they are greatly dependent upon school policy decisions, e.g., the grade at which English as a foreign language is to be first introduced. Despite the fact that these time factors are school related, it was felt that they should be entered in the regression analysis prior to the school variables in order to determine the impact of the non-time-factor school variables on achievement.

Block 4 included *school-related variables,* that is, those variables that characterized the conditions under which the student was learning at the time of the survey. These conditions include learning both at school and when doing lessons at home. Because the variables in this block are specifically thought of as school-learning variables, they are generally referred to in this chapter as the school variables and include the following:

- Total auxiliary staff, including school librarian, foreign language
    assistants, foreign language laboratory technician (SQ)
- Classes conducted in English (SQ)
- Students select English as a subject (SQ)
- Total time English taught per week at
    Beginning level
    Intermediate level
    Advanced level (SQ)
- Hours per week teacher spends marking papers (TQ)

- Sex of teacher (TQ)
- Teacher teaching other foreign languages in addition to English (TQ)
- Teacher's perceived skill for
    listening
    speaking
    reading
    writing
    pronunciation (TQ)
- Time teacher resided or studied in an English-speaking country (TQ)
- Years teacher taught a (any) foreign language (TQ)
- Method of teaching grammar (TQ)
- Hours per week student spends doing homework in all subjects (PQ)
- Student sometimes speaks English to the teacher in the classroom (PQ)
- Student listens to the teacher sometimes speak English in the classroom (PQ)
- Student writes exercises in English in the classroom (PQ)
- Student sometimes reads English for pleasure in the classroom (PQ)

These variables are based upon the school (SQ), teacher (TQ), and student (PQ) questionnaires, and the sources for each are indicated in the parentheses following each variable.

Kindred variables comprised Block 5. These variables are those attitudes and practices—all based upon student responses to questionnaires—that were related to achievement, but whose causal influence was partly in doubt. That is, the school and/or home might well affect these variables, e.g., the educational level a student expects to attain might well be determined by his parents' attitudes and desires as well as by his school achievement record. The kindred variables include the following:

- Hours per week student spends doing English homework
- Student's expected education
- Like school scale
- Student's aspiration to
    speak English
    understand English
    read English
    write English

274

- Frequency student is exposed to English, including reading books, seeing movies and television programs, listening to radio programs
- Interest in English scale
- English activities outside of school scale
- Perceived utility of English scale

Since information was available on several hundred different measures, the choice of variables for inclusion in Blocks 4 and 5 of the regression analysis was not simple. To select these variables, several steps were followed. In the first step, the variables of English Reading and English Listening (where available) were selected as the criterion variables, as measures of success or achievement in English. These variables were selected because the greatest number of students in each national sample took the achievement tests in Reading and Listening. In fact, the entire national sample in each country took the Reading test.

For the second step, standardized partial regression coefficients of each criterion variable on each of the remaining variables—the predictor or independent variables—with the School Handicap Score partialled out were determined. These partial regression coefficients were displayed visually for each population with the values for each country being plotted on a single scale. These plots enabled the investigators to see, after having controlled for the School Handicap Score, which variables were related to a criterion in more than one country. To pick the final set of predictor variables for the regression analysis, lists were made of those student predictors which had a partial coefficient greater than 0.1 and those school and teacher predictors which had a partial coefficient greater than 0.2 in at least two countries having the coefficient with the same sign (positive or negative) or at least three countries having the coefficient vary in sign (both positive and negative). These lists were then shortened using the following guidelines:

1. Predictors where low reliabilities had been calculated were omitted.
2. Where more than 20 % of the data was missing, the variable was left out.
3. The criterion of sensibility was used, in that some variables of particular importance, as viewed by the investigators in terms of past research and experience in the field, were included in spite of

the small partial regression coefficients. It was felt that the inclusion of such variables added meaningfulness to the analysis.

The same list of variables was used for each population with the exception of the three variables in Block 4 entitled Total time English taught per week. The Total time—beginning level and Total time—intermediate level were used only for Population II analyses while the Total time—advanced level was used only for Population IV analyses. The reason for this was that few schools with Population II students had data available for the Total time—advanced level, and few schools with Population IV students had data available for the Total time—beginning and intermediate levels.

Block 6, the last block, contained the score on the Word Knowledge test. Although this is generally looked upon as a surrogate of *intellectual ability,* being a verbal aptitude test in the student's mother tongue, it was not entered until last in the regression analysis because it was a test taken at the same time as the other cognitive tests and did not precede them on the time scale. Further, it is likely that the scores on the Word Knowledge test are somewhat affected by school learning.

The Regression Analysis

As has been noted, the regression analysis followed the procedure of adding six blocks of variables successively in an order that would reflect the chronology of impact upon the student. Of course, this is not the only valid way of examining the data and it is hoped that future research, including the use of other approaches to the regression analysis as well as other methods of data analysis, will provide greater knowledge concerning these data which are part of an IEA data bank.

Within each block in the regression analysis a step-wise procedure was used. That is, for each block the variables were allowed to enter the regression equation in the order in which they contributed to a reduction in the unexplained variance. The method of regression analysis depends on wide variation (variance) in both the predictor and criterion variables to allow the relationship between them to be estimated at all accurately. To limit the entry of variables into the regression equation an F-test was applied, and only variables with F-values above 2.0 were allowed to enter. Such a low F value was used to permit a search for variables with coefficients of the same sign (although they might well be small) that appeared in the regression equation in as many countries as possible rather than to attempt to identify statistically significant variables in only a few countries. As has been indicated earlier in this volume, the main intention of the investigators has been to draw inferences from the general results across countries rather than to emphasize the results in any one country. National Centers will be reporting the results of particular significance in their countries.

As blocks are added in the regression analysis, the achievement of a student is divided into two parts, (1) the part predicted by that block as well as any others preceding it and (2) a residue. The residue represents the effects of all the unmeasured variables to that point of time in the analysis. As each block is added, the predicted part (multiple correlation or R) becomes larger and the residue smaller.

After the addition of each block, the multiple correlation and the percentage of predicted variance added by the block were determined. Further, the percent of total variance accounted for by all six blocks was also determined. For some countries, the percentage of total variance accounted for is quite high while in others it is relatively low. Where it is low, it may be that there are many unmeasured variables yet to be accounted for in predicting student achievement in English or that the instruments used in this survey were not such that they completely or adequately reflected the variables derived from them in a universal manner across countries.

In the section that follows, the results of the regression analysis will be examined in terms of the contributions of the blocks with comments on the contributions of specific variables. Where the pattern of prediction is radically different in one country as compared to the pattern in others, an attempt will be made to seek plausible explanations for the difference.

RESULTS OF THE ANALYSIS

It is to be noted that although Israel did participate in the English as a Foreign Language study, and some Israeli data have been cited earlier in this volume, gaps in the data dealing with school and teacher variables pertinent to the regression analyses were so great that the results and discussion of the regression analyses for Israel are excluded.

Tables 9.1 through 9.4 present a summary of results of the regression analyses for both populations. As has been indicated, the criterion variables selected were English Reading and English Listening (where available).

Correlation coefficients for all variables which were included in the regression analyses are not presented here because of space limitations. However, correlation coefficients for some of the variables in the regression analyses can be found in the earlier section of this volume in which the relationships of selected variables with Reading and Listening achievement are discussed.

Total Variance Accounting for Achievement

With English reading as the criterion, regression analyses were carried out for seven countries with both Population II and IV students as well as for two more countries having only Population IV students taking part in the study. Because fewer countries had data available for English listening than for English reading, regression analyses with English listening as the criterion were carried out for only four countries with both Population II and IV students and for the two countries where only Population IV students participated. As was seen earlier in the case of the correlation coefficients for selected variables, there are appreciable variations from country to country as well as between populations in the regression analyses. However, certain general trends do stand out.

With respect to the regression analyses using English reading as the criterion, it appears that the variables entered in the six blocks accounted for more of the total variance for achievement at the Population II level than at the Population IV level. The median values for percentages of total variance accounted for by all blocks are 55.7 % and 42.0 % for Populations II and IV respectively. In general, the exceptions being Italy and Thailand, the variables in the regression analyses for Population II account for over half the variation in English reading achievement, whereas for Population IV this is true only in Italy.

When English listening is used as the criterion, the median values of variance accounted for are 47.0 % and 45.3 % for Populations II and IV respectively. Unlike the regression analyses with English reading as the criterion, the variables entered for Population II account for less than half the variation in English listening achievement, except for Finland. For Population IV, there appears to be no general trend, but note should be made of the Swedish results. In Sweden, 95.1 % of the variation in English listening achievement of Population IV students is accounted for by the variables in the regression analyses, half by the Kindred variables alone.

Block 1, which is intended to represent home circumstances and sex, appears to be of greater importance for Population II than for Population IV. For Population II, in terms of the percentage of English reading and listening variance accounted for by this block, it is generally second in importance. Block 2 usually contributes more to the total variance accounted for in the various countries. Looking at all analyses, both the School Handicap Score and Sex consistently show positive weights across countries and populations, the only exception being for two of the Population IV analyses where the Sex variable has a negative weight. Why these two were the exception is uncertain, but girls from Population IV in Chile do not follow the general pattern of excelling boys on English reading, nor do girls from Population IV in Hungary follow the general pattern of doing better than boys on English listening.

As indicated, of greater importance at the Population II level than at the Population IV level is Block 2, representing Type of school and Type of program. Further, for both populations this block tends to account for more variation in English reading than in English listening scores. In four of the seven countries with Population II students, this block contributes most to account for the variation in achievement in English reading. The importance of Type of school and Type of program for the Population II students is to be expected since generally there is greater variation in these variables for Population II than for Population IV. The general trend seems to be for the Population IV students to attend "academic" types of schools. Furthermore, even when they are in other types of schools, such as the comprehensive schools, Population IV students of English are likely to be in "academic" programs. Type of school is the more consistently entering variable of the two in the block, Type of program entering less frequently. It is to be noted that in Sweden Type of school does not even enter the regression analysis for Population II students since there is only one type of school at this level. However, it does enter for Population IV students since some of these attend vocational/technical schools, although most (90 %) are in a type of school that provides a variety of course. The only case in which Type of school shows a negative weight is for the Population IV students in Thailand, in the analysis using English Reading as the criterion. The fact that the majority of schools in the sample have only an academic type of program, raising the possibility that a greater number of less able students may be found in such schools, may be one explanation for this result. Another explanation might be that the curricular emphasis is not on English reading but rather tends to be on English listening comprehension, as has been noted in the chapter on teacher characteristics.

As expected, Block 3, which is comprised of time factors, tends to contribute substantially to the prediction of English reading and listening scores. Variation in scores both within and between countries and populations may be accounted for by the amount of time the student has spent studying English. Countries vary in their educational policies: they differ in the average amount of time allotted to English and the grade at which students may begin studying English. The variation in scores, then, may be viewed as a reflection of the variations in educational policy rather than evidence that some countries are superior to others because of the way in which English is taught. Yet, many other factors enter into the prediction of English reading and listening scores and some of these other factors may be more important than some time factors.

Taking Sweden as a case in point, it can be seen from reviewing the results of the univariate analyses, presented in the tables in the chapter on school characteristics, that in terms of the number of minutes devoted to teaching English per week Sweden would rank quite low—in fact, lowest—for beginning and advanced courses. Yet looking at the mean scores for English reading, presented in the chapter dealing with some aspects of student performance, Sweden ranks quite high as compared with other countries. Obviously, factors other than this time factor are operating. One time factor that does appear to be operating in Sweden is the number of years English is studied. The tables in Chapter 8 on student characteristics as well as the figure giving mean scores and range of years studied English in Chapter 4, both based on univariate analyses, show that the Swedish students tend to have studied English for a greater number of years than those in other countries in the survey. However, for the regression analyses in Sweden, Years studied English is not a strong factor at the Population IV level. For these students some relatively strong kindred variables, such as Interest in English, Frequent exposure to English, Aspiration to speak, read and write English, are operating. It would appear that the Years studied English may no longer be as strong a contributor to the prediction of English reading and listening scores as these other factors are. Further analysis of the survey data and more research are certainly needed to fully comprehend the situation in Sweden as well as in the other countries.

However, with the exception of Population IV in Sweden, the Years studied English consistently appears in the analyses for all countries. Further, this variable shows positive weights in all cases but one, thus indicating that in general, the greater the number of years a student studies English, the better he performs on the achievement tests. The case in which Years studied English shows a negative weight is for the Population IV students in Chile with English listening as the criterion. This is difficult to explain, particularly since Chile does not have Population II students on which to base a comparison. It may be that achievement in English reading is of greater importance than is achievement in English listening, although the information obtained from the univariate analyses does not appear to indicate that this would be the case. It would seem that the situation calls for a more complex explanation that the National Center will have to deal with in its report.

For Population II students, Grade, consistently showing positive weights, generally appears to contribute to the total variance accounted for by Block 3. The higher the grade, the better tend to be the English reading and listening achievement scores for Population II students in general. However, Grade is not an entering variable in the regression analyses for Population IV students, the Netherlands being the only exception. This lack of influence of Grade as a predictor of achievement for Population IV students is not unexpected since Population II students generally represent a wider range of grade levels than do those who are in Population IV.

Grade beginning English enters the analyses for some countries, but the direction of the weights is not consistent from country to country or population to population. Age tends to be a strong factor only for Population IV students and consistently shows a negative relationship with achievement in English reading in all countries except Hungary where it did not enter the analysis. The general implication is that the better performing students tend to be the younger ones in the Population IV sample. In examining the mean age and standard deviations for age of students across countries, it is obvious that, again with the exception of students in Hungary, Population IV tends to be comprised mostly of 17 to 19-year-olds. In Hungary, the students appear to center around 18 years of age. It may be that for countries other than Hungary, the older students are repeaters or slower learning than the younger ones, which may account for their tendency to have a lower level of achievement as compared with the younger students in the sample. For many, English is the second foreign language, and others had ceased to study English.

Block 4, composed of those variables characterizing school-related learning conditions, tends to account for the greatest percentage of variance in English Reading and Listening scores for the Population IV students. The median values are 15.2 % and 25.4 % for English reading and listening respectively. For the Population II students, this block accounts for a considerable amount of the variance in scores but is much less important than for the Population IV students. Perhaps this reflects the fact that Population IV students have spent more time in school than those in Population II and, therefore, may be more sensitive to the effects of the school variables than are Population II students. Further, it might be expected that for an almost entirely school-learned subject like English, Population IV students who have been in school longer and possibly studied English longer than those in Population II would be more influenced by the factors (school) that characterize the place where that subject is learned. The variables entering the regression analyses and the direction in which they are weighted to predict achievement are listed in Tables 9.5 and 9.6.

For the analyses with English reading as the criterion, the most consistently appearing variables, both across countries and populations, are those that are concerned with student activities in the classroom: Student sometimes speaks English to the teacher, Student writes exercises in English, and Student sometimes reads English for pleasure. These generally carry positive weights, implying that such activities tend to lead to greater achievement in English reading. None of the other variables is entirely consistent from country to country or population to population in the sign of its weight, and a number divide almost evenly between positive and negative weights. The most consistent for Population II are the Students select English as a subject, Teacher's perceived listening skill, and Years teacher taught a foreign language. These all tend to have more positive than negative weights. For Population IV, the most consistent variables are Total auxiliary staff, Classes conducted in English, Teacher's perceived speaking skill, Time teacher resided or studied in an English-speaking country, and Years teacher taught a foreign language. As with Population II, these variables tend to have more positive than negative weights.

When English listening is a criterion, there tends to be inconsistency from country to country and from population to population regarding the direction in which the variables are weighted. For Population II, the most consistent variable with a positive weight is Student writes exercises in English in the classroom. The most consistent variables with positive weights for Population IV are Total auxiliary staff, Time teacher resided or studied in an English-speaking country, Years teacher taught a foreign language, and Teacher's perceived reading skill—which seems to indicate specialized teaching at this level. It is interesting to note that the Teacher's perceived reading skill generally carries a negative weight for Population II. Why this is so is uncertain; nor is it clear why the Student listens to the teacher sometimes speak English in the classroom carries a negative weight for two of the four Population II countries and three of the six Population IV countries. However, that the Teacher teaching other foreign language(s) in addition to English carries a negative weight in four of the six Population IV countries is not surprising. This may be due to the fact that the teacher of English may have another language as her "first teaching language," or that when one must teach more than one language at a time chances of being proficient in any one of them may not be as high as if one taught only a single language.

It appears that the general conclusion regarding Block 4 must be that although the variables collectively account for a considerable proportion of the variance in the English reading and listening scores, the general inconsistency in the behavior of the variables from country to country and population to population leaves very little to be said regarding the general trend for the prediction of achievement. Only with regard to achievement in English reading can it be said that a general trend appears to exist. In the case of English reading, it would seem that students speaking English, writing exercises in English, and reading in English for pleasure, all classroom activities, tend to lead to higher achievement. Encountering the same consistent and strong predictors of achievement for both English reading and listening might have been a surprise, since one might expect certain variables to be more important for predicting achievement in English reading and certain other variables to be more important for predicting achievement in English listening. Perhaps the instruments of this study were not refined enough to entirely answer the questions concerning which variables serve as the best predictors of achievement for each of the four aspects of language learning—listening comprehension, speaking, reading and writing. Certainly more research in this area is needed. When the National Centers examine their data from this survey, they may be able to provide some clues as to the best way to approach further research studies and which variables appear to be the most promising predictors.

Block 5, consisting of the kindred variables, tends to be of greater importance for Population IV than for Population II. Again, this is not really surprising since these variables represent attitudes and practices related to achievement and Population IV students have certainly had more time and opportunity than those in Population II to develop well-established attitudes and practices to affect their achievement. The kindred variables to enter the regression analyses and the direction in which they are weighted to predict are given in Tables 9.5 and 9.6, along with the variables that entered in Block 4.

For the analyses using English reading as the criterion, there are two consistent variables both across countries and populations: Student's expected education and Interest in English scale. Both of these variables have positive weights, implying that the greater the number of years a student expects to further his education and the greater his interest in learning English, the greater tends to be his achievement in English reading. The other variables entering the analyses tend to be inconsistent from population to population, and frequently from country to country. Of these variables, the one that consistently receives positive weights whenever it enters the analyses for Population II students is Student's aspiration to understand English. For Population IV students, there are two variables that consistently carry positive weights in the analyses in four of the nine countries: Student's aspiration to read English and English activities outside of school. The implication is that the higher these aspirations and/or activities, the greater tends to be the achievement. It is interesting to note that for some Population II students a rather important variable is to understand English, considered by many the first step in language acquisition, while for some Population IV students an important variable is to read English, which is considered by many to come later than *understanding* in the language learning process. It should be further noted that Student's Aspiration to Speak English has a positive weight when it appears in the analyses; there is only one exception to this and that is in the Population II analyses.

When English listening is used as the criterion, the most consistent variables across countries and populations are Student's aspiration to understand English and the English activities outside of school scale, both having positive weights. Two other important variables for both populations of students are the Student's aspiration to read English and the Interest in English scale. These variables tend to have positive weights, but for each there is one exception to this in the Population II analyses. The overall impression is that aspiring to understand and read English, having an interest in English and participating in English activities outside the classroom tend to result in greater achievement in English listening.

In considering a general trend for Block 5, Interest in English appears to be the only relatively consistent predictor for both English reading and listening. This implies that motivation might be a strong factor in learning English.

One would expect variables related to student aspirations to learn English, the Interest in English scale, the Perceived utility of English scale, and the Number of hours per week student spends doing English homework to behave in a somewhat similar manner, as they all tend to be generally considered as possible indicators of motivation to learn English. It may be noted in the Tables 9.5 and 9.6 that two variables, the Hours per week student spends doing English homework and the Perceived utility of English scale, tend to carry negative weights in the analyses they enter, whether the criterion is English reading or listening. However, since the tendency for these variables is for negative standardized partial regression coefficients that are very small to be recorded at the same time as positive correlation coefficients, there is a question as to whether or not these variables do predict in the direction in which they are weighted in the regression analyses. The fact that they enter the analyses at all may be due to the very low F value used, the reason for using such a low F value having been discussed earlier. It is to be further noted here that because of the low F value, and the occurrence sometimes of mixed signs (both a positive and a negative sign, one for the standardized partial regression coefficient and the other for the correlation coefficient), caution needs to be taken (and was in this report) in interpreting results that may appear to be questionable in some countries or for some populations. Reports from the National Centers will be helpful in providing further direction. Also, future analyses and research are called for where the results appear doubtful.

Block 6, containing only Word Knowledge,[3] is the least important block in the regression analyses for both Populations. However, with both English reading and listening used as the criterion measures, achievement on the Word Knowledge test appears to be a good predictor of achievement in English reading and listening. This is not surprising, since both the English tests and the Word Knowledge Test deal with achievement in the "verbal domain."

SUMMARY

A quantity of detail has been presented on the variables in the home, in the school, and other current characteristics of students that are associated with student achievement on English reading and listening measures. An attempt to summarize the findings therefore seems appropriate.

Although there are appreciable variations from country to country, certain general trends stand out. First, the data about the home environment allow a fairly good prediction of a 14-year old student's achievement in English reading and listening. However, the ability of these variables to predict achievement for a student at the end of secondary education falls considerably. This may be a result of selection processes on the basis of academic ability and/or economic level which tend to take place in many countries. However, since English students generally may be in a somewhat select group to begin with, and since the variables related to school characteristics and student attitudes and practices are very important predictors of achievement for students at the end of secondary school, it is more likely that the effects of schooling well outweigh home background factors in predicting achievement for the older students who are learning a subject that is generally learned only at school.

For 14-year olds, placement by type of school or program seems to be an important predictor of achievement. Again, however, this is not the case for the group at the end of secondary education. It seems reasonable to think that this may result from the tendency of 14-year olds to be in various kinds of schools or programs where a factor of placement could be important, whereas the older students who take English tend to be concentrated in academic type programs to which they have been admitted on the basis of past achievement or ability.

As expected, the amount of time a student has studied English seems to be an important predictor of achievement in English reading and listening. National policy frequently plays a major role in determining the amount of time allotted to English in the curriculum as well as the grade at which the study of English may begin, and, to this extent, achievement is likely to reflect the policy decisions.

Although the school factors collectively are very important for students at the end of secondary school, very little consistent pattern is found in the data. For both populations, certain variables do emerge in a few countries, often predicting in the positive direction in some but in the negative direction in others. However, certain classroom activities such as speaking and writing English as well as reading English for pleasure tend to lead to higher achievement in English Reading.

Of the other current characteristics of students, the kindred variables, which like the school variables are important predictors collectively for the older students but not for the 14-year-olds, only a motivational factor tends to emerge as a consistent predictor. Having an interest in English tends to lead to higher achievement in both English reading and listening.

Finally, Word Knowledge tends to be a predictor of achievement in English although it is the least important of the groups of variables in the regression analyses.

The results reported in this chapter should be looked at as only a beginning in a series of analyses and further research in the areas under study here. Reports of the National Centers, further analyses of the data collected in the Data Bank as well as additional research studies will certainly contribute more to providing guidance for the improvement of the educational enterprise.

REFERENCE

Beaton, A. E. "Some Mathematical and Empirical Properties of Criterion Scaled Variables." In G. W. Mayeske *et.al.*, *A Study of Our Nation's Schools*. Washington, U.S. Department of Health, Education and Welfare, 1969.

NOTES

[2] In the case of Sweden, only four variables could be used. The two excluded were Father's education and Mother's education due to ambiguities in the wording of questions for these variables.

[3] It is to be noted that in Belgium, there is no Word Knowledge score available; therefore, the Belgian analyses have only five blocks for the regression analyses.

Table 9.1. *Multiple Correlations and Added Percentages of Variance for the Reading Regression Six Blocks of Variables.—Population II*

Blocks	Belgium (Fr.)	FRG	Finland	Italy	Netherlands	Sweden	Thailand
1—School Handicap Score and Sex							
R	.38	.39	.51	.11	.33	.35	.29
% Added Variance	14.2	15.1	25.7	1.2	10.6	12.5	8.2
2—Type of School and Program							
R	.59	.68	.81	.30	.79	.35	.31
% Added Variance	21.0	30.7	40.4	7.5	51.7	0.0	1.4
3—Time Factors							
R	.65	.77	.85	.38	.84	.46	.49
% Added Variance	6.5	14.0	5.8	5.4	8.4	8.6	14.5
4—School Variables							
R	.72	.85	.86	.52	.85	.50	.58
% Added Variance	9.8	13.0	2.2	13.2	2.1	4.2	9.9
5—Kindred Variables							
R	.75	.87	.88	.55	.87	.68	.67
% Added Variance	5.5	3.2	3.2	2.8	2.6	21.5	10.3
6—Word Knowledge							
R	.75	.89	.88	.60	.88	.74	.69
% Added Variance	0.0	2.5	0.9	6.0	2.1	7.6	2.8
% Total Variance Accounted for	57.0	78.5	78.2	36.1	77.5	54.4	47.1

Table 9.2. *Multiple Correlations and Added Percentages of Variance for the Listening Regression Six Blocks of Variables—Population II*

Blocks	Belgium (Fr.)	Finland	Italy	Sweden
1—School Handicap Score and Sex				
R	.33	.52	.05	.34
% Added Variance	11.0	27.3	0.3	11.6
2—Type of School and Program				
R	.46	.77	.34	.34
% Added Variance	10.5	32.7	11.0	0.0
3—Time Factors				
R	.50	.81	.37	.44
% Added Variance	3.5	5.6	2.5	7.5
4—School Variables				
R	.66	.82	.51	.48
% Added Variance	18.1	1.8	12.6	4.1
5—Kindred Variables				
R	.68	.84	.53	.64
% Added Variance	3.8	3.0	1.5	17.5
6—Word Knowledge				
R	.68	.84	.54	.69
% Added Variance	0.0	0.8	1.5	6.3
% Total Variance Accounted for	46.9	71.2	29.4	47.0

Table 9.3. *Multiple Correlations and Added Percentages of Variance for the Reading Regression Six Blocks of Variables—Population IV*

Blocks	Belgium (Fr.)	Chile	FRG	Finland	Hungary	Italy	Netherlands	Sweden	Th... la...
1—School Handicap Score and Sex									
R	.24	.29	.10	.21	.17	.41	.08	.18	
% Added Variance	6.0	8.2	1.0	4.3	2.9	16.4	0.6	3.1	1
2—Type of School and Program									
R	.31	.41	.12	.21	.39	.69	.13	.48	
% Added Variance	3.4	8.5	0.5	0.2	12.7	30.8	1.2	19.5	
3—Time Factors									
R	.45	.46	.30	.49	.42	.73	.21	.49	
% Added Variance	10.7	4.7	7.5	19.3	2.1	5.8	2.8	1.5	
4—School Variables									
R	.60	.60	.42	.51	.59	.83	.32	.51	
% Added Variance	15.6	15.2	8.9	2.3	17.5	15.3	5.8	2.3	1
5—Kindred Variables									
R	.65	.63	.49	.61	.64	.86	.43	.61	
% Added Variance	6.2	3.7	5.7	11.6	5.6	6.2	8.5	11.0	
6—Word Knowledge									
R	.65	.65	.58	.66	.64	.87	.47	.69	
% Added Variance	0.0	1.7	10.4	5.4	0.8	1.0	3.5	9.6	
% Total Variance Accounted for	41.9	42.0	34.0	43.1	41.6	75.5	22.4	47.0	4

Table 9.4. *Multiple Correlations and Added Percentages of Variance for the Listening Regression Six Blocks of Variables—Population IV*

Blocks	Belgium (Fr.)	Chile	Finland	Hungary	Italy	Sweden
1—School Handicap Score and Sex						
R	.16	.18	.23	.15	.29	.17
% Added Variance	2.6	3.2	5.4	2.2	8.2	3.0
2—Type of School and Program						
R	.17	.24	.23	.15	.49	.37
% Added Variance	0.2	2.4	0.0	0.0	16.1	10.4
3—Time Factors						
R	.32	.34	.42	.16	.53	.46
% Added Variance	7.5	5.6	12.1	0.5	3.7	8.2
4—School Variables						
R	.58	.67	.48	.55	.85	.61
% Added Variance	23.0	33.3	5.7	27.8	44.1	16.0
5—Kindred Variables						
R	.61	.73	.58	.58	.87	.94
% Added Variance	3.8	8.8	10.2	3.0	4.3	51.4
6—Word Knowledge						
R	.61	.73	.60	.59	.88	.98
% Added Variance	0.0	0.1	2.7	1.5	0.7	7.1
% Total Variance Accounted for	37.1	53.4	36.1	35.0	77.1	95.1

Table 9.5. *Variables Entering Blocks 4 and 5 in the Reading Regression Analyses and the Direction in which They Are Weighted*

(*Population II, N = 7; Population IV, N = 9*)

Block	Variable	Population	Number of countries in which the sign is +	Number of countries in which the sign is −
4	Total auxiliary staff	II	2	2
		IV	5	2
	Classes conducted in English	II	2	3
		IV	4	2
	Students select English as a subject	II	4	1
		IV	−	−
	Sex of teacher	II	2	2
		IV	−	−
	Hours per Week teacher spends marking papers	II	3	1
		IV	−	−
	Teacher teaching other foreign language(s) in Addition to English	II	2	3
		IV	−	−
	Teacher's perceived listening skill	II	3	1
		IV	−	−
	Teacher's perceived speaking skill	II	−	−
		IV	4	2
	Teacher's perceived pronunciation skill	II	−	−
		IV	2	3
	Time teacher resided or studied in an English-speaking country	II	−	−
		IV	6	1
	Years teacher taught a foreign language	II	5	1
		IV	4	2
	Method of teaching grammar	II	2	2
		IV	−	−
	Hours per week student spends doing homework in all subjects	II	−	−
		IV	2	3
	Student sometimes speaks English to the teacher in the classroom	II	5	−
		IV	7	−
	Student writes exercises in English in the classroom	II	5	−
		IV	4	1
	Student sometimes reads English for pleasure in the classroom	II	4	−
		IV	7	−

Table 9.5. *(Cont.)*

Block	Variable	Popul-tion	Number of countries in which the sign is	
			+	−
5	Hours per week student spends doing English homework	II	1	3
		IV	1	5
	Student's expected education	II	6	−
		IV	6	−
	Student's aspiration to speak English	II	3	1
		IV	5	−
	Student's aspiration to understand English	II	5	−
		IV	−	−
	Student's aspiration to read English	II	−	−
		IV	4	−
	Student's aspiration to write English	II	−	−
		IV	4	1
	Frequency of student exposure to English	II	−	−
		IV	4	2
	Interest in English scale	II	7	−
		IV	8	−
	English activities outside of school scale	II	−	−
		IV	4	−
	Perceived utility of English scale	II	−	4
		IV	−	−

Table 9.6. *Variables Entering Blocks 4 and 5 in the Listening Regression Analyses and the Direction in which They Are Weighted*

(*Population II, N=4; Population IV, N=6*)

Block	Variable	Population	Number of countries in which the sign is	
			+	−
4	Total auxiliary staff	II	2	2
		IV	5	−
	Classes conducted in English	II	2	2
		IV	3	2
	Students select English as a subject	II	−	−
		IV	3	2
	Sex of teacher	II	2	2
		IV	3	1
	Hours per week teacher spends marking papers	II	2	−
		IV	2	3
	Teacher teaching other foreign language(s) in addition to English	II	−	−
		IV	−	4
	Teacher's perceived listening skill	II	−	−
		IV	3	3
	Teacher's perceived speaking skill	II	−	−
		IV	3	1
	Teacher's perceived reading skill	II	1	3
		IV	5	1
	Teacher's perceived writing skill	II	−	−
		IV	1	3
	Teacher's perceived pronunciation skill	II	−	−
		IV	1	3
	Time teacher resided or studied in an English-speaking country	II	−	−
		IV	4	1
	Years teacher taught a foreign language	II	−	−
		IV	4	1
	Method of teaching grammar	II	−	−
		IV	2	2
	Hours per week student spends doing home work in all subjects	II	−	−
		IV	−	5
	Student sometimes speaks English to the teacher in the classroom	II	2	−
		IV	3	2

Table 9.6. *(Cont.)*

| Block | Variable | Population | Number of countries in which the sign is | |
			+	−
	Student listens to the teacher sometime speak English in the classroom	II	−	2
		IV	−	3
	Student writes exercises in English in the classroom	II	2	−
		IV	−	−
5	Hours per week student spends doing English homework	II	−	3
		IV	2	2
	Student's expected education	II	2	−
		IV	−	−
	Student's aspiration to speak English	II	−	−
		IV	4	−
	Student's aspiration to understand English	II	2	−
		IV	3	−
	Student's aspiration to read English	II	2	1
		IV	4	−
	Frequency of student exposure to English	II	2	−
		IV	−	−
	Interest in English scale	II	3	1
		IV	3	−
	English activities outside of school scale	II	2	−
		IV	5	−
	Perceived utility of English scale	II	−	2
		IV	−	3

Chapter 10

Conclusions, Implications and Recommendations

The purpose of a study such as this is, of course, to provide some insight into factors influencing the teaching of English as a Foreign Language in the participating countries. But perhaps of even greater importance, one would hope to arrive at some definite conclusions and recommendations. This chapter, the last in the volume, is an attempt to supply this information.

CONCLUSIONS

One major finding of the study is that cross-national comparisons of achievement in English as a Foreign Language are possible provided that great care is taken in the construction of the instruments. A general consensus, so to speak, was arrived at by the participating countries in the selection of questions to be used in the study. As a result, the achievement measures and the questionnaires were generally valid instruments in the countries in which they were tested. Further, those measures for which reliabilities were determined appear to be reasonably precise.

Differences in achievement between-countries do appear. However, these differences seem to reflect the variations among countries in regard to the program offered and the attitude toward the teaching/learning of English. For example, when student errors on the achievement tests were examined and the total results of the study considered, it appeared that the native language of the student did affect responses but that, in addition, sources of error other than the mother tongue may have been more influential. Some of the sources of error appear to be a simple lack of knowledge about English, the inherent inconsistencies of the English language, not making semantic associations in responding to questions, and weaknesses in the fundamental operation of some skills such as drawing inferences. Such errors are likely to be a result of the curriculum and other school variables. That is, if certain skills in English—such as drawing inferences from materials written in English—are not an objective of the teaching program, it is likely that students would have difficulty with test questions that focus on this.

The factors that stand out across countries as important predictors of success in the study of English as a Foreign Language appear to be Time, Classroom practice, and Student attitude and aspirations. Of course, there are differences between the two populations studied. English students may be in a generally select group to begin with and those who have stayed on to study English until the end of secondary school are likely to be an even more select group. Since English is a subject generally learned only at school, it was not unexpected that the Home background factors would be outweighed by the school determined factors. For this reason, educational planning and curricular provisons has a great effect on the outcome of student achievement in English.

IMPLICATIONS AND RECOMMENDATIONS

Generally speaking, achievement is affected by educational policy. Therefore, educational planning must take into account what outcomes are desired.

Since time is shown by this study to be an important factor in determining achievement, educational planners need to determine first the levels of performance that are *satisfactory* at given points in the educational program of English as a Foreign Language. Such levels of performance need not be the same for all students but could vary for different groups of students.

Student aspirations and needs are shown to be important predictors of achievement in English and should be considered at the same time as the performance objectives. Together, they should constitute the *educational objectives* of the English program. That is, whenever possible, the educational program should reflect the various needs and aspirations of the students. Are they more interested in reading; or is it understanding and speaking? Of course, a common core of knowledge is needed, but the requirements for specific levels of expertise in the receptive and productive modes may vary depending upon the students' aspirations and needs.

Once the levels of performance are specified, if possible in terms of groups of students, the optimum age of entry and the length of time needed to attain various levels of performance can be determined. Since the analyses for this report do not provide information for such decision-making, further study of the data in the IEA Data Bank is necessary.

In addition to the further analyses of the IEA data, it seems appropriate that field testing of curriculum decisions be made. Perhaps using the current IEA measures as a resource base, tests that focus on the specific performance objectives deemed as desirable can be developed to determine if given levels of achievement have been attained. Naturally, there should be questionnaires and, if possible, school and classroom observations that carefully seek to determine the degree of adherence to the curriculum as well as what other factors may be affecting achievement.

The findings indicate that perceived teacher competence in English makes a difference in student achievement. However, the amount of training or travel and residence in an English-speaking country do not appear to make any particular difference. Therefore, in considering teacher selection and training, it would seem that any measure to improve perceived teacher competence would have positive effects. Perhaps future research can identify what specific measures these might be.

The length of teaching experience and the effort put into preparation for classes show some effect on student achievement. A teacher who may not have many years of experience teaching but does invest a great deal of time in preparation for classes may do as well as an effective teacher with lengthy service. Apparently, time is needed to perfect methods of teaching. This suggests that teachers be given adequate time to prepare for classes as well as opportunity to continue teaching over the years.

With regard to classroom practice, the use of English in reading, writing and speaking seems to have a positive effect on achievement. It would appear that when students are placed in a classroom situation requiring substantial use of English, the students are likely to have a decided advantage over students in classrooms where the mother tongue prevails. It is important to note, however, that this does not imply that the mother tongue should be completely withdrawn from English classrooms; rather, there is a need to strike a balance in the use of the two languages that maximizes achievement in English. For example, at some levels it may be more economical in terms of time as well as more efficient in terms of student comprehension and learning to teach certain things by using the mother tongue. Perhaps additional research can provide greater insight as to exactly what degree the mother tongue should be used at the various student performance levels.

SOME ADDITIONAL SUGGESTIONS FOR FUTURE RESEARCH

For those who have been engaged in this study a great deal of interest has arisen from indications of ways in which further research may be pursued. The suggestions offered are linked in almost equal measure to the desirability of profiting from new approaches regarding the analysis of the data available and to the need to clarify inconsistencies and ambiguities in the present study. For some studies an abundance of information is available in the IEA Data Bank while for other studies additional information is required. Such information might be sought either in national studies or in coordinated cross-national studies such as this one. It should be stressed that the suggestions offered are only a few that might arise from the present study and that there is no intention to argue in the context of foreign language learning as a general problem that they are the most urgent or the most likely to be productive to the students of language pedagogy.

Suggestions for Instruments

The International English Committee regretted the absence of a single coherent instrument for use in describing teaching method and in producing a profile of method which could be compared with differences in achievement. Related to this, a single instrument to describe student classroom activities was also found to be needed. Such an instrument might be used to determine the relative importance of various activities to achievement in English.

Linguists have long been interested in questions of "linguistic distance" between languages. Since this study showed that to some extent the mother tongue influenced achievement in the foreign language, an instrument to measure "linguistic distance" might prove helpful. This might be approached either by contrasting the features of the languages with the intention of producing a weighted profile or by examining a detailed item analysis of responses by students from different countries on the same tests.

Perhaps, so far as the present study is concerned, the most valuable research would involve the replication of the study in those countries where English is a second language rather than a foreign language, and where relative importance of school and non-school influences (home, neighborhood, mass media, etc.) may be found to be very different from what was found in this study. Such research would add substantially to our knowledge about foreign language learning.

In addition, studying achievement at age levels other than those studied here might help educational planners determine objectives for the English program. In such studies, as well as for the further analyses of the IEA data, consideration should be given to the analysis of sex differences with respect to both student achievement and teacher effectiveness.

FINAL REMARKS

Was the study worthwhile in terms of the tremendous efforts required to accomplish it? In the eyes of these investigators, the answer can only be "yes." The study served to substantiate other research at national or local levels as well as the intuition and observations of the members of the International English Committee. Further, and perhaps of greatest importance, the proper interpretation of the results of the study at the national levels should provide a firm basis for determining educational policies and practices regarding instruction of English as a Foreign Language. This is not to say that all the answers are here. They are not. Much more needs to be done, but here we have a beginning.